The Nystrom

Atlas *of* World History

SECOND EDITION

NYSTROM
EDUCATION

v2.01

Table of Contents

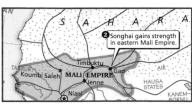
2014 Update of Names and Boundaries
© 2013, 2004 Nystrom Education
10200 Jefferson Blvd., Culver City, CA 90232

Printed in U.S.A.

v2.01

Print: ISBN: 978-0-7825-2183-2   Product Code: NYS183_9AWH-2
E-book: ISBN: 978-0-7825-2188-7   Product Code: SL5-AWH-2-NA

To order: www.nystromeducation.com or 800-421-4246

EDUCATIONAL CONSULTANTS

Michael Bruner, History Teacher, Chanute High School, Chanute, Kansas

Melissa Green, 6th Grade Teacher, Haven Middle School, Evanston School District #65, Evanston, Illinois

Lawrence W. McBride, Professor, Department of History, Illinois State University, Normal, Illinois

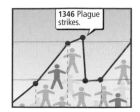

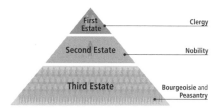
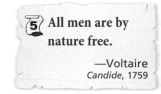
PHOTO CREDITS
Credit Abbreviations: **AI/C** Archivo Iconographico, S.A./Corbis **ART** Art Resources, NY **B/C** Bettmann/Corbis **BAL** Bridgeman Art Library
BrM Trustees of the British Museum **BPK/ART** Bildarchiv Preussischer Kulturbesitz/Art Resources, NY **C** Corbis **EL/ART** Erich Lessing/
Art Resources, NY **FL** First Light **GI** Getty Images **GC** Granger Collection, New York **MF** Masterfile **RA/GC** Rue des Archives/
Granger Collection, New York **RMN/ART** Reunion des Musees Nationaux/Art Resources, NY **S/ART** Scala/Art Resources, NY

front cover top RA/GC; **front cover bottom** British Library/HIP/ART; **back cover** GI; **2** GC; **3** BAL; **7C** B/C; **7D** Vaka Taumako Project, 2002;
10A Fernando Fernández/A.G.E. Fotostock/FL; **12B** Francoise de Mulder/C; **16B** 2003 C; **17E** C; **19C** BrM; **19D** DEA/S. VANNINI/GI; **20A** Daryl
Benson/MF; **21E** Corbis Asian Arts & Archaeology/C; **22B** Dallas & John Heaton/C; **26A** Greg Stott/MF; **28A** Adalberto Rios Szalay/Sexto Sol/
Photodisc/GI; **29D** M.L. Sinibaldi/C; **31C** RA/GC; **33E** Brigida Soriano/123RF.com; **34A** EL/ART; **36A** The Gallery Collection/C; **38A** Richard T
Nowitz/C; **41D** BAL; **42A** S/ART; **43D** GC; **44A** GC; **45C** Brian A. Vikander/C; **45D** GC; **45E** BrM; **46A** Bojan Brecelj/C; **47D** Nabeel Turner/GI;
48A EL/ART; **49C** RMN/ART; **50B** Werner Forman/ART; **51D** BAL/GI; **52A** Elena Roman Durante/GI; **53C** Victoria & Albert Museum/ART;
55D BAL; **57C** Dave Bartruff/C; **58A** AI/C; **60A** Nik Wheeler/C; **61D** British Library/HIP/ART; **62A** Desmond Kwande/AFP/GI; **64B** Archive Photos/
GI; **66B** Vittoriano Rastelli/C; **67D** painting by Michael P Frase, Swartz City, Michigan; **68B** Stapleton Collection/C; **70B** AI/C; **72B** BAL/GI; **74B**
BPK/ART; **75D** S/ART; **76A** GC; **77D** GI; **78A** GI; **78B** BPK/ART; **80A** Schalkwijk/ART; **81E** GC; **83B** BAL; **84A** David Muench/C; **86A** Robbie
Jack/C; **86B** GC; **86C** GC; **87D** RMN/ART; **87E** Andrew Ward/Life File/GI; **87F** Chris Ward Jones/Bloomberg via GI; **88A** SuperStock/GI;
89D S/ART; **90A** Chris Hellier/C; **91E** Imagno/GC; **94A** 1543 GC; **94A** 1610 Gustavo Tomsich/C; **94A** 1662 Hulton Archives/GI; **94A** 1665 GC;
94B GC; **97B** B/C; **98B** Giraudon/ART; **99D** B/C; **101C** Stock Montage/GI; **102B** ullstein bild/GC; **104B** B/C; **106A** AI/C; **109C** GC; **110B** B/C;
112B GC; **113E** GC; **115C** GC; **116A** Popperfoto, GI; **116B** C; **118B** GC; **120A** RA/GC; **121D** B. Press/Picture Quest; **122A** Adel Karroum/epa/C;
123E Bruno Morandi/GI; **124A** Mike Hill/GI; **125E** Sophia Paris/MINUSTAH via GI; **134 top** GC; **134 middle** RA/GC; **134 bottom** Popperfoto/GI;
135 top Nabeel Turner/GI; **135 middle** Stock Montage/GI; **135 bottom** DEA/S. VANNINI/GI; **136** RMN/ART

How does this atlas work?

1 First read the **unit title**, which tells what the unit is about and what time period it covers.

2 Then read the **topic title** which tells what these two pages are about.

3 Next read the **introduction**, for more about the topic.

4 Now follow the **A B C D** markers for the clearest path through the pages.

The **A B C D captions** help you understand each map, graph, and picture.

Maps show places, movement, people, and events.

The **legend** gives the title of the map and explains what its colors and other symbols mean. Read the legend before studying the map.

Pictures show how people and places looked in the past.

UNIT 6 Europe in the Middle Ages
418 to 1492

711–1492 Moors rule Spain.

400	600	800

418 Visigoths start a kingdom in Spain.

432 St. Patrick introduces Christianity to Ireland.

789 Vikings' first raid strikes Portland, England.

800 Charlemagne is crowned "Emperor of the West."

Early Kingdoms of Medieval Europe

During the Middle Ages or medieval era, many Europeans were poor, uneducated, and violent.

- Early in the Middle Ages, barbarian tribes settled in Western Europe and established their own kingdoms.

- Barbarian kings, wanting to be as civilized as the Romans, became Roman Catholic.

- One Frankish king, Charlemagne, conquered much of Western Europe and launched education reforms.

B Charlemagne, a Frank, conquered the Bavarians, Lombards, and Avars. He hoped to restore the Roman Empire in the West. Here his army battles the Saxons.

A Compare the barbarian invasions on page 43 with the kingdoms on this map.

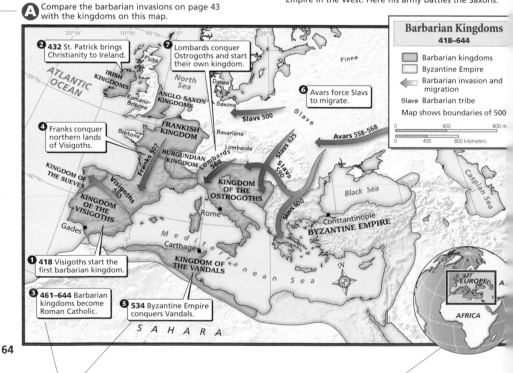

2 432 St. Patrick brings Christianity to Ireland.

7 Lombards conquer Ostrogoths and start their own kingdom.

6 Avars force Slavs to migrate.

4 Franks conquer northern lands of Visigoths.

1 418 Visigoths start the first barbarian kingdom.

3 461–644 Barbarian kingdoms become Roman Catholic.

5 534 Byzantine Empire conquers Vandals.

Barbarian Kingdoms
418–644

- Barbarian kingdoms
- Byzantine Empire
- → Barbarian invasion and migration
- *Slavs* Barbarian tribe

Map shows boundaries of 500

| 0 | 400 | 800 miles |
| 0 | 400 | 800 kilometers |

ATLANTIC OCEAN
IRISH KINGDOMS
Picts
Finns
North Sea
Danes
Saxons
Romano-Britons
ANGLO-SAXON KINGDOMS
Slavs 500
Slavs
Bretons
FRANKISH KINGDOM
Bavarians
Franks 507
BURGUNDIAN KINGDOM
Lombards 568
Slavs 625
Avars 558–568
Slavs 510
KINGDOM OF THE SUEVES
Visigoths 585
KINGDOM OF THE OSTROGOTHS
Slavs 600
Black Sea
Caspian Sea
KINGDOM OF THE VISIGOTHS
Gades
Rome
Constantinople
BYZANTINE EMPIRE
Mediterranean Sea
Carthage
KINGDOM OF THE VANDALS
SAHARA

EUROPE
AFRICA

64

Call-outs are mini-captions right on the map.

Locator maps explain what part of the world is shown.

4

The **unit timeline** shows key events from this time period. Use it to preview the unit.

At the end of the unit, use the timeline to review the sequence of key events.

This symbol lets you know that the website **WorldHistoryAtlas.com** has more maps, graphs, photos, and/or primary sources on the topic.

1066
Normans take control of England.

1095
First Crusade is called by Pope Urban II.

1347
Plague-infected rats arrive in Sicily.

1453
Ottomans conquer Constantinople.

1000　　　　**1200**　　　　**1400**　　　　**1600**

936
Otto I creates what will be the Holy Roman Empire.

1215
Magna Carta gives rights to free men in England.

1337–1453
Hundred Years' War fought between England and France.

more at NWHatlas.com

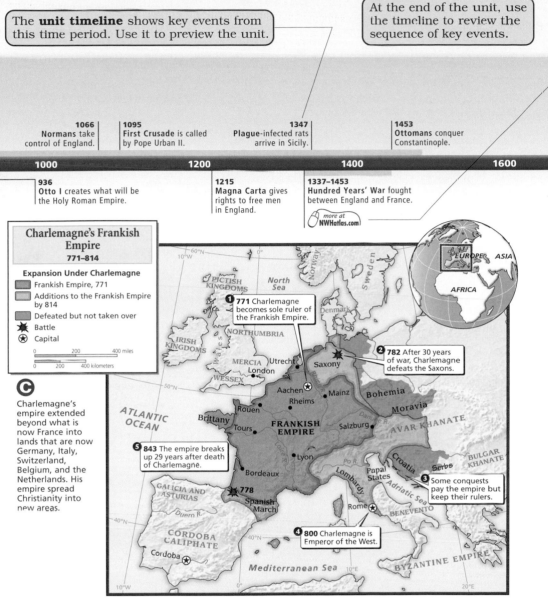

Charlemagne's Frankish Empire
771–814

Expansion Under Charlemagne
- Frankish Empire, 771
- Additions to the Frankish Empire by 814
- Defeated but not taken over
- ✷ Battle
- ✪ Capital

0　　200　　400 miles
0　　200　　400 kilometers

C Charlemagne's empire extended beyond what is now France into lands that are now Germany, Italy, Switzerland, Belgium, and the Netherlands. His empire spread Christianity into new areas.

❶ **771** Charlemagne becomes sole ruler of the Frankish Empire.

❷ **782** After 30 years of war, Charlemagne defeats the Saxons.

❸ Some conquests pay the empire but keep their rulers.

❹ **800** Charlemagne is Emperor of the West.

❺ **843** The empire breaks up 29 years after death of Charlemagne.

778

CULTURE
Education in the Frankish Empire

Before Charlemagne		Charlemagne's Education Reform
Boys studying to be clergy Some children of aristocrats	**Students**	All boys
Grammar, Rhetoric*	**Subjects taught**	Grammar, Rhetoric, Logic, Geometry, Arithmetic, Astronomy, Music
Monasteries Schools founded by bishops	**Location of schools**	Palace School in Aachen Primary schools in every city and village

*involved reading, rereading, commenting on, and imitating the classics

D At that time, lessons were taught in Latin. Charlemagne brought in teachers from England, Ireland, Spain, and Italy. But, without money or enough teachers, Charlemagne's education reform was largely a dream.

65

Who can read?
After the fall of Rome, education in most of Western Europe collapsed. Monks saved and copied books and taught a few students to read. Monasteries remained the center of European learning for almost 1000 years.

History Questions help you understand key words or ideas.

Charts and graphs organize information visually.

What else can you find in this atlas?

Milestones of World History on the inside front cover are a short list of key events.

Reference Maps on pages 126–129 show the world today.

Timetables of World History on 130–133 show what was happening in different places at the same time.

Glossary on 134–136 defines special words and names used in the atlas.

Index on 137–144 lists all the pages where people, places, or events are mentioned.

Thematic Index on the inside back cover lists all the pages related to certain big topics.

Abbreviations are explained on the inside front cover too.

100,000 B.C. (B.C.E.)	10,000 B.C. (B.C.E.)	8000 B.C. (B.C.E.)	6000 B.C. (B.C.E

7000 B.C.
Symbols, earliest ancestors of writing, are first used.

100,000 B.C.
People migrate beyond East Africa.

9000 B.C.
Farming and herding begin in Fertile Crescent.

8000 B.C.
Jericho is one of the first cities.

By 6000 B.C.
Farming begins in Egypt, India, and China.

People Migrate Across the Earth

About 100,000 B.C. early people began migrating from their African homeland.

- For thousands of years, people moved into new areas in search of food. They hunted animals and gathered wild plants.

- Ice ages killed much of their food, forcing people to move. They migrated on foot or in small boats.

- By 9000 B.C. people had migrated to most regions of the world.

A People first migrated to regions that had plenty of food and comfortable climates. Which continents had been reached by 25,000 B.C.?

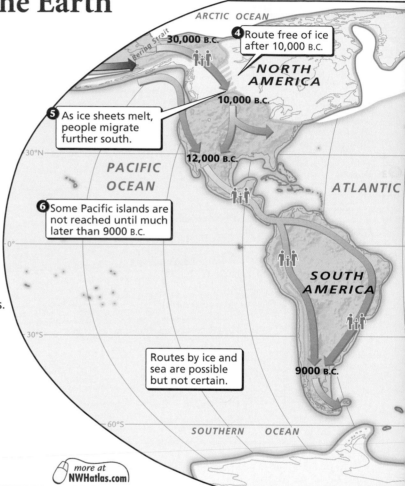

ARCTIC OCEAN

30,000 B.C.

4 Route free of ice after 10,000 B.C.

NORTH AMERICA

10,000 B.C.

5 As ice sheets melt, people migrate further south.

12,000 B.C.

30°N

PACIFIC OCEAN

ATLANTIC

6 Some Pacific islands are not reached until much later than 9000 B.C.

0°

SOUTH AMERICA

30°S

Routes by ice and sea are possible but not certain.

9000 B.C.

60°S

SOUTHERN OCEAN

ENVIRONMENT
Sea Level at the Bering Strait

more at **NWHatlas.com**

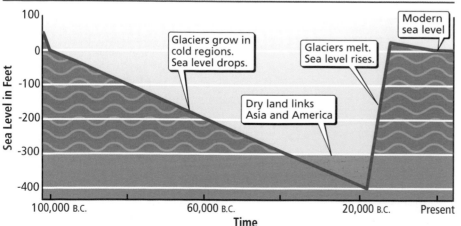

Glaciers grow in cold regions. Sea level drops.

Glaciers melt. Sea level rises.

Modern sea level

Dry land links Asia and America

Sea Level in Feet: 100, 0, -100, -200, -300, -400

Time: 100,000 B.C. — 60,000 B.C. — 20,000 B.C. — Present

B The earth's temperature began to fall around 100,000 B.C. Rivers froze, so water could not flow back to the sea. The sea level dropped. Areas that had been underwater were exposed as dry land.

What was the ice age?

Large parts of the earth were once covered by thick layers of ice called ice sheets. They formed during the cold periods known as **ice ages**, which lasted thousands of years.

5000 B.C.
Irrigation is used in farming.

3500 B.C.
First civilization rises in Sumer. Bronze tools are made.

2350 B.C.
First empire rises in Akkad.

By 1200 B.C.
Hebrews live in Canaan.

539 B.C.
Cyrus of Persia conquers Babylon.

4000 B.C. (B.C.E.)   **2000 B.C. (B.C.E.)**   B.C. (B.C.E.) ◀ | ▶ A.D. (C.E.)

4000 B.C.
Sahara gets drier, soon becomes desert.

1800–1600 B.C.
Assyria and Babylonia create empires in Mesopotamia.

900 B.C.
Phoenicians sail to the Atlantic Ocean.

ARCTIC   OCEAN

EUROPE
40,000 B.C.

45,000 B.C.

50,000 B.C.

ASIA

30,000 B.C.

90,000 B.C.

30°N

❸ 30,000 B.C. First cave art appears.

PACIFIC

OCEAN

60,000 B.C.

AFRICA

OCEAN

100,000 B.C.

❶ 100,000 B.C. People begin to migrate out of East Africa.

0°

OCEANIA

55,000 B.C.

30,000 B.C.

❷ 55,000 B.C. People cross open ocean to reach Australia.

AUSTRALIA

30°S

INDIAN

OCEAN

33,000 B.C.

N

SOUTHERN   OCEAN

60°S

ANTARCTICA

Early Human Migrations
100,000–9000 B.C.

Spread of Humans

- 100,000–75,000 B.C.
- 75,000–50,000 B.C.
- 50,000–25,000 B.C.
- 25,000–9000 B.C.

12,000 B.C. Approximate date of arrival in region

Ice Age

- Sea ice, 16,000 B.C.
- Glacier or ice sheet
- Ice Age coastline
- Coastline today

Equatorial Scale

0   1000   2000 miles

0   1000   2000 kilometers

C One early form of expression was cave painting. Many cave paintings show animals that people hunted.

D About 2000 B.C. people with advanced skills and improved boats began sailing to distant islands in the Pacific Ocean.

Agriculture and Early Settlements

Agriculture, or growing plants and raising animals for food, changed human society forever. Agriculture was more reliable than hunting and gathering.

■ People began to herd or keep wild animals in pens. They became farmers, planting seeds from wild grasses using hoes and digging sticks.

■ Settlements became permanent. Farming communites grew into villages. A surplus of food allowed people to **specialize** and work other jobs.

■ Specialists improved metalworking, making stronger tools and weapons. These advances in technology are used to name the Bronze and Iron Ages.

 more at NWHatlas.com

SCIENCE & TECHNOLOGY
Earliest Domestic Plants and Animals

PLANTS		ANIMALS
Barley, lentils, peas, wheat	**Middle East**	Cattle, goats, pigs, sheep
Millet, rice	**China**	Chicken, pigs, water buffalo
Cotton, millet, rice, soybeans, sweet potatoes, taro	**South and Southeast Asia**	Cattle, chicken, pigs, water buffalo
Barley, millet, sorghum, wheat, yams	**Africa**	Cattle, sheep
Barley, rye, wheat	**Europe**	Cattle, dogs, pigs
Beans, peppers, potatoes, squash	**Americas**	Dogs, turkeys

B Agriculture started with resources found in the environment. What were the most common domestic plants and animals?

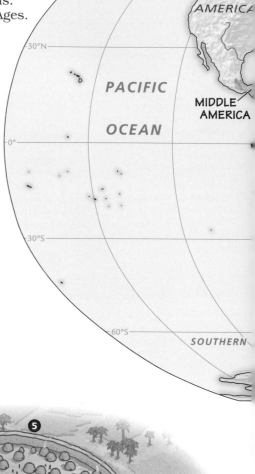

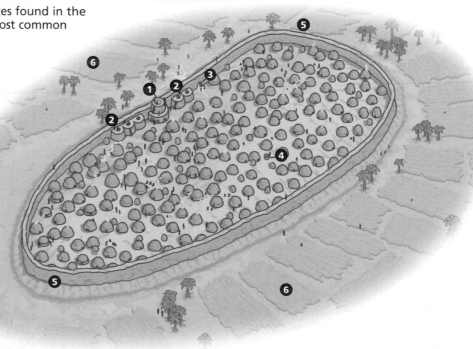

Jericho
7000 B.C.

❶ Tower
❷ Grain storage
❸ Gate
❹ Spring
❺ City wall
❻ Grain field

Other buildings are houses.

C About 1,000 people lived in Jericho, one of the world's oldest cities. What clues does this illustration give you about their society?

A Agriculture developed in several different regions of the world at about the same time. In some areas, people used irrigation to direct river water to their crops. In areas unsuitable for farming, people continued to hunt and gather.

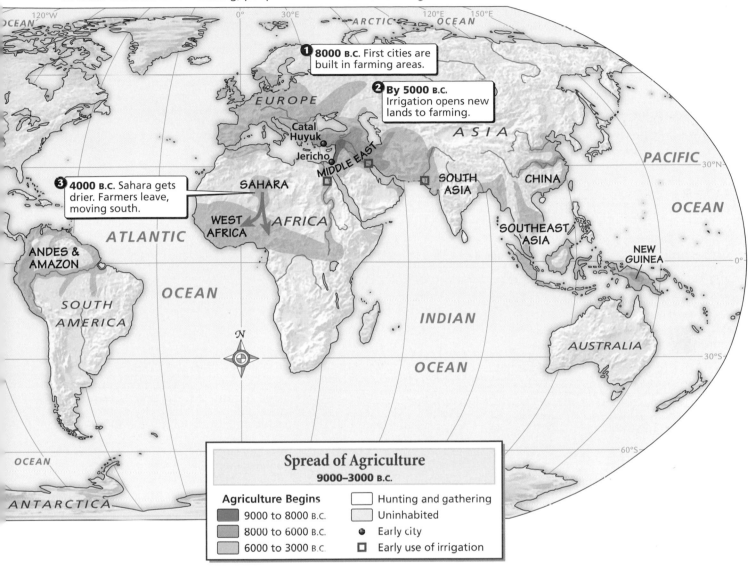

1 8000 B.C. First cities are built in farming areas.

2 By 5000 B.C. Irrigation opens new lands to farming.

3 4000 B.C. Sahara gets drier. Farmers leave, moving south.

Spread of Agriculture
9000–3000 B.C.

Agriculture Begins

■ 9000 to 8000 B.C.	☐ Hunting and gathering
■ 8000 to 6000 B.C.	☐ Uninhabited
■ 6000 to 3000 B.C.	◉ Early city
	☐ Early use of irrigation

SCIENCE & TECHNOLOGY
Tool-Making Technology

■ Stone and Copper Ages (Neolithic and Chalcolithic)　　■ Bronze Age　　■ Iron Age

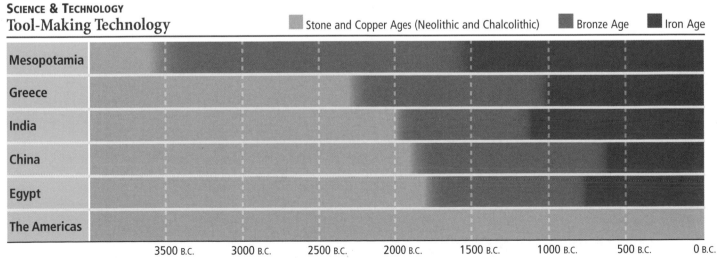

	3500 B.C.	3000 B.C.	2500 B.C.	2000 B.C.	1500 B.C.	1000 B.C.	500 B.C.	0 B.C.
Mesopotamia								
Greece								
India								
China								
Egypt								
The Americas								

D Metal replaced stone for making tools and weapons at different times around the world. Bronze, a mixture of copper and tin, replaced copper and stone when more tin was found. Iron, a cheaper and stronger metal, replaced bronze when improved heating methods were developed.

Civilization in Ancient Mesopotamia

The earliest known civilization, Sumer, and the world's first empire, the Akkadian Empire, both developed in Mesopotamia.

- The Sumerians developed the first written language and the first laws. They also traded with places as far away as Egypt and India.

- Each Sumerian city-state was independent. Each had its own ruler, own special god, and own army.

- People from the neighboring region of Akkad later conquered Sumer and the rest of the area around the Tigris and Euphrates Rivers. Once conquered, city-states were simply cities.

A During the Bronze Age, Sumerians fought using bronze weapons and chariots pulled by donkeys. This image is of Sumerians crushing an enemy.

WRITING & LANGUAGE
Sumerians Develop Writing, 7000–3000 B.C.

Word	Token 7000 B.C.	Pictograph 3500 B.C.	Cuneiform 3000 B.C.
Sheep			
Metal			

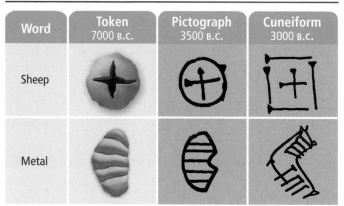

B People in Mesopotamia first used objects, or tokens, to record trades. Sumerians then scratched the same shapes on clay tablets. Later they used triangular reeds to scratch these shapes. These wedge shapes, or cuneiform, became the basis of written languages in Mesopotamia.

Is it a city or is it a state?

Early civilizations weren't part of a large country. Instead, people were governed by their own **city-state**. A city-state included a city and the surrounding countryside. There are a few city-states today, such as Monaco in Europe and Singapore in Asia.

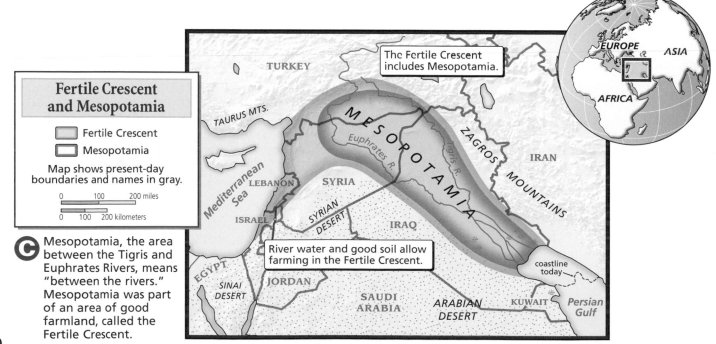

Fertile Crescent and Mesopotamia

- Fertile Crescent
- Mesopotamia

Map shows present-day boundaries and names in gray.

0   100   200 miles
0   100   200 kilometers

The Fertile Crescent includes Mesopotamia.

River water and good soil allow farming in the Fertile Crescent.

coastline today

C Mesopotamia, the area between the Tigris and Euphrates Rivers, means "between the rivers." Mesopotamia was part of an area of good farmland, called the Fertile Crescent.

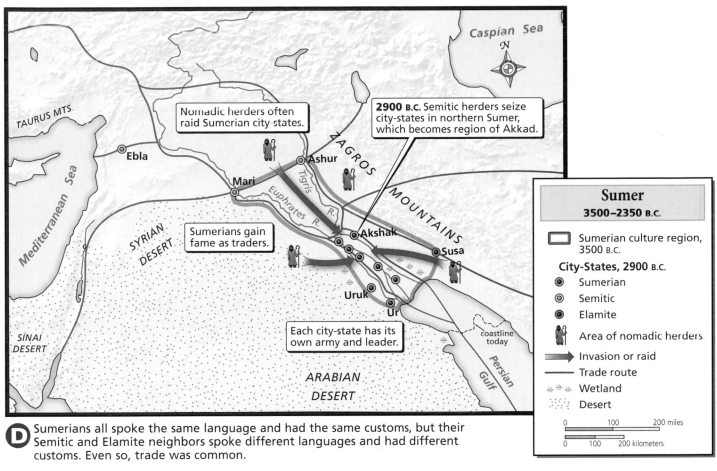

Caspian Sea

Nomadic herders often raid Sumerian city-states.

2900 B.C. Semitic herders seize city-states in northern Sumer, which becomes region of Akkad.

TAURUS MTS.

Ebla

Ashur

Mari

Tigris R.

Euphrates R.

ZAGROS MOUNTAINS

Sumerians gain fame as traders.

Akshak

Susa

Mediterranean Sea

SYRIAN DESERT

Uruk

Ur

coastline today

Each city-state has its own army and leader.

SINAI DESERT

ARABIAN DESERT

Persian Gulf

Sumer
3500–2350 B.C.

▢ Sumerian culture region, 3500 B.C.

City-States, 2900 B.C.

◉ Sumerian
◉ Semitic
◉ Elamite
⛏ Area of nomadic herders
➤ Invasion or raid
— Trade route
⸬ Wetland
⸬ Desert

0 — 100 — 200 miles
0 — 100 — 200 kilometers

D Sumerians all spoke the same language and had the same customs, but their Semitic and Elamite neighbors spoke different languages and had different customs. Even so, trade was common.

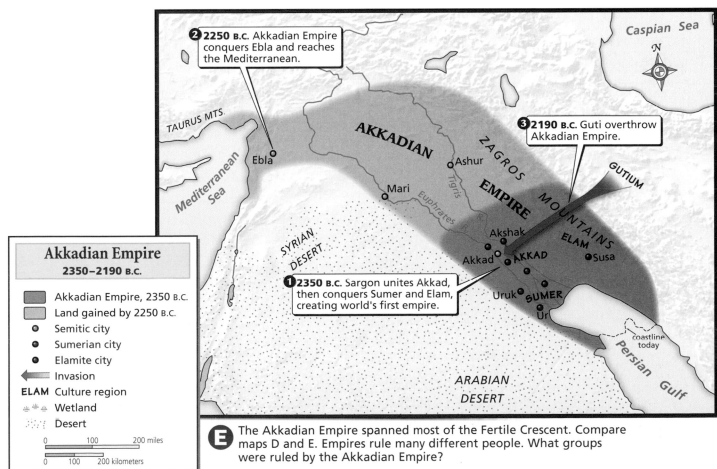

2 **2250 B.C.** Akkadian Empire conquers Ebla and reaches the Mediterranean.

Caspian Sea

AKKADIAN

3 **2190 B.C.** Guti overthrow Akkadian Empire.

TAURUS MTS.

Ebla

Ashur

ZAGROS

GUTIUM

Mari

Tigris

EMPIRE

MOUNTAINS

ELAM

Mediterranean Sea

SYRIAN DESERT

Euphrates R.

Akshak

Akkad

AKKAD

Susa

Uruk

SUMER

Ur

coastline today

Akkadian Empire
2350–2190 B.C.

▨ Akkadian Empire, 2350 B.C.
▨ Land gained by 2250 B.C.
◉ Semitic city
◉ Sumerian city
◉ Elamite city
➤ Invasion
ELAM Culture region
⸬ Wetland
⸬ Desert

0 — 100 — 200 miles
0 — 100 — 200 kilometers

1 **2350 B.C.** Sargon unites Akkad, then conquers Sumer and Elam, creating world's first empire.

ARABIAN DESERT

Persian Gulf

E The Akkadian Empire spanned most of the Fertile Crescent. Compare maps D and E. Empires rule many different people. What groups were ruled by the Akkadian Empire?

11

Babylonia and Assyria

After the Akkadian Empire fell, two groups struggled for control of the Fertile Crescent. Babylonians from Babylon and Assyrians from Ashur became the major powers in the region.

- Babylon was long known as a center of learning. Babylonian science and literature were admired and imitated throughout the Fertile Crescent.

- In contrast, Assyria was known for its fierce army.

- Babylonia and Assyria fought each other often over the course of a thousand years. Each conquered the other more than once.

B The Babylonians and Assyrians built monuments to show their wealth and power. Above is a replica of Babylon's Ishtar Gate. The wealth came from conquests and taxes.

A The Babylonian Empire expanded under Hammurabi, one of Babylonia's most important kings. He is also remembered for his extensive law code.

Why do empires fail?

Akkad, Babylon, and Ashur all produced **empires**, ruling distant lands with languages and customs unlike their own. Such differences make empires hard to govern.

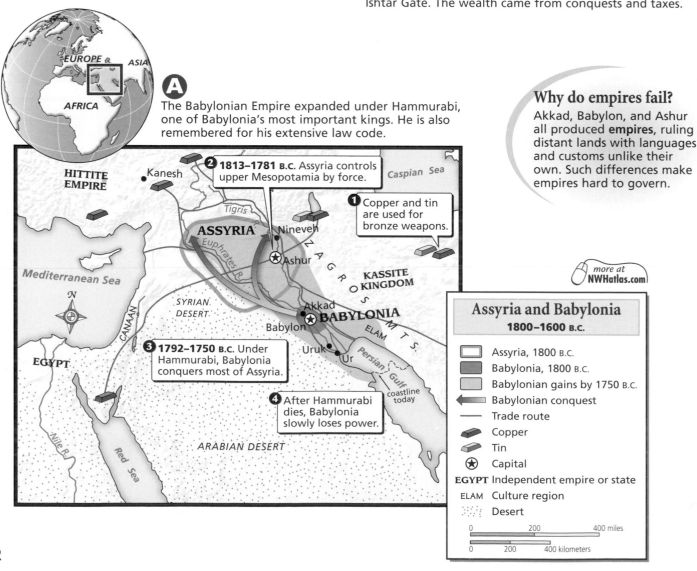

2 1813–1781 B.C. Assyria controls upper Mesopotamia by force.

1 Copper and tin are used for bronze weapons.

3 1792–1750 B.C. Under Hammurabi, Babylonia conquers most of Assyria.

4 After Hammurabi dies, Babylonia slowly loses power.

more at NWHatlas.com

Assyria and Babylonia
1800–1600 B.C.

☐	Assyria, 1800 B.C.
☐	Babylonia, 1800 B.C.
☐	Babylonian gains by 1750 B.C.
←	Babylonian conquest
—	Trade route
	Copper
	Tin
✪	Capital
EGYPT	Independent empire or state
ELAM	Culture region
	Desert

0   200   400 miles

0   200   400 kilometers

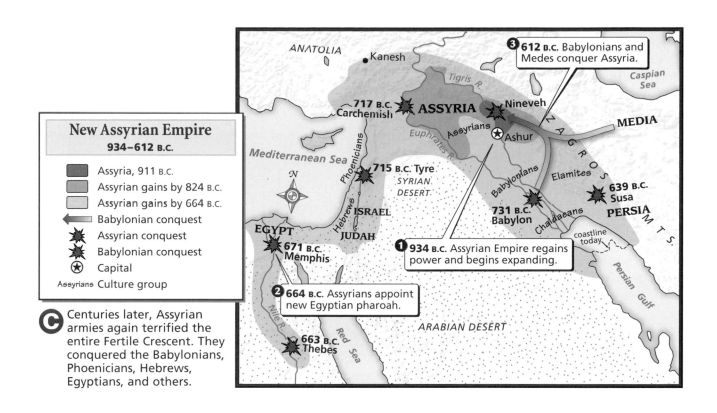

New Assyrian Empire
934–612 B.C.

- Assyria, 911 B.C.
- Assyrian gains by 824 B.C.
- Assyrian gains by 664 B.C.
- Babylonian conquest
- ✸ Assyrian conquest
- ✸ Babylonian conquest
- ★ Capital
- Assyrians Culture group

3 612 B.C. Babylonians and Medes conquer Assyria.

717 B.C. Carchemish

715 B.C. Tyre

731 B.C. Babylon

639 B.C. Susa

1 934 B.C. Assyrian Empire regains power and begins expanding.

671 B.C. Memphis

2 664 B.C. Assyrians appoint new Egyptian pharoah.

663 B.C. Thebes

C Centuries later, Assyrian armies again terrified the entire Fertile Crescent. They conquered the Babylonians, Phoenicians, Hebrews, Egyptians, and others.

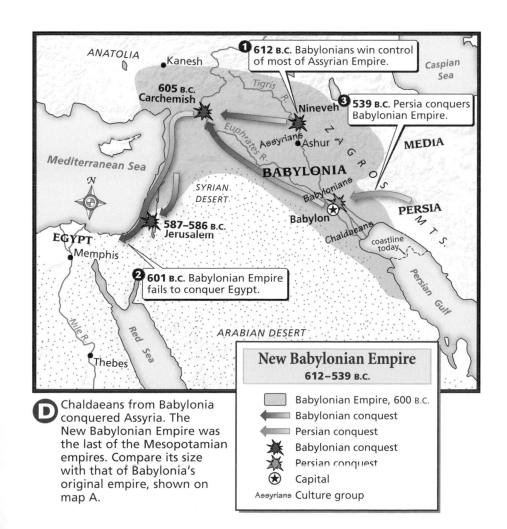

1 612 B.C. Babylonians win control of most of Assyrian Empire.

3 539 B.C. Persia conquers Babylonian Empire.

605 B.C. Carchemish

587–586 B.C. Jerusalem

2 601 B.C. Babylonian Empire fails to conquer Egypt.

New Babylonian Empire
612–539 B.C.

- Babylonian Empire, 600 B.C.
- Babylonian conquest
- Persian conquest
- ✸ Babylonian conquest
- ✸ Persian conquest
- ★ Capital
- Assyrians Culture group

D Chaldaeans from Babylonia conquered Assyria. The New Babylonian Empire was the last of the Mesopotamian empires. Compare its size with that of Babylonia's original empire, shown on map A.

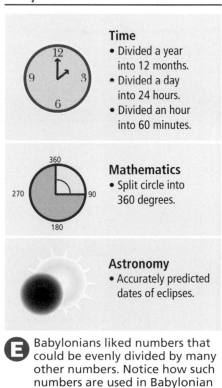

SCIENCE & TECHNOLOGY
Babylonian Contributions

Time
- Divided a year into 12 months.
- Divided a day into 24 hours.
- Divided an hour into 60 minutes.

Mathematics
- Split circle into 360 degrees.

Astronomy
- Accurately predicted dates of eclipses.

E Babylonians liked numbers that could be evenly divided by many other numbers. Notice how such numbers are used in Babylonian contributions to time and mathematics.

ebrew Kingdoms

According to the Hebrew Bible (Tanakh), Hebrews came from southeastern Mesopotamia near the Persian Gulf. Around 1800 B.C., they migrated west to the Mediterranean coast.

- They are said to have settled in Canaan, which they believed their god had given them.

- A Hebrew kingdom was formed by 1200 B.C. Later it split into Israel and Judah.

- Wars and famine often forced Hebrews to leave their "Promised Land."

- The Hebrews came to be called **Jews** and their religion **Judaism**.

HITTITE EMPIRE

1 1800 B.C. Abraham and relatives move from Ur to Canaan.

2 1700 B.C. Famine forces Hebrews to move to Egypt. They become slaves.

FERTILE

ASSYRIA

Tigris R.

Euphrates R.

ZAGROS MTS.

CANAAN

Bethel

Jericho

SYRIAN DESERT

BABYLONIA

5 Hebrews reach Canaan and form a kingdom.

EGYPT

Succoth

Mediterranean Sea

Ur

Persian Gulf

coastline today

4 Moses gets divine Ten Commandments. Hebrews accept one god.

Mt. Sinai

Nile R.

3 1200 B.C. Moses leads freed Hebrews from Egypt back to Canaan.

ARABIAN DESERT

Red Sea

Biblical Migrations to Canaan
1800–1200 B.C.

- Fertile land
- ← Hebrew migration
- ASSYRIA Culture region
- ⋯⋯ Desert

0   100   200 miles
0 100 200 kilometers

A In the biblical accounts, leaders such as Abraham and Moses led the Hebrews to Canaan. Archaeologists have not been able to confirm these accounts.

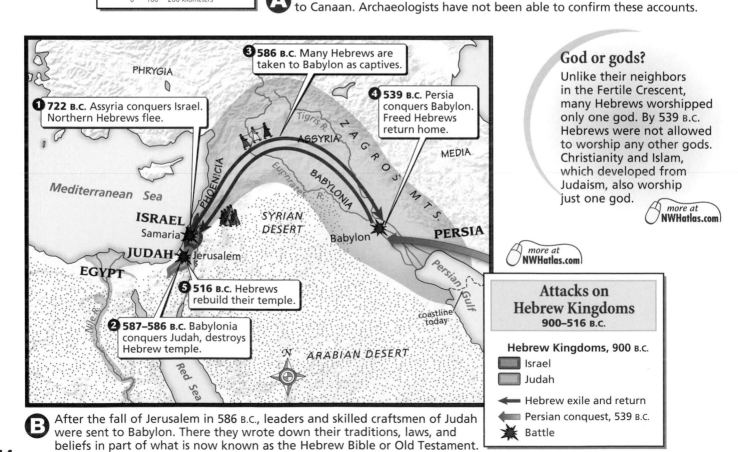

3 586 B.C. Many Hebrews are taken to Babylon as captives.

1 722 B.C. Assyria conquers Israel. Northern Hebrews flee.

PHRYGIA

4 539 B.C. Persia conquers Babylon. Freed Hebrews return home.

Tigris R.

ASSYRIA

ZAGROS MTS.

MEDIA

Euphrates R.

PHOENICIA

BABYLONIA

Mediterranean Sea

ISRAEL
Samaria

SYRIAN DESERT

Babylon

PERSIA

JUDAH Jerusalem

EGYPT

Persian Gulf

coastline today

5 516 B.C. Hebrews rebuild their temple.

2 587–586 B.C. Babylonia conquers Judah, destroys Hebrew temple.

Nile R.

ARABIAN DESERT

Red Sea

God or gods?

Unlike their neighbors in the Fertile Crescent, many Hebrews worshipped only one god. By 539 B.C. Hebrews were not allowed to worship any other gods. Christianity and Islam, which developed from Judaism, also worship just one god.

more at NWHatlas.com

more at NWHatlas.com

Attacks on Hebrew Kingdoms
900–516 B.C.

Hebrew Kingdoms, 900 B.C.

- Israel
- Judah

- ← Hebrew exile and return
- ← Persian conquest, 539 B.C.
- ✹ Battle

B After the fall of Jerusalem in 586 B.C., leaders and skilled craftsmen of Judah were sent to Babylon. There they wrote down their traditions, laws, and beliefs in part of what is now known as the Hebrew Bible or Old Testament.

Phoenician Trade

The Phoenician civilization, like that of the Hebrews, developed along the eastern edge of the Mediterranean Sea.

- By 2900 B.C. the Phoenicians had become the first major sea-going civilization. Their ships could travel long distances using either sails or oars.

- The Phoenicians established a large trade network. They also established colonies in North Africa, southern Spain, and on islands in the Mediterranean Sea.

- To make trade easier, the Phoenicians developed a simple writing system that used symbols for sounds instead of symbols for words or ideas.

WRITING & LANGUAGE
Development of Our Alphabet

Phoenician 1000 B.C.	Greek 600 B.C.	Roman A.D. 300
K	Λ	A
◁	B	B
◁	Δ	D
ⅎ	F	E

C Sumerians used over 500 symbols in their writing; Phoenicians used only 22. Other cultures adopted the Phoenician symbols, on which our modern alphabet is based.

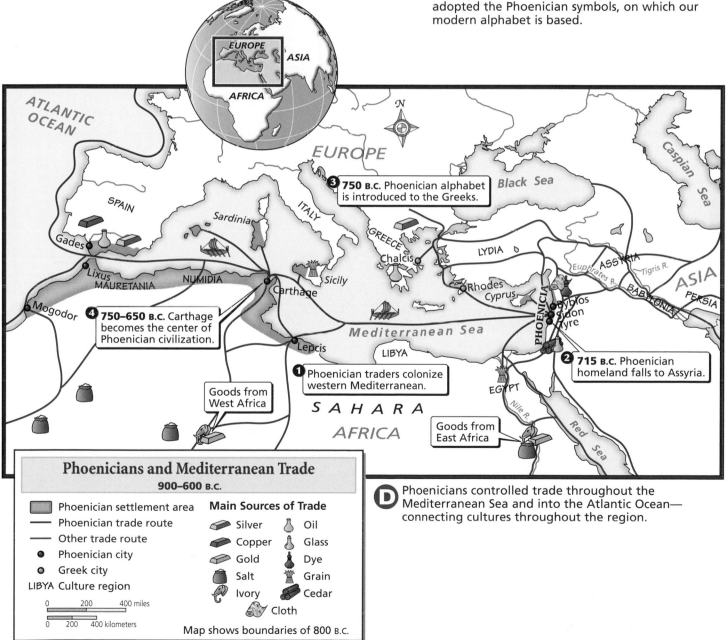

3 750 B.C. Phoenician alphabet is introduced to the Greeks.

4 750–650 B.C. Carthage becomes the center of Phoenician civilization.

1 Phoenician traders colonize western Mediterranean.

2 715 B.C. Phoenician homeland falls to Assyria.

Goods from West Africa

Goods from East Africa

Phoenicians and Mediterranean Trade
900–600 B.C.

- ▨ Phoenician settlement area
- — Phoenician trade route
- — Other trade route
- ● Phoenician city
- ◉ Greek city
- LIBYA Culture region

Main Sources of Trade
- Silver
- Copper
- Gold
- Salt
- Ivory
- Oil
- Glass
- Dye
- Grain
- Cedar
- Cloth

0   200   400 miles
0   200   400 kilometers

Map shows boundaries of 800 B.C.

D Phoenicians controlled trade throughout the Mediterranean Sea and into the Atlantic Ocean—connecting cultures throughout the region.

2500 B.C.
Planned cities are built in India.

6000 B.C. (B.C.E.)	5000 B.C. (B.C.E.)	4000 B.C. (B.C.E.)	3000 B.C. (B.C.E.)

6000 B.C.
Farming begins in western India.

5000 B.C.
Yangshao culture begins in China.

3100 B.C.
Upper and Lower Egypt unite.

Civilization in Ancient Egypt

Ancient Egypt is one of the oldest and longest lasting civilizations in the world. This civilization began in a river valley more than 5,000 years ago.

- Ancient Egypt arose along the Nile River in northeastern Africa.

- The first 2,000 years of Egyptian history are divided into three periods: the Old, Middle, and New Kingdoms.

- The ancient Egyptians developed an advanced civilization. They built cities, invented hieroglyphics (a form of writing), and created large monuments.

A During the Old Kingdom, a strong central government was established and the building of pyramids began. During the Middle Kingdom, Egypt expanded south along the Nile and conquered Lower Nubia.

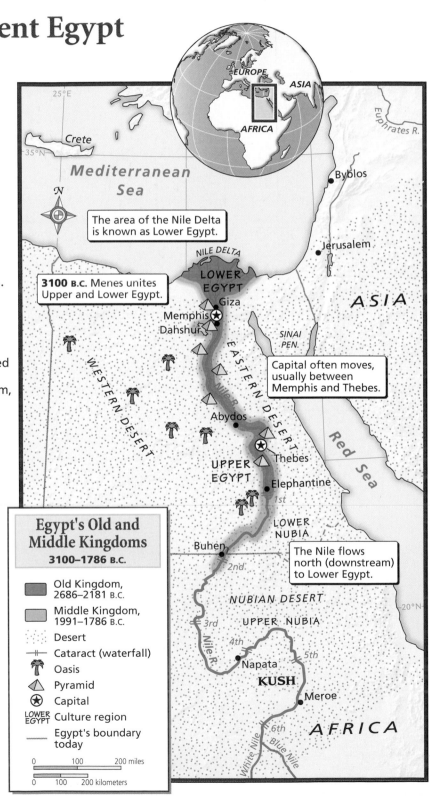

The area of the Nile Delta is known as Lower Egypt.

3100 B.C. Menes unites Upper and Lower Egypt.

Capital often moves, usually between Memphis and Thebes.

The Nile flows north (downstream) to Lower Egypt.

Egypt's Old and Middle Kingdoms
3100–1786 B.C.

- Old Kingdom, 2686–2181 B.C.
- Middle Kingdom, 1991–1786 B.C.
- Desert
- Cataract (waterfall)
- Oasis
- Pyramid
- Capital
- LOWER EGYPT Culture region
- Egypt's boundary today

0   100   200 miles
0   100   200 kilometers

B Thousands of workers built huge pyramids as tombs for Egyptian rulers. Farmers helped when the Nile flooded.

1766 B.C.
Shang dynasty, China's first, begins.

1570 B.C.
New Kingdom of Egypt begins.

1200 B.C.
Olmecs build the earliest cities in the Americas.

563 B.C.
Siddhartha Gautama (Buddha) is born.

212 B.C.
Great Wall of China construction begins.

A.D. 500
Gupta Empire collapses after Hun invasions.

A.D. 900
Lowland Maya leave their cities.

1000 B.C.
Hindus write down world's oldest scriptures.

551 B.C.
Confucius is born.

321 B.C.
Mauryan Empire begins in India.

A.D. 350
Kingdom of Kush falls.

C After the Middle Kingdom broke apart, Egypt was ruled by the Hyksos people of Asia. Then the Egyptians overthrew the Hyksos and began the New Kingdom. This new Egyptian empire became the strongest and wealthiest in the world.

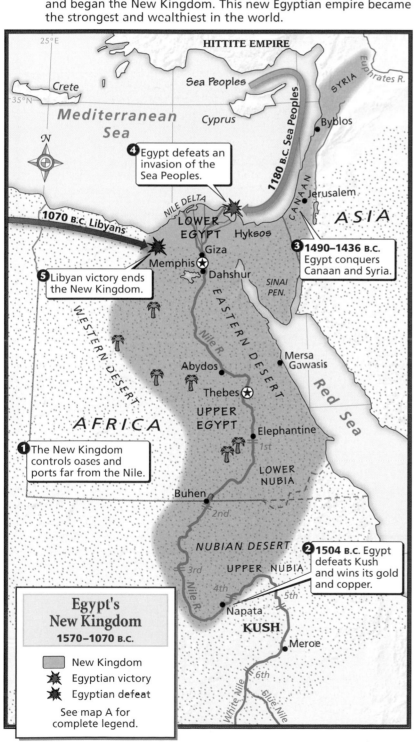

4 Egypt defeats an invasion of the Sea Peoples.

1070 B.C. Libyans

5 Libyan victory ends the New Kingdom.

3 1490–1436 B.C. Egypt conquers Canaan and Syria.

1 The New Kingdom controls oases and ports far from the Nile.

2 1504 B.C. Egypt defeats Kush and wins its gold and copper.

HITTITE EMPIRE

Sea Peoples

1180 B.C. Sea Peoples

Crete

Mediterranean Sea

Cyprus

Byblos

Jerusalem

ASIA

SYRIA

Euphrates R.

NILE DELTA

LOWER EGYPT

Hyksos

CANAAN

Giza

Memphis

Dahshur

SINAI PEN.

EASTERN DESERT

Nile R.

Abydos

Mersa Gawasis

Red Sea

Thebes

UPPER EGYPT

Elephantine

1st

WESTERN DESERT

AFRICA

LOWER NUBIA

Buhen

2nd

NUBIAN DESERT

3rd

UPPER NUBIA

4th

5th

Napata

KUSH

Meroe

6th

White Nile

Blue Nile

Egypt's New Kingdom
1570–1070 B.C.

New Kingdom
✳ Egyptian victory
✸ Egyptian defeat
See map A for complete legend.

ENVIRONMENT
Flooding of the Nile

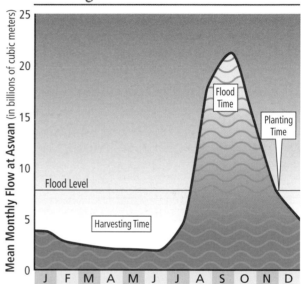

Mean Monthly Flow at Aswan (in billions of cubic meters)

25

20

15

10

5

0

Flood Level

Flood Time

Planting Time

Harvesting Time

J F M A M J J A S O N D

D The Nile flooded around the same time every year, depositing rich soil for farming. The data for this graph is from a more recent time. Exact water levels may have been different in ancient Egypt.

E Most Egyptians lived in the Nile River Valley. This husband and wife are plowing fields, preparing the soil for planting. Look at graph D. In which months would they be plowing?

Ancient Egypt and Kush

At the end of the New Kingdom, nobles and priests began to compete for power. The Egyptian empire weakened and began to lose territory.

- Egypt was invaded by neighboring Libyans. The Libyans were among the first foreigners to rule Egypt.

- As Egypt fell under foreign rule, the kingdom of Kush formed its own civilization based on Egyptian and local cultures.

- Kush ruled Egypt for almost 100 years. Later it defended itself from the foreign rulers of Egypt.

- Kush and later kingdoms remained centers of trade between southern Africa and the Mediterranean region.

A

Kush invaded Egypt from the south and gradually conquered Egyptian territory to the Mediterranean Sea. Kushites ruled Egypt until they were defeated by Assyrians.

B

Compare the amount of time that Egyptians ruled Egypt with the amount of time that foreign powers ruled. Which foreign power ruled Egypt the longest?

more at NWHatlas.com

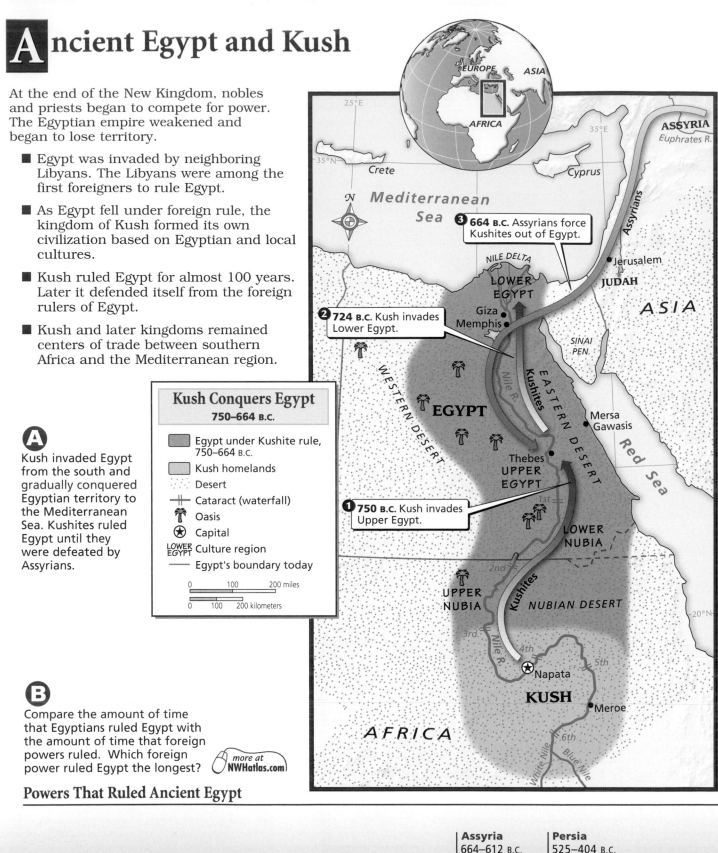

3 664 B.C. Assyrians force Kushites out of Egypt.

2 724 B.C. Kush invades Lower Egypt.

1 750 B.C. Kush invades Upper Egypt.

Kush Conquers Egypt
750–664 B.C.

- Egypt under Kushite rule, 750–664 B.C.
- Kush homelands
- Desert
- Cataract (waterfall)
- Oasis
- Capital
- LOWER EGYPT Culture region
- Egypt's boundary today

0   100   200 miles
0   100   200 kilometers

Powers That Ruled Ancient Egypt

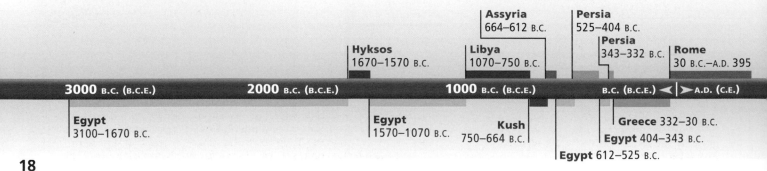

| | | | | | Assyria 664–612 B.C. | | Persia 525–404 B.C. | | |
| Hyksos 1670–1570 B.C. | | Libya 1070–750 B.C. | | | Persia 343–332 B.C. | Rome 30 B.C.–A.D. 395 |

| 3000 B.C. (B.C.E.) | 2000 B.C. (B.C.E.) | 1000 B.C. (B.C.E.) | B.C. (B.C.E.) ◄ | ► A.D. (C.E.) |

Egypt 3100–1670 B.C.

Egypt 1570–1070 B.C.

Kush 750–664 B.C.

Greece 332–30 B.C.

Egypt 404–343 B.C.

Egypt 612–525 B.C.

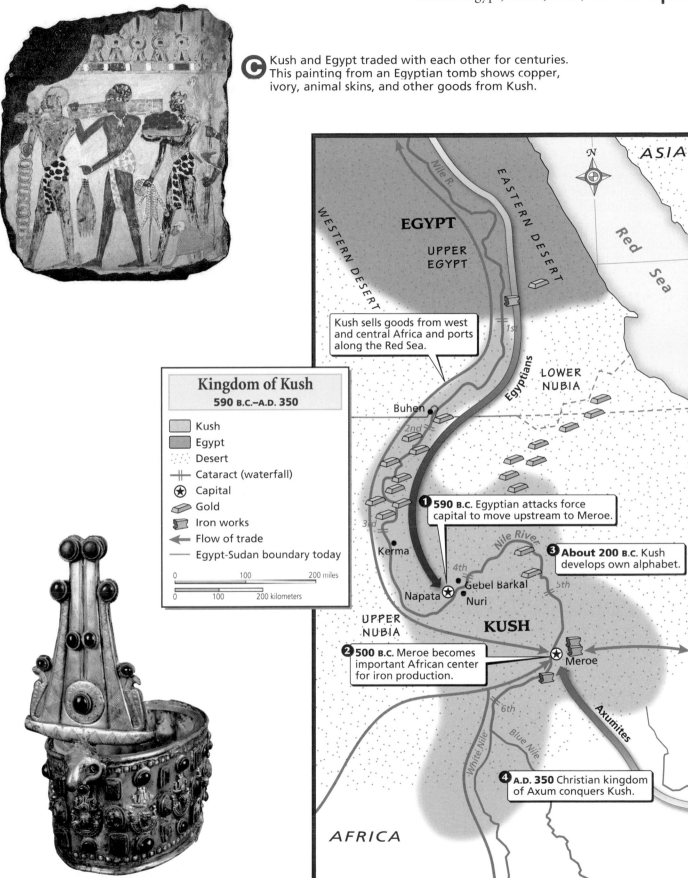

C Kush and Egypt traded with each other for centuries. This painting from an Egyptian tomb shows copper, ivory, animal skins, and other goods from Kush.

Kingdom of Kush
590 B.C.–A.D. 350

- Kush
- Egypt
- Desert
- Cataract (waterfall)
- ★ Capital
- Gold
- Iron works
- ← Flow of trade
- Egypt-Sudan boundary today

0   100   200 miles
0   100   200 kilometers

Kush sells goods from west and central Africa and ports along the Red Sea.

❶ 590 B.C. Egyptian attacks force capital to move upstream to Meroe.

❸ About 200 B.C. Kush develops own alphabet.

❷ 500 B.C. Meroe becomes important African center for iron production.

❹ A.D. 350 Christian kingdom of Axum conquers Kush.

EGYPT
UPPER EGYPT
ASIA
Red Sea
EASTERN DESERT
WESTERN DESERT
Nile R.
1st
Egyptians
LOWER NUBIA
Buhen
2nd
3rd
Kerma
4th
Napata
Gebel Barkal
Nuri
5th
UPPER NUBIA
KUSH
Nile River
Meroe
Axumites
6th
White Nile
Blue Nile
AFRICA

D Kush took Egyptian culture and adapted it. For example, this Kush crown has cobras, similar to those on an Egyptian pharoah's crown. Where are the cobras?

E After withdrawing from Egypt, Kush moved its capital farther south to Meroe. They controlled trade along the Nile and became the main source of iron for much of eastern Africa.

Civilization in Ancient China

China has one of the oldest continuous civilizations in the world. Chinese civilization developed from two early cultures living in two river valleys.

- The earliest Chinese culture was the Yangshao. It developed 7,000 years ago in the Huang He Valley, in what is now northern China.

- The Longshan culture developed about 2,000 years later and eventually replaced the Yangshao.

- China's first dynasty or family of rulers emerged from the Longshan culture. It is known as the Shang dynasty.

- The Shang dynasty ruled a portion of what is now China for more than 600 years.

A Rice was first grown in the Yangtze Valley around 5000 B.C. It became the main crop of southern China.

B

The development and spread of early farming cultures advanced Chinese civilization. Compare what was grown in northern China with what was grown farther south.

Early Chinese Civilizations
5000–1700 B.C.

- Yangshao, 5000–3000 B.C.
- Longshan, 3000–1700 B.C.
- ○ Farming settlement
- Millet
- Rice
- Spread of rice farming
- Thais Culture group
- Desert
- China's boundary today

0   200   400   600 miles
0   200   400   600 kilometers

1 **5800 B.C.** Farming begins in China.

2 Yangshao culture grows millet and raises pigs.

3 **3000 B.C.** Rice farming spreads to Huang He Valley.

4 Longshan culture grows rice, raises cattle, and carves jade.

ASIA
AUSTRALIA

Xiongnu

GOBI

TAKLIMAKAN DESERT

Huang He

CHINA

Tibetans

Cishan

YANGSHAO
Banpo

Peiligang

Daxi

LONGSHAN

Yangtze R.

HIMALAYAS

INDIA

Bay of Bengal

Thais

Hainan

Koreans

Yellow Sea

coastline today

coastline today

Hemudu

East China Sea

Taiwan

South China Sea

30°N

15°N

90°E

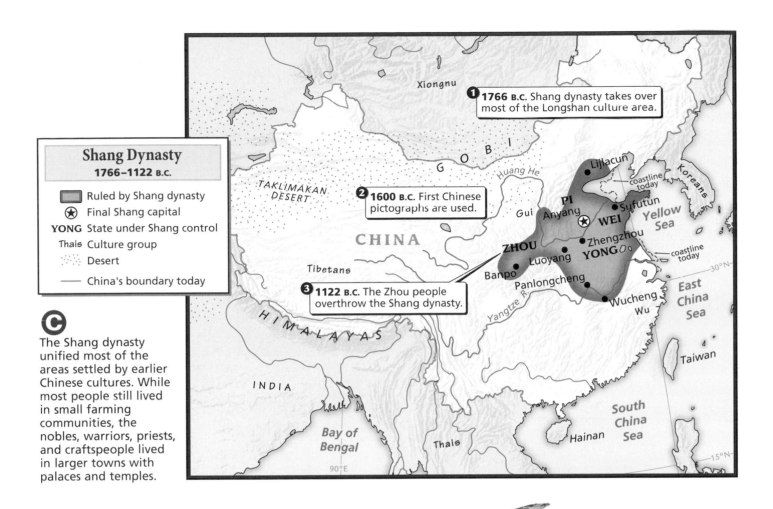

Shang Dynasty
1766–1122 B.C.

▨	Ruled by Shang dynasty
★	Final Shang capital
YONG	State under Shang control
Thais	Culture group
∷	Desert
—	China's boundary today

❶ 1766 B.C. Shang dynasty takes over most of the Longshan culture area.

❷ 1600 B.C. First Chinese pictographs are used.

❸ 1122 B.C. The Zhou people overthrow the Shang dynasty.

C The Shang dynasty unified most of the areas settled by earlier Chinese cultures. While most people still lived in small farming communities, the nobles, warriors, priests, and craftspeople lived in larger towns with palaces and temples.

WRITING & LANGUAGE
Development of Chinese Characters
1600 B.C.–Today

Object	Pictograph 1600 B.C.	Ancient Character 200 B.C.	Present Character A.D. 200
Ear	𠂆	耳	耳
Moon	D	𠩵	月
Rain	⻖	雨	雨

D Writing developed during the Shang dynasty. Chinese characters represented ideas, not sounds. Everyone used the same characters so people could communicate through writing even if they spoke different languages.

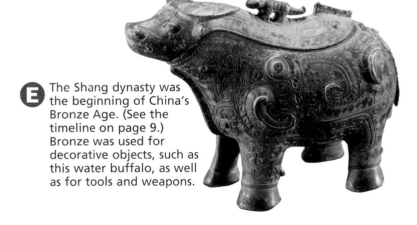

E The Shang dynasty was the beginning of China's Bronze Age. (See the timeline on page 9.) Bronze was used for decorative objects, such as this water buffalo, as well as for tools and weapons.

Can we keep it in the family?
When the rule of a kingdom or an empire is passed down from one family member to another, usually from a father to a son, it is sometimes called a **dynasty**. Ancient China was ruled by a series of dynasties, as was ancient Egypt.

21

Dynasties of Ancient China

After the Shang dynasty was overthrown, three other dynasties helped expand, unify, and develop ancient China.

- The Zhou dynasty ruled for 900 years. However, the Zhou had difficulty controlling their territory.

- The Qin established China's first unified empire. The name **China** comes from **Qin**, which is also spelled **Chin**.

- The Qin were overthrown, and the Han dynasty rose to power. The first Han emperor reduced taxes and changed harsh laws.

What did Confucius say?

The Chinese philosopher Confucius (born around 551 B.C.) developed a guide to living a moral life. His teachings apply to everyday life, as well as to political rule. They became the ruling philosophy of China.

more at
NWHatlas.com

B The Qin dynasty began the Great Wall of China to keep out barbarian invaders. Later dynasties added to the wall. This section was built during the Ming dynasty (see page 53). The Great Wall is more than 4,000 miles long.

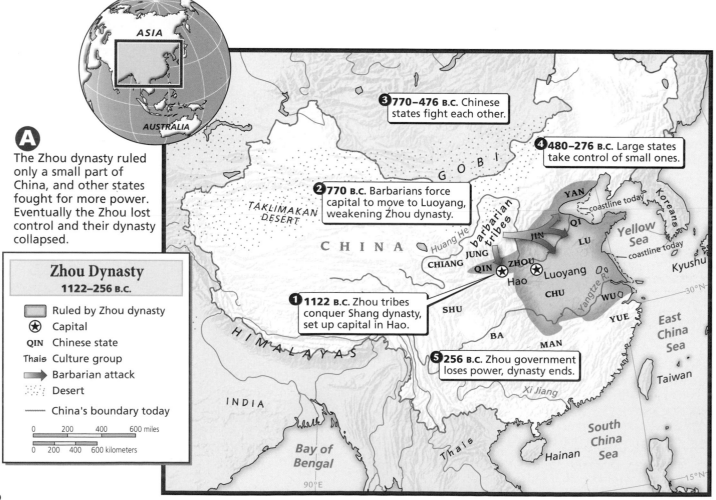

A The Zhou dynasty ruled only a small part of China, and other states fought for more power. Eventually the Zhou lost control and their dynasty collapsed.

3 770–476 B.C. Chinese states fight each other.

4 480–276 B.C. Large states take control of small ones.

2 770 B.C. Barbarians force capital to move to Luoyang, weakening Zhou dynasty.

1 1122 B.C. Zhou tribes conquer Shang dynasty, set up capital in Hao.

5 256 B.C. Zhou government loses power, dynasty ends.

Zhou Dynasty
1122–256 B.C.

- Ruled by Zhou dynasty
- ⊛ Capital
- QIN Chinese state
- Thais Culture group
- ➡ Barbarian attack
- ⋯ Desert
- —— China's boundary today

0   200   400   600 miles
0   200   400   600 kilometers

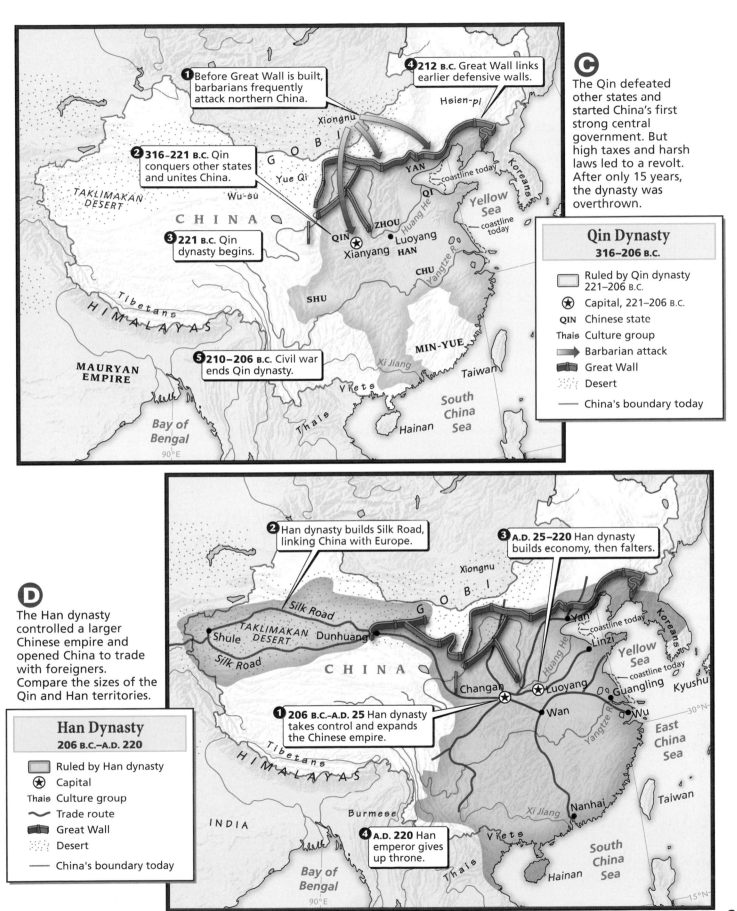

C The Qin defeated other states and started China's first strong central government. But high taxes and harsh laws led to a revolt. After only 15 years, the dynasty was overthrown.

1 Before Great Wall is built, barbarians frequently attack northern China.

4 212 B.C. Great Wall links earlier defensive walls.

2 316–221 B.C. Qin conquers other states and unites China.

3 221 B.C. Qin dynasty begins.

5 210–206 B.C. Civil war ends Qin dynasty.

Qin Dynasty
316–206 B.C.

- Ruled by Qin dynasty 221–206 B.C.
- ⊛ Capital, 221–206 B.C.
- QIN Chinese state
- Thais Culture group
- Barbarian attack
- Great Wall
- Desert
- China's boundary today

D The Han dynasty controlled a larger Chinese empire and opened China to trade with foreigners. Compare the sizes of the Qin and Han territories.

2 Han dynasty builds Silk Road, linking China with Europe.

3 A.D. 25–220 Han dynasty builds economy, then falters.

1 206 B.C.–A.D. 25 Han dynasty takes control and expands the Chinese empire.

4 A.D. 220 Han emperor gives up throne.

Han Dynasty
206 B.C.–A.D. 220

- Ruled by Han dynasty
- ⊛ Capital
- Thais Culture group
- Trade route
- Great Wall
- Desert
- China's boundary today

23

Ancient India and the Spread of Hinduism

One of the first civilizations and one of the world's oldest religions developed in ancient India.

- People began to settle in the Indus River Valley in south Asia about 6,000 years ago. Farming and herding communities developed.

- An advanced civilization with carefully planned cities developed in the valley. The Indus Valley Civilization thrived for 900 years.

- A large group of nomads, the Aryans, migrated to India. Their religious beliefs helped form a new religion called **Hinduism**.

What do Hindus believe?

Hindus believe that all living things have many lives. If you do good things in this life, you will come back as someone wiser and better in your next life. If you do bad things in this life, you could come back as a rat or even a gnat!

more at NWHatlas.com

How Big Is The Indian Subcontinent?

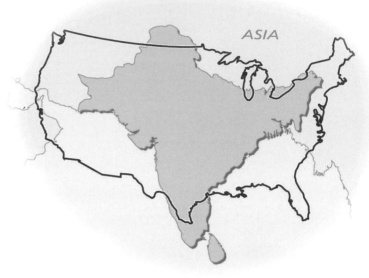

A India is part of a subcontinent that includes the modern countries of India, Pakistan, Bangladesh, Nepal, Sri Lanka, and Bhutan. (See their boundaries on page 127.) Compare it to the size of the United States.

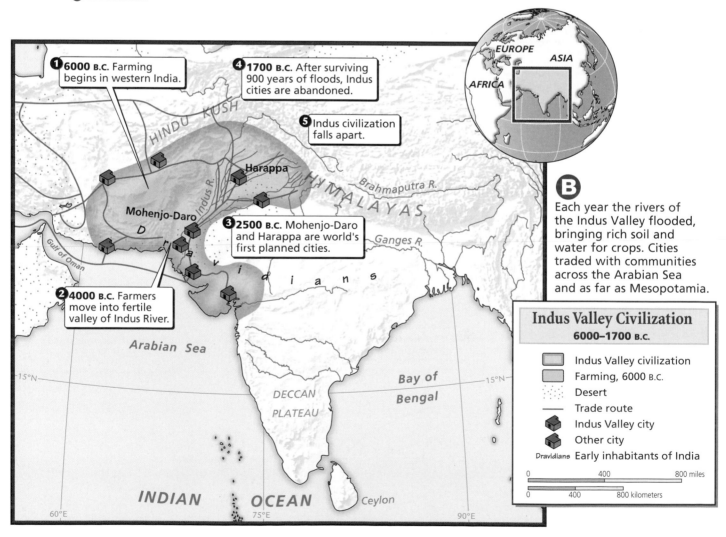

❶ 6000 B.C. Farming begins in western India.

❹ 1700 B.C. After surviving 900 years of floods, Indus cities are abandoned.

❺ Indus civilization falls apart.

❸ 2500 B.C. Mohenjo-Daro and Harappa are world's first planned cities.

❷ 4000 B.C. Farmers move into fertile valley of Indus River.

Harappa

Mohenjo-Daro

HINDU KUSH

HIMALAYAS

Brahmaputra R.

Indus R.

Ganges R.

Gulf of Oman

D r a v i d i a n s

Arabian Sea

DECCAN PLATEAU

Bay of Bengal

INDIAN OCEAN

Ceylon

15°N

60°E   75°E   90°E

B Each year the rivers of the Indus Valley flooded, bringing rich soil and water for crops. Cities traded with communities across the Arabian Sea and as far as Mesopotamia.

Indus Valley Civilization
6000–1700 B.C.

	Indus Valley civilization
	Farming, 6000 B.C.
	Desert
—	Trade route
	Indus Valley city
	Other city
Dravidians	Early inhabitants of India

0   400   800 miles

0   400   800 kilometers

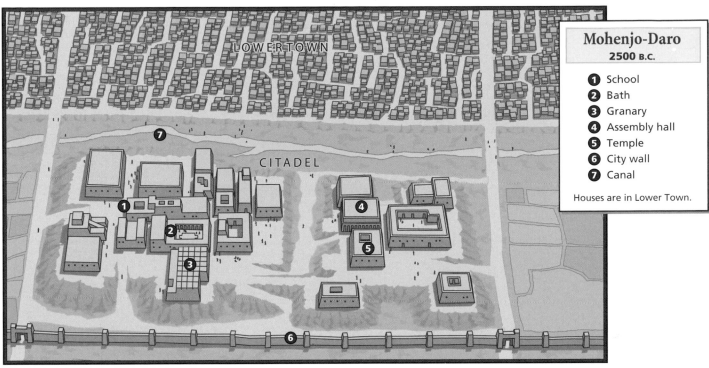

Mohenjo-Daro
2500 B.C.

1 School
2 Bath
3 Granary
4 Assembly hall
5 Temple
6 City wall
7 Canal

Houses are in Lower Town.

C Mohenjo-Daro had straight streets and large public buildings and meeting places. Its two-story houses were built of baked bricks, and many included rooms for bathing.

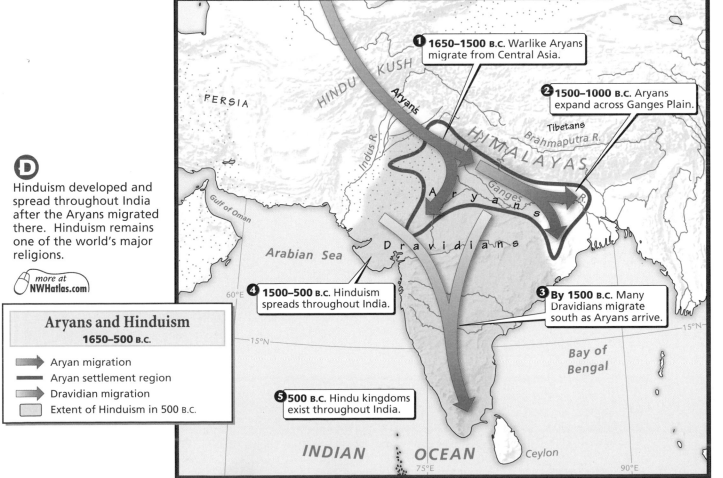

D Hinduism developed and spread throughout India after the Aryans migrated there. Hinduism remains one of the world's major religions.

more at NWHatlas.com

Aryans and Hinduism
1650–500 B.C.

➡ Aryan migration
— Aryan settlement region
➡ Dravidian migration
▢ Extent of Hinduism in 500 B.C.

1 **1650–1500 B.C.** Warlike Aryans migrate from Central Asia.

2 **1500–1000 B.C.** Aryans expand across Ganges Plain.

3 **By 1500 B.C.** Many Dravidians migrate south as Aryans arrive.

4 **1500–500 B.C.** Hinduism spreads throughout India.

5 **500 B.C.** Hindu kingdoms exist throughout India.

Ancient India and the Spread of Buddhism

In addition to Hinduism, another major world religion developed in ancient India—**Buddhism**.

- Buddhism was based on the teachings of Siddhartha Gautama. He preached a new way of life to end suffering.

- The Mauryas united India and created the first Indian empire. During their reign, Buddhism spread throughout India.

- Later the Gupta Empire emerged. They started a golden age in India when culture and science thrived.

What's nirvana?

Imagine having great wisdom and compassion and being free from suffering. This state of peacefulness is called **nirvana**. Reaching nirvana is the goal of Buddhism.

more at
NWHatlas.com

A The name **Buddha** means "the Enlightened One." Siddhartha Gautama was called Buddha because of his wise teachings on how to live a good life.

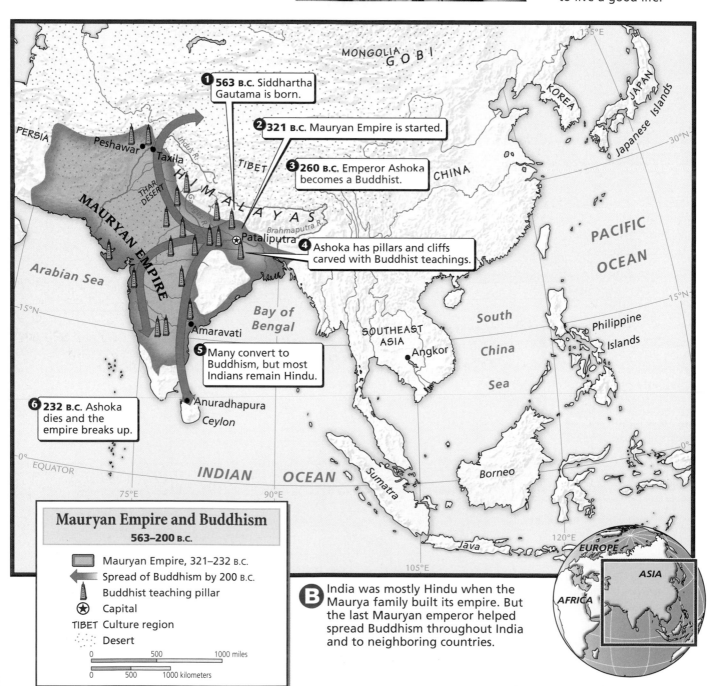

1 **563 B.C.** Siddhartha Gautama is born.

2 **321 B.C.** Mauryan Empire is started.

3 **260 B.C.** Emperor Ashoka becomes a Buddhist.

4 Ashoka has pillars and cliffs carved with Buddhist teachings.

5 Many convert to Buddhism, but most Indians remain Hindu.

6 **232 B.C.** Ashoka dies and the empire breaks up.

Mauryan Empire and Buddhism
563–200 B.C.

- Mauryan Empire, 321–232 B.C.
- ← Spread of Buddhism by 200 B.C.
- Buddhist teaching pillar
- ⊛ Capital
- TIBET Culture region
- Desert

0   500   1000 miles
0   500   1000 kilometers

B India was mostly Hindu when the Maurya family built its empire. But the last Mauryan emperor helped spread Buddhism throughout India and to neighboring countries.

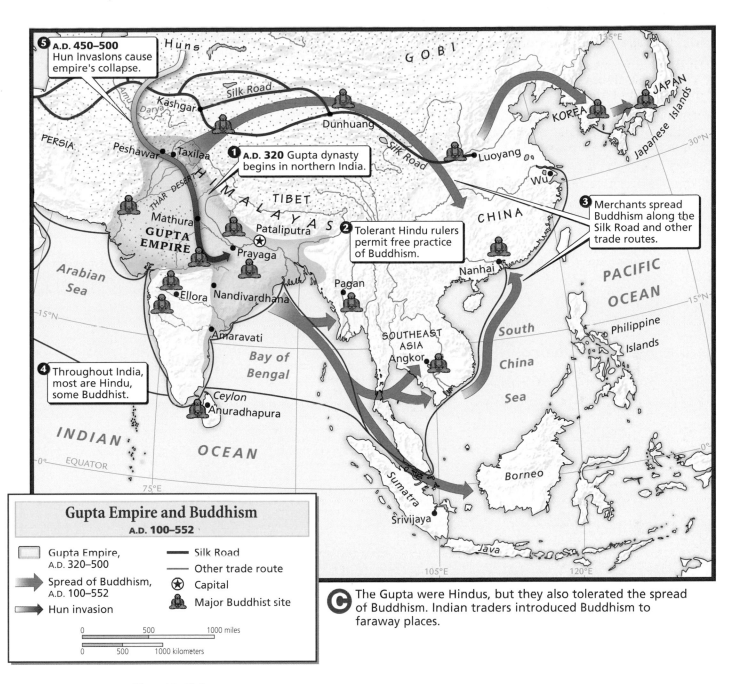

5 A.D. 450–500 Hun Invasions cause empire's collapse.

1 A.D. 320 Gupta dynasty begins in northern India.

2 Tolerant Hindu rulers permit free practice of Buddhism.

3 Merchants spread Buddhism along the Silk Road and other trade routes.

4 Throughout India, most are Hindu, some Buddhist.

Gupta Empire and Buddhism
A.D. 100–552

Gupta Empire, A.D. 320–500

Spread of Buddhism, A.D. 100–552

Hun invasion

Silk Road

Other trade route

★ Capital

Major Buddhist site

0   500   1000 miles
0   500   1000 kilometers

C The Gupta were Hindus, but they also tolerated the spread of Buddhism. Indian traders introduced Buddhism to faraway places.

Top 10 Cities, A.D.100

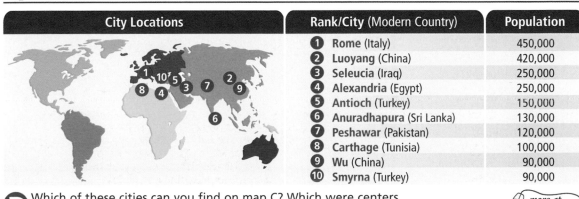

City Locations	Rank/City (Modern Country)	Population
	1 Rome (Italy)	450,000
	2 Luoyang (China)	420,000
	3 Seleucia (Iraq)	250,000
	4 Alexandria (Egypt)	250,000
	5 Antioch (Turkey)	150,000
	6 Anuradhapura (Sri Lanka)	130,000
	7 Peshawar (Pakistan)	120,000
	8 Carthage (Tunisia)	100,000
	9 Wu (China)	90,000
	10 Smyrna (Turkey)	90,000

D Which of these cities can you find on map C? Which were centers of Buddhism?

more at NWHatlas.com

Civilization in Ancient Mexico

The Olmec and the Maya were the earliest major Native American civilizations. Both developed in Middle America.

- The Olmec civilization developed along the coast of the Gulf of Mexico.

- The Olmec built large sculptures and were the first people in the Americas to build pyramids. Their art and religion influenced later cultures of Middle America, including the Maya.

- The Maya civilization developed east of the Olmec. It was one of the longest lasting civilizations in the Americas.

- The Maya used pictographs to record major events in their history on large stone sculptures. Many of these sculptures still stand today.

A Giant carvings like this one were used in ceremonies at Olmec religious centers. The largest heads were up to 10 feet tall and weighed several tons.

Why the difference?

Asians, Africans, and Europeans learned from one another. Without this contact, Native American civilizations never developed bronze or iron. They also never domesticated animals larger than dogs, except in Peru.

more at NWHatlas.com

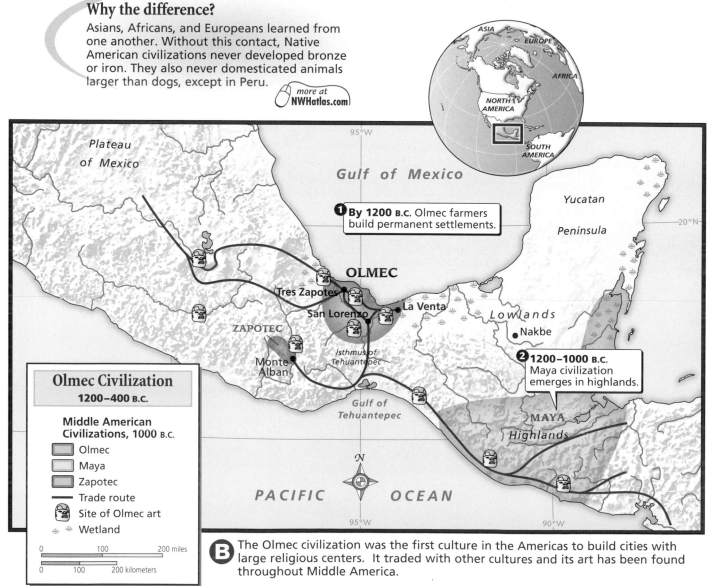

1 By **1200 B.C.** Olmec farmers build permanent settlements.

2 1200–1000 B.C. Maya civilization emerges in highlands.

OLMEC
Tres Zapotes
San Lorenzo
La Venta
ZAPOTEC
Monte Alban
Isthmus of Tehuantepec
Nakbe
Gulf of Tehuantepec
MAYA
Highlands
Lowlands
Yucatan Peninsula
Plateau of Mexico
Gulf of Mexico
PACIFIC OCEAN

Olmec Civilization
1200–400 B.C.

Middle American Civilizations, 1000 B.C.

- Olmec
- Maya
- Zapotec
- —— Trade route
- Site of Olmec art
- Wetland

0   100   200 miles
0   100   200 kilometers

B The Olmec civilization was the first culture in the Americas to build cities with large religious centers. It traded with other cultures and its art has been found throughout Middle America.

SCIENCE & TECHNOLOGY
Maya Contributions

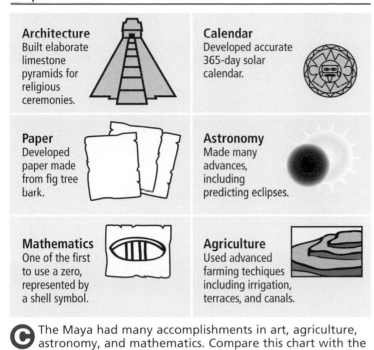

Architecture
Built elaborate limestone pyramids for religious ceremonies.

Calendar
Developed accurate 365-day solar calendar.

Paper
Developed paper made from fig tree bark.

Astronomy
Made many advances, including predicting eclipses.

Mathematics
One of the first to use a zero, represented by a shell symbol.

Agriculture
Used advanced farming techiques including irrigation, terraces, and canals.

C The Maya had many accomplishments in art, agriculture, astronomy, and mathematics. Compare this chart with the one for Babylon on page 13.

D Large limestone pyramids with temples at the top were built by the Maya for religious ceremonies. This pyramid is located in the Maya city of Tikal. Find Tikal on map E.

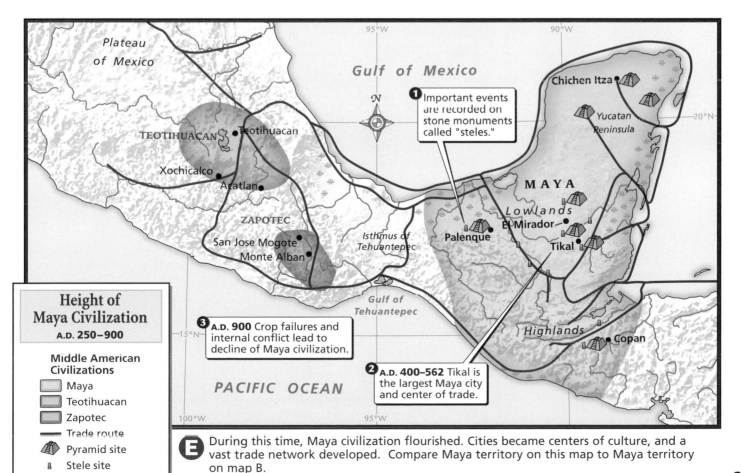

Height of Maya Civilization
A.D. 250–900

Middle American Civilizations
- Maya
- Teotihuacan
- Zapotec
- Trade route
- Pyramid site
- Stele site

1 Important events are recorded on stone monuments called "steles."

3 A.D. 900 Crop failures and internal conflict lead to decline of Maya civilization.

2 A.D. 400–562 Tikal is the largest Maya city and center of trade.

E During this time, Maya civilization flourished. Cities became centers of culture, and a vast trade network developed. Compare Maya territory on this map to Maya territory on map B.

1200–800 B.C.
Early Greek civilizations are destroyed.

3000 B.C. (B.C.E.)	**1500 B.C. (B.C.E.)**	**1000 B.C. (B.C.E.)**

3000 B.C.
Minoan civilization emerges in Crete.

1600 B.C.
Mycenaean civilization develops in Greece.

750–550 B.C.
Greek colonies founded around the Mediterranean Sea.

Civilizations of Ancient Greece

The Minoans and the Mycenaeans developed civilizations in the region of present-day Greece. Their achievements became the foundation of Greek culture.

- The Minoans were known as great artisans. Legends of their cleverness became part of Greek myths.

- The Mycenaeans were fierce warriors. Through conquest, they spread their culture around the Aegean Sea.

- Both civilizations produced expert sailors. Around 1200 B.C., they were destroyed by invasion.

- Greek city-states recovered before 750 B.C. As the city-states grew, they established new colonies along the sea coasts.

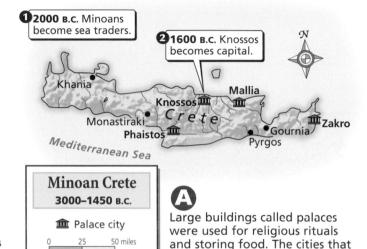

1 **2000 B.C.** Minoans become sea traders.

2 **1600 B.C.** Knossos becomes capital.

Khania

Knossos

Mallia

Crete

Monastiraki

Phaistos

Gournia · Zakro

Pyrgos

Mediterranean Sea

Minoan Crete
3000–1450 B.C.

🏛 Palace city

0   25   50 miles

0   25   50 kilometers

A Large buildings called palaces were used for religious rituals and storing food. The cities that developed around these places were known as palace cities.

EUROPE   ASIA

AFRICA

15°E   30°E

Adriatic Sea

BALKAN PENINSULA

Black Sea

2 **1250 B.C.** Trojan War (according to legend)

ITALY

PINDUS MTS.

GREECE

Aegean Sea

Troy

3 **1200 B.C.** Invading Sea Peoples destroy palaces.

Tyrrhenian Sea

Thebes

Mycenae   Athens

ANATOLIA

· Miletus

4 **about 1200 B.C.** Mycenaean civilization collapses.

Mediterranean Sea

Rhodes

35°N

Knossos

Crete

1 **1450 B.C.** Mycenaeans conquer Minoans.

20°E   25°E   30°E

35°N

Mycenaean Greece
2000–1200 B.C.

▨ Mycenaean civilization
— Minoan civilization until 1450 B.C.
⇨ Mycenaean migration, 2000 B.C.
⇨ Mycenaean conquest, 1450 B.C.
⇨ Sea Peoples invasion, 1200 B.C.
⊛ Capital
🏛 Palace city
GREECE Culture region

0   100   200 miles

0   100   200 kilometers

B The Myceneans took control of the region and conquered Minoan Crete. Afterwards they were shaped by the Minoan culture.

more at NWHatlas.com

431 B.C. Athens and Sparta go to war.	399 B.C. Socrates is executed. 336–323 B.C. Alexander the Great conquers the Persian Empire.	27 B.C. Rome becomes an empire.	A.D. 305 Constantine becomes emperor.	A.D. 476 Western Roman Empire falls.

500 B.C. (B.C.E.) B.C. (B.C.E) ◄ | ► A.D. (C.E.) **A.D. (C.E.) 500**

509–508 B.C. Rome becomes a republic. Democracy begins in Athens.	146 B.C. Romans conquer Greeks.	A.D. 392 Christianity becomes the official religion of the Roman Empire.

C The Mycenaeans were known for their elaborate bronze and gold work. Great wealth and labor was spent on royal graves filled with treasures such as this gold mask.

What is a colony?

Greek "mother-cities" founded new cities, or colonies, throughout the Mediterranean region. Most colonies were independent city-states, while others were only trading posts.

2 Saguntum becomes the westernmost Greek colony.

1 750 B.C. Greeks from ten city-states begin forming colonies to increase farmland and expand trade.

Greece and Its Colonies
750–550 B.C.

- Greece, 750 B.C.
- Greek colonial area, 550 B.C.
- ● City-state with colonies
- ○ Other city-state
- Phoenician lands, 750 B.C.
- — Trade route
- GREECE Culture region

0 — 250 — 500 miles
0 — 250 — 500 kilometers

D The Greeks and the Phoenicians were trading partners and rivals. Compare this map with the map on page 15. Which areas did both Greeks and Phoenicians settle?

more at NWHatlas.com

31

Growth of Greek City-States

Ancient Greece was a culture region, not a country. It was made up of independent city-states.

- Although Greek city-states shared the same language and religion, they had different forms of government.

- The Persian Empire threatened to conquer Greece. The most powerful Greek city-states united to overcome Persian forces.

- The city-state of Athens was the birthplace of democracy and a leading cultural center of the Greek world. Its ideas influenced later civilizations.

- Wars between the two most powerful city-states, Athens and Sparta nearly destroyed Greece.

SOCIAL STRUCTURE
Athens 510–338 B.C.

Citizens
- Have two Athenian parents.
- Can own land, if men.
- Serve in the Assembly, hold offices, and vote, if men.
- Work as land-owning aristocrats, farmers, craftsmen, merchants, and rowers.

Metics
- Have at least one non-Athenian or foreign parent.
- Cannot own land or vote.
- Work as business owners and merchants.

Slaves
- Are prisoners of war or foreign captives.
- Cannot own land or vote.
- Work as house servants, miners, and policemen.

A In Athens, a man's place in society was based on his parents. All women in Athens were considered the property of their fathers, husbands, or owners. Athenian women were rarely seen outside the home.

B After Athens and Eretria helped the Ionian revolts, Persia invaded European Greece twice. Athens and Sparta organized the city-states to resist the invasions. Incredibly the Greeks defeated the Persian Empire.

The Persian War
499–449 B.C.

- Persian Empire
- ◉ Greek city against Persia
- ○ Neutral Greek city
- → Persian campaigns
- ✸ Greek victory
- ✸ Persian victory
- IONIA Culture region

0   100   200 miles
0   100   200 kilometers

2 **492 B.C.** Macedonia submits to Persian control.

3 **490 B.C.** Persians destroy Eretria but lose to Athenians.

4 **480 B.C.** A small Spartan army delays Persian invasion.

1 **499–493 B.C.** Greek cities in Ionia unsuccessfully rebel against Persia.

6 **480–449 B.C.** Fighting continues for the next 30 years.

5 **480 B.C.** Athenians lead a Greek navy that destroys Persian fleet.

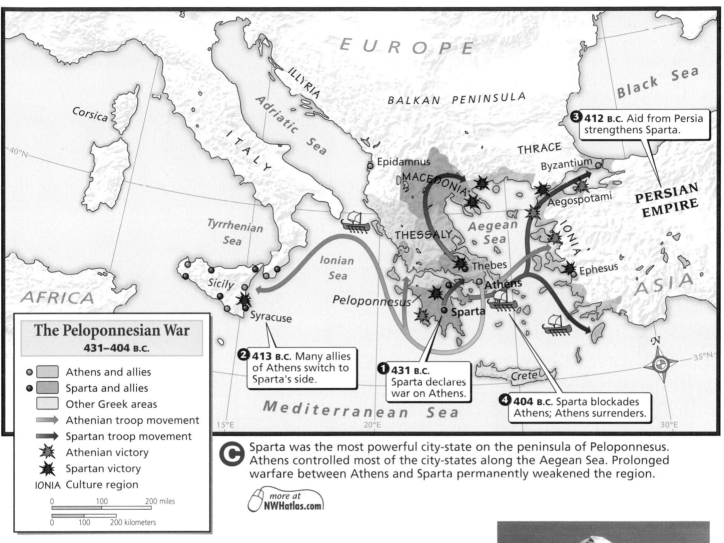

The Peloponnesian War
431–404 B.C.

- ○ ▨ Athens and allies
- ● ▨ Sparta and allies
- ▢ Other Greek areas
- → Athenian troop movement
- → Spartan troop movement
- ✹ Athenian victory
- ✸ Spartan victory
- IONIA Culture region

```
0        100        200 miles
0    100    200 kilometers
```

❸ **412 B.C.** Aid from Persia strengthens Sparta.

❷ **413 B.C.** Many allies of Athens switch to Sparta's side.

❶ **431 B.C.** Sparta declares war on Athens.

❹ **404 B.C.** Sparta blockades Athens; Athens surrenders.

C Sparta was the most powerful city-state on the peninsula of Peloponnesus. Athens controlled most of the city-states along the Aegean Sea. Prolonged warfare between Athens and Sparta permanently weakened the region.

more at NWHatlas.com

GOVERNMENT
Democracy in Athens

more at NWHatlas.com

Assembly

Members: All citizens over age 20

Role: Made decisions and passed laws by majority vote.

Council of 500

Members: 500 randomly chosen citizens over age 30

Role: Proposed laws and carried out decisions made by the Assembly.

Court

Members: 6,000 randomly chosen citizens assigned to specific panels

Role: Decided on cases by majority vote. A tie vote acquitted. Verdicts could not be appealed.

Generals

Members: Ten elected citizens (the only elected office)

Role: Commanded armies and navies. Decisions made by a majority.

E Socrates of Athens encouraged his students to question everything to find truth and live by that truth. This **Socratic method** would become the basis of all later Greek philosophy.

more at NWHatlas.com

D The Athenian government was a direct democracy. Any male citizen could personally serve in the government, rather than through representatives.

The Conquests of Alexander the Great

Alexander the Great, king of ancient Macedonia, built an empire that stretched from Greece to India.

- Years of fighting had weakened the Greek city-states. Macedonia, a kingdom in northern Greece, conquered the entire region.

- Then Alexander turned to the east and conquered the Persian Empire.

- When Alexander died, his generals divided his empire into separate kingdoms.

- Alexander's conquests led to the mixing of Greek culture with the cultures of conquered lands.

A Alexander's conquests spread Greek society across western Asia. This Greek-style relief of him was found in Sidon, a major Phoenician city in Lebanon.

How Big Was Alexander's Empire?

more at NWHatlas.com

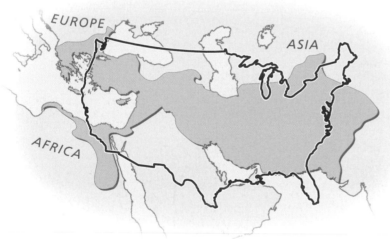

B Alexander's vast empire included land on Europe, Africa, and Asia. Compare it to the size of the United States.

How do you show your culture?

Culture is what makes a group of people unique, or different from other groups. The religion we follow, the language we speak, even what we eat or drink, can all be part of our culture.

1 **336** B.C. Alexander becomes ruler of Greece.

EUROPE

ASIA

AFRICA

MACEDONIA
Pella ★ THRACE
GREECE
334 B.C. Granicus

334– 333 B.C.

Mediterranean Sea

CYRENAICA
Alexandria
333– 332 B.C.

EGYPT

SAHARA

Nile R.

Alexander Conquers Persia
336–323 B.C.

- Alexander's Empire, 323 B.C.
- ➔ Route of conquest
- Persian road
- ✴ Major battle
- ★ Capital
- PERSIA Culture region
- ⋰ Desert area

0   300   600 miles

0   300   600 kilometers

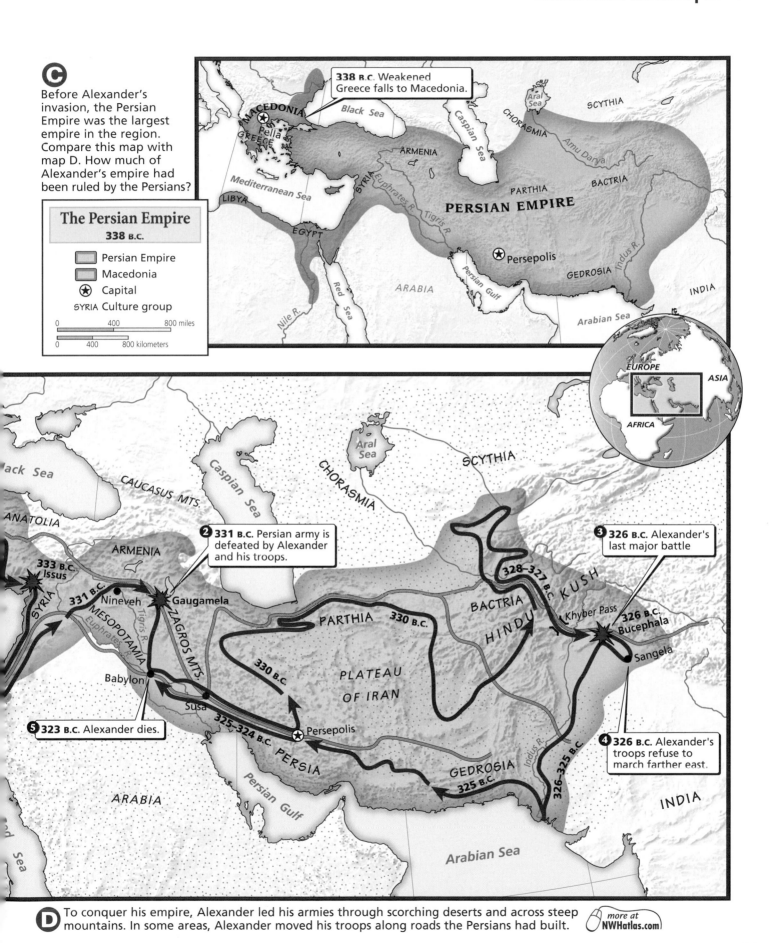

C Before Alexander's invasion, the Persian Empire was the largest empire in the region. Compare this map with map D. How much of Alexander's empire had been ruled by the Persians?

The Persian Empire
338 B.C.

- Persian Empire
- Macedonia
- ⊛ Capital
- SYRIA Culture group

0   400   800 miles
0   400   800 kilometers

338 B.C. Weakened Greece falls to Macedonia.

MACEDONIA
Pella
GREECE
Black Sea
SCYTHIA
Aral Sea
CHORASMIA
Caspian Sea
ARMENIA
Amu Darya
PARTHIA
BACTRIA
Mediterranean Sea
SYRIA
Euphrates R.
Tigris R.
PERSIAN EMPIRE
LIBYA
EGYPT
Nile R.
Red Sea
ARABIA
Persian Gulf
⊛ Persepolis
Indus R.
GEDROSIA
INDIA
Arabian Sea

EUROPE
ASIA
AFRICA

2 **331 B.C.** Persian army is defeated by Alexander and his troops.

3 **326 B.C.** Alexander's last major battle

Aral Sea
Black Sea
CAUCASUS MTS.
Caspian Sea
CHORASMIA
SCYTHIA
ANATOLIA
ARMENIA
333 B.C. Issus
SYRIA
331 B.C.
Nineveh
Gaugamela
ZAGROS MTS.
MESOPOTAMIA
Tigris R.
Euphrates R.
PARTHIA
330 B.C.
328–327 B.C.
BACTRIA
HINDU KUSH
Khyber Pass
326 B.C. Bucephala
Babylon
330 B.C.
PLATEAU OF IRAN
Sangela
Susa
5 **323 B.C.** Alexander dies.
325–324 B.C.
⊛ Persepolis
PERSIA
Indus R.
326–325 B.C.
4 **326 B.C.** Alexander's troops refuse to march farther east.
ARABIA
Persian Gulf
GEDROSIA
325 B.C.
INDIA
Arabian Sea

D To conquer his empire, Alexander led his armies through scorching deserts and across steep mountains. In some areas, Alexander moved his troops along roads the Persians had built.

more at NWHatlas.com

From Roman Republic to Roman Empire

Rome was founded as a small city-state, then became a republic, and eventually grew into a powerful empire.

- Rome became a republic in 509 B.C. The republic came to have a democratic government.

- The Roman Republic gained land through conquest. As the republic grew, so did its army.

- Civil wars destroyed the Roman Republic. The republic became an empire by 27 B.C., led by a single ruler.

- The capital of the republic and the empire was the city of Rome.

A Julius Caesar, in red, was a popular general and politician. His conquest of Gaul allowed him to overthrow the Senate and become dictator.

more at NWHatlas.com

B

The republic first expanded beyond Italy during wars with its neighboring rival, Carthage. After Carthage was defeated, the Romans conquered former allies of Carthage.

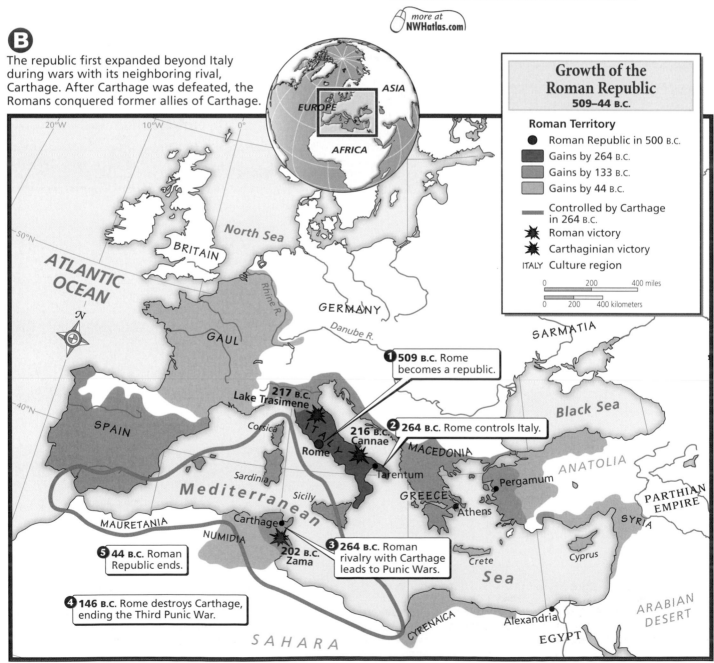

Growth of the Roman Republic
509–44 B.C.

Roman Territory
- ● Roman Republic in 500 B.C.
- Gains by 264 B.C.
- Gains by 133 B.C.
- Gains by 44 B.C.
- ▬ Controlled by Carthage in 264 B.C.
- ✸ Roman victory
- ✸ Carthaginian victory
- ITALY Culture region

0   200   400 miles
0   200   400 kilometers

❶ 509 B.C. Rome becomes a republic.

❷ 264 B.C. Rome controls Italy.

❸ 264 B.C. Roman rivalry with Carthage leads to Punic Wars.

❹ 146 B.C. Rome destroys Carthage, ending the Third Punic War.

❺ 44 B.C. Roman Republic ends.

217 B.C. Lake Trasimene

216 B.C. Cannae

202 B.C. Zama

ATLANTIC OCEAN

North Sea

BRITAIN

GERMANY

Danube R.

Rhine R.

GAUL

SPAIN

Corsica

Sardinia

ITALY
Rome

Sicily

Tarentum

MACEDONIA

GREECE
Athens

Pergamum

ANATOLIA

PARTHIAN EMPIRE

SYRIA

Cyprus

Crete

Black Sea

SARMATIA

Mediterranean Sea

MAURETANIA

NUMIDIA

Carthage

CYRENAICA

SAHARA

Alexandria

EGYPT

ARABIAN DESERT

EUROPE

ASIA

AFRICA

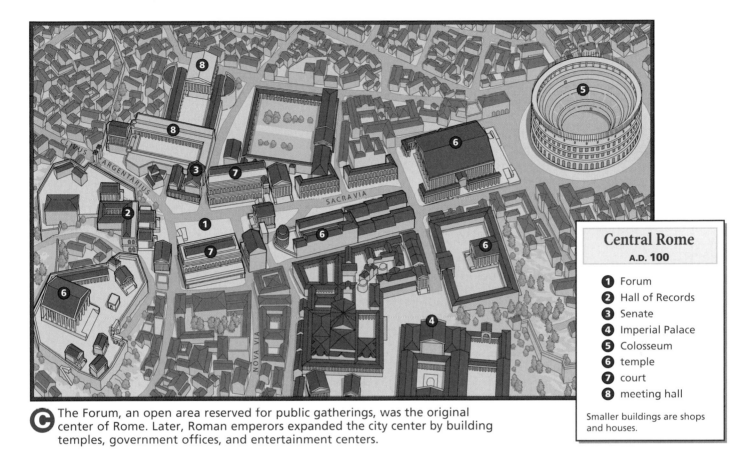

Central Rome A.D. 100	
❶	Forum
❷	Hall of Records
❸	Senate
❹	Imperial Palace
❺	Colosseum
❻	temple
❼	court
❽	meeting hall

Smaller buildings are shops and houses.

C The Forum, an open area reserved for public gatherings, was the original center of Rome. Later, Roman emperors expanded the city center by building temples, government offices, and entertainment centers.

GOVERNMENT
From Republic to Empire

Roman REPUBLIC 509–44 B.C.		Roman EMPIRE 44 B.C.–A.D. 476
Elected officials (two consuls)	Who leads?	Emperor (also later known as Caesar)
One year	How long do they rule?	For life, although many were assassinated
Appointed by Senate	How do new leaders take power?	By inheritance or by force
It was the most powerful government body	What is the role of the Senate?	It had very little real power under the emperor

D Julius Caesar's great-nephew, later called Augustus Caesar, eliminated the Senate's power by 27 B.C. As emperor, he and his successors held supreme power. However by A.D. 41 the Roman Army began overthrowing emperors.

WARFARE
Battle Casualties

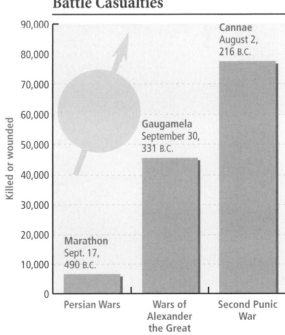

Killed or wounded

- Marathon Sept. 17, 490 B.C.
- Gaugamela September 30, 331 B.C.
- Cannae August 2, 216 B.C.

Persian Wars | Wars of Alexander the Great | Second Punic War

E Ancient armies fought using hand-to-hand combat. The Greeks and Macedonians used spears and the Romans used swords. An army would charge at the enemy trying to break its formations.

Height of the Roman Empire

After the change from republic to empire, Roman territory continued to expand. At its height, the Roman Empire ruled the entire Mediterranean region.

- Strong Roman rulers brought peace and wealth to the region during a period called "Pax Romana."

- Roman roads and sea routes connected the empire. Long distance trade thrived.

- The Roman Empire included many different cultures. Trade and a common language helped unite the empire.

A Roman coins were used throughout the empire, making trade easier. Coins also announced an emperor's achievements, similar to newspaper headlines.

B The Roman Empire was rich with important resources, such as grain and metal. As the empire grew, the variety of trade goods increased.

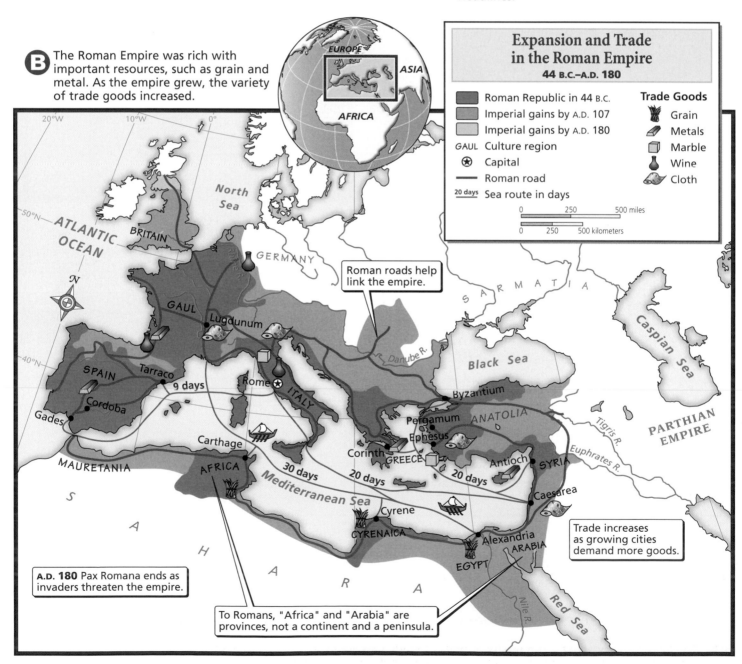

Expansion and Trade in the Roman Empire
44 B.C.–A.D. 180

- Roman Republic in 44 B.C.
- Imperial gains by A.D. 107
- Imperial gains by A.D. 180
- GAUL Culture region
- ✪ Capital
- — Roman road
- 20 days Sea route in days

Trade Goods
- Grain
- Metals
- Marble
- Wine
- Cloth

Roman roads help link the empire.

Trade increases as growing cities demand more goods.

A.D. 180 Pax Romana ends as invaders threaten the empire.

To Romans, "Africa" and "Arabia" are provinces, not a continent and a peninsula.

38

SCIENCE & TECHNOLOGY
Contributions of Rome

Sanitation
- Built aqueducts, large structures to carry water.
- Built public baths and sewer systems.

Architecture
- Designed large, stone domes.
- Created large, indoor spaces in palaces, temples, and public baths.

Construction
- Built large outdoor stadiums capable of elaborate shows.
- Organized entrances and seating for efficient crowd movement.

Transportation
- Built a system of straight, paved roads over 50,000 miles long.
- Designed roads using strong materials and effective drainage.

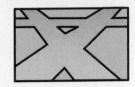

C The Romans were experts in construction. They developed concrete, a strong, durable building material. Many Roman buildings are still standing today, and many roads are still in use.

 more at NWHatlas.com

How Big Was the Roman Empire?

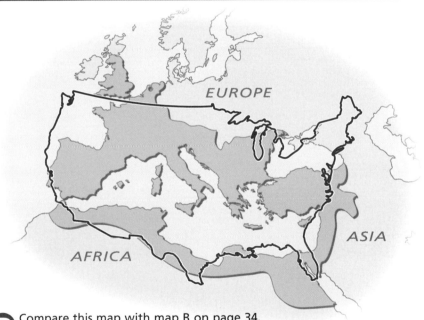

EUROPE

ASIA

AFRICA

Why is Latin a dead language?
When Roman education collapsed along with the Roman Empire, simpler, less formal dialects of Latin replaced official, formal Latin. As time went on, these versions became different Romance languages.

D Compare this map with map B on page 34. The Romans ruled the Mediterranean region and Western Europe for centuries. Also compare it to the size of the United States. *more at* NWHatlas.com

WRITING & LANGUAGE
Latin Origins of Modern Languages

LATIN	MODERN ROMANCE LANGUAGES					MODERN ENGLISH
	Portuguese	Spanish	French	Italian	Romanian	
tres	tres	tres	trois	tre	trei	three
nota	nota	nota	note	notazione	nota	note
ferrum	ferro	hierro	fer	ferro	fier	iron

E Latin is no longer spoken, but modern Romance languages are based on Latin. English is not a Romance language. Many of its words have Latin roots, but many others do not.

 more at NWHatlas.com

Judaism and Christianity in the Roman Empire

Judaism and Christianity expanded throughout the Roman Empire.

- The king of Judea voluntarily joined the Roman Empire in 63 B.C. However, many Jews objected to foreign rule.

- Many Jews left Judea for greater economic opportunities.

- Christianity began as a branch of Judaism. After Jesus died, his followers spread through the empire. As non-Jews joined, Christianity became its own religion.

- Both Jews and Christians were persecuted by the Romans. After two major revolts, the surviving Jews were expelled from their homeland.

Jews and Christians Under Roman Rule

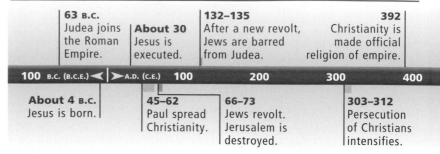

| 63 B.C. Judea joins the Roman Empire. | About 30 Jesus is executed. | 132–135 After a new revolt, Jews are barred from Judea. | 392 Christianity is made official religion of empire. |

100 B.C. (B.C.E.) ◄ ► A.D. (C.E.)   100   200   300   400

| About 4 B.C. Jesus is born. | 45–62 Paul spread Christianity. | 66–73 Jews revolt. Jerusalem is destroyed. | 303–312 Persecution of Christians intensifies. |

A Roman leaders persecuted both Jews and Christians, but Jewish and Christian communities continued to spread. Eventually Christianity became the official religion in the Roman Empire.

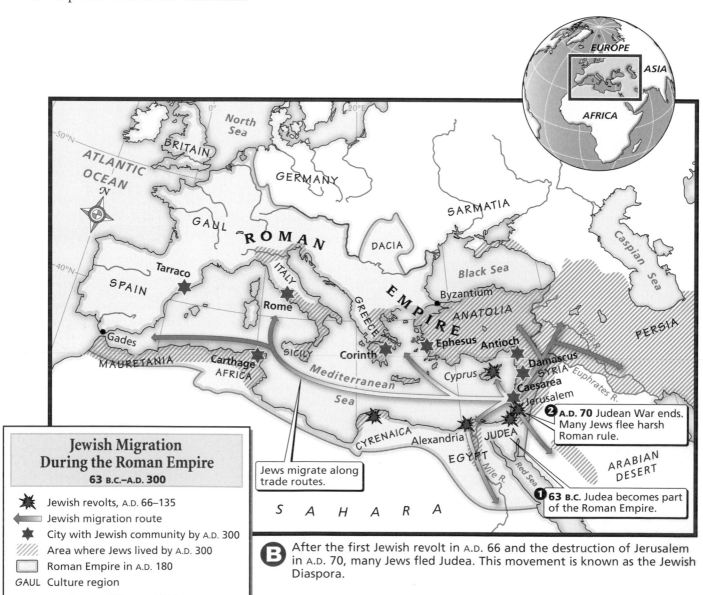

Jews migrate along trade routes.

2 A.D. 70 Judean War ends. Many Jews flee harsh Roman rule.

1 63 B.C. Judea becomes part of the Roman Empire.

Jewish Migration During the Roman Empire
63 B.C.–A.D. 300

- ✸ Jewish revolts, A.D. 66–135
- ← Jewish migration route
- ★ City with Jewish community by A.D. 300
- ▨ Area where Jews lived by A.D. 300
- ▢ Roman Empire in A.D. 180
- GAUL Culture region

0   250   500 miles
0   250   500 kilometers

B After the first Jewish revolt in A.D. 66 and the destruction of Jerusalem in A.D. 70, many Jews fled Judea. This movement is known as the Jewish Diaspora.

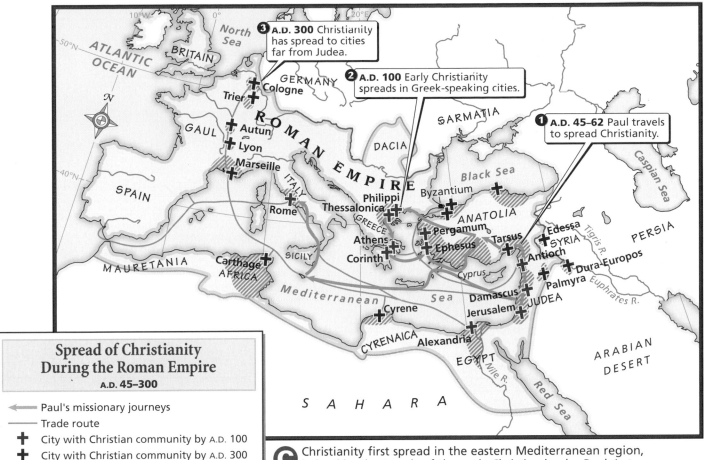

Spread of Christianity During the Roman Empire
A.D. 45–300

- ← Paul's missionary journeys
- — Trade route
- ✝ City with Christian community by A.D. 100
- ✚ City with Christian community by A.D. 300
- ▨ Area where Christians lived by A.D. 300
- ▭ Roman Empire in A.D. 180
- GAUL Culture region

0   250   500 miles
0   250   500 kilometers

3 A.D. 300 Christianity has spread to cities far from Judea.

2 A.D. 100 Early Christianity spreads in Greek-speaking cities.

1 A.D. 45–62 Paul travels to spread Christianity.

C Christianity first spread in the eastern Mediterranean region, helped by the travels of the early Christian leader Paul. Later Christian communities were established along important trade routes in other parts of the Roman Empire.

What Is Christianity?

Christianity is based on the teachings of Jesus Christ, whom Christians believe is the son of God. Today Christianity, which began as a branch of Judaism, has more followers than any other religion in the world.

more at NWHatlas.com

D Paul was a Jew from Tarsus who converted to Christianity. He traveled through the empire as far as Rome, preaching Christian ideas to non-Jews and establishing Christian communities. Here he is shown in Athens.

more at NWHatlas.com

Decline of the Roman Empire

Corrupt rulers and constant wars weakened the Roman Empire. By the end of the 400s, only the eastern half of the empire had survived.

- Civil wars, disease, and famine created disorder throughout the empire.

- At the same time, migrating barbarians from Europe and Asia invaded the empire. They claimed land for their own kingdoms.

- In 395 Roman territory was divided into the Western Empire and the Eastern Empire.

- By 476 the western lands were no longer under Roman control. The Eastern Empire continued to thrive.

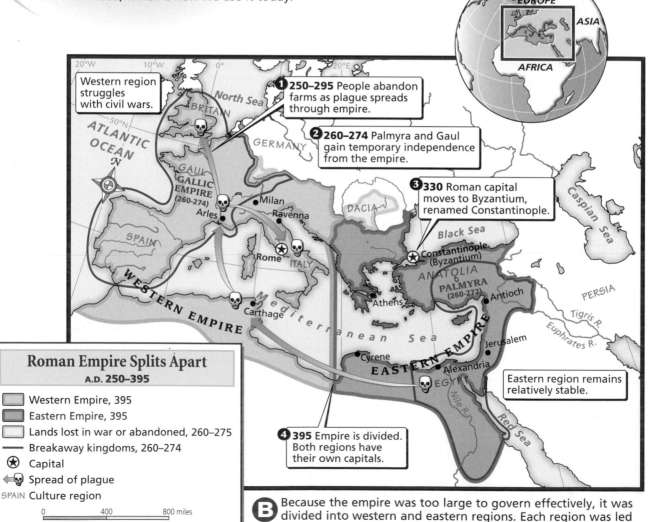

A Constantine, shown here being baptized, is known as the first Christian emperor. He was the last major emperor to rule the united Roman Empire.

What is a barbarian?

The word **barbarian** comes from a Greek insult to non-Greek speakers. To the Greeks, other languages were just "bar-bar," or nonsense. The Romans used the word to describe people who were uncivilized, which is how we use it today.

Western region struggles with civil wars.

1 **250–295** People abandon farms as plague spreads through empire.

2 **260–274** Palmyra and Gaul gain temporary independence from the empire.

3 **330** Roman capital moves to Byzantium, renamed Constantinople.

4 **395** Empire is divided. Both regions have their own capitals.

Eastern region remains relatively stable.

Roman Empire Splits Apart
A.D. 250–395

- ☐ Western Empire, 395
- ☐ Eastern Empire, 395
- ☐ Lands lost in war or abandoned, 260–275
- — Breakaway kingdoms, 260–274
- ★ Capital
- ☠ Spread of plague
- SPAIN Culture region

0   400   800 miles

0   400   800 kilometers

B Because the empire was too large to govern effectively, it was divided into western and eastern regions. Each region was led by its own emperor. The empire was never reunited.

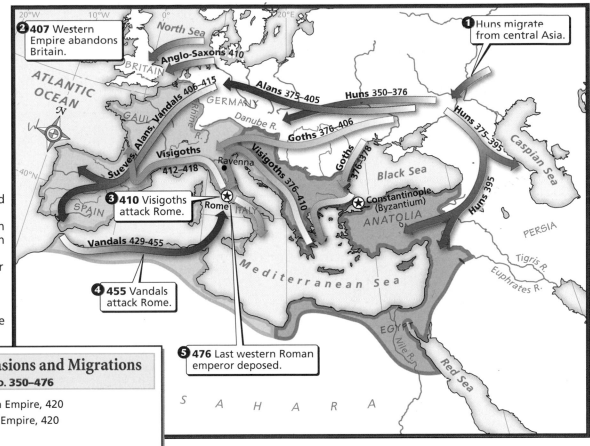

❶ Huns migrate from central Asia.

❷407 Western Empire abandons Britain.

Anglo-Saxons 410

Alans 375–405

Huns 350–376

Huns 375–395

Sueves, Alans, Vandals 406–415

Goths 376–406

Visigoths 376–410

Goths 376–378

Huns 395

Visigoths 412–418

❸410 Visigoths attack Rome.

Constantinople (Byzantium)

❹455 Vandals attack Rome.

Vandals 429-455

❺476 Last western Roman emperor deposed.

North Sea · BRITAIN · ATLANTIC OCEAN · GAUL · GERMANY · Rhine R. · Danube R. · Ravenna · Rome · ITALY · SPAIN · Black Sea · ANATOLIA · PERSIA · Caspian Sea · Tigris R. · Euphrates R. · Mediterranean Sea · EGYPT · Nile R. · Red Sea · SAHARA

C By 476 invaders had conquered most of the Western Roman Empire. The Eastern Roman Empire was stronger and better organized. It continued to resist invaders long after the Western Empire collapsed.

Barbarian Invasions and Migrations
A.D. 350–476

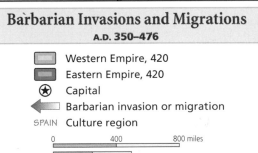

	Western Empire, 420
	Eastern Empire, 420
⊛	Capital
⬅	Barbarian invasion or migration
SPAIN	Culture region

0   400   800 miles
0   400   800 kilometers

D The Huns terrified both Romans and other barbarians. Tribes fled from the Huns by invading the empire. A Roman-barbarian alliance stopped the Huns, but the Western Empire was effectively destroyed.

Top 10 Cities, A.D.500

City Locations

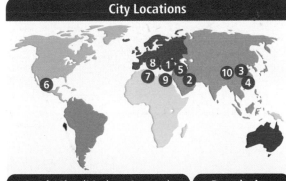

Rank/City (Modern Country)	Population
❶ Constantinople (Turkey)	400,000
❷ Ctesiphon (Iraq)	400,000
❸ Luoyang (China)	200,000
❹ Nanjing (China)	150,000
❺ Antioch (Turkey)	150,000
❻ Teotihuacan (Mexico)	125,000
❼ Carthage (Tunisia)	100,000
❽ Rome (Italy)	100,000
❾ Alexandria (Egypt)	100,000
❿ Changan (China)	100,000

E By 500 Constantinople had become one of the world's great cities.

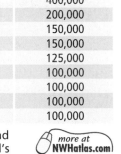 more at NWHatlas.com

Empires and Cultures of Asia

395 to 1641

622
Islam begins to spread.

500

395
Byzantine Empire separates from Western Roman Empire.

By 620
Hindu-Arabic numbers used in India.

Ideas Travel the Silk Road

Between A.D. 400 and 1500, cultures of Asia, Africa, and Europe came into closer contact with one another.

- The Silk Road and other trade routes helped link distant areas. Trade and travel increased.

- Traders and armies brought ideas and inventions from one region to another.

- Religions such as Christianity, Islam, and Buddhism linked large regions.

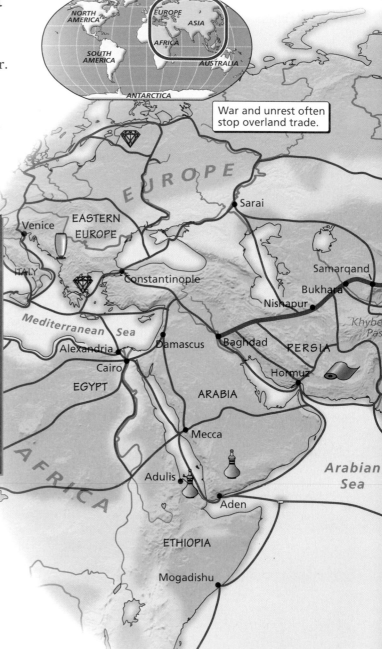

War and unrest often stop overland trade.

Silk Road and Other Trade Routes
400–1500

Tundra or ice   Forest   Grass   Shrub or desert

—— Silk Road   —— Other trade route

PERSIA   Culture region

Sources of Trade Goods

Frankincense   Cotton   Horses

Gems   Silk   Glassware

Spices   Wool   Porcelain

0   500   1000 miles
0   500   1000 kilometers

more at NWHatlas.com

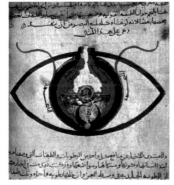

A
From the 700s to the 1400s, the **Arab world** was the center of scientific discovery. Many advances were made in science and medicine, as shown by this text on the human eye.

B The digits 0–9 that are used by people all over the world today are called Hindu-Arabic numerals. This system was developed in **India** over hundreds of years and then spread westward.

| 800–1200 Khmer kingdoms flourish in Southeast Asia. | 1054 Eastern and Western Christianity split into two separate churches. | 1398 Mongol ruler Timur invades Delhi. | 1453 Ottoman Turks conquer Byzantine Empire. |

1000 **1500**

| 751 Chinese expansion into Islamic lands is halted. | 1180–1603 Japan is engulfed by civil wars. | 1279–1368 Mongols conquer and rule China. | 1640 Japan expels European traders. |

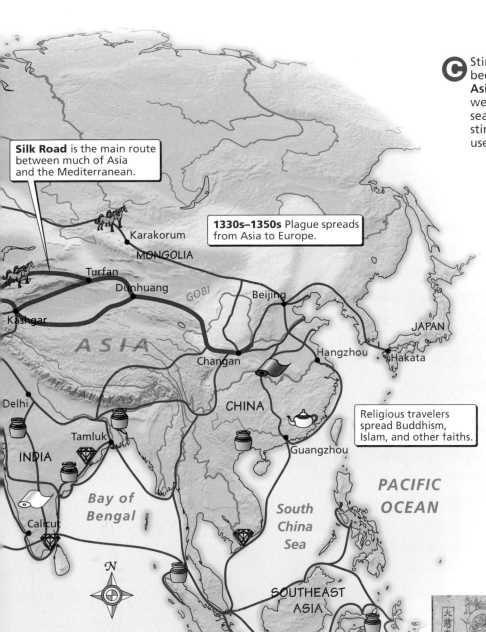

Silk Road is the main route between much of Asia and the Mediterranean.

1330s–1350s Plague spreads from Asia to Europe.

Religious travelers spread Buddhism, Islam, and other faiths.

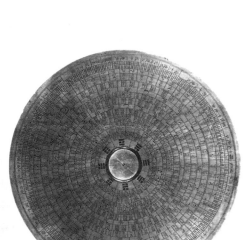

C Stirrups, thought to have been developed in **Central Asia**, changed how horses were used in war. A rider seated in a saddle with stirrups was better able to use a weapon.

D Chinese sailors were the first to use magnetic compasses. Unlike navigating by the stars, a compass could be used any time of day in any weather conditions and allowed for more accurate navigation.

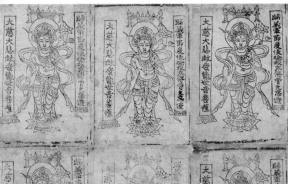

E Printing, invented in **China**, allowed many copies to be produced quickly, making information more widely available. Printing used paper, also invented in China, which was much cheaper than other writing materials.

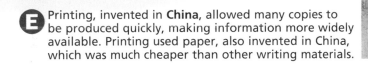

The Spread of Islam

Islam emerged in Arabia in the 600s and grew into a major world religion.

- Muhammad was the founder of Islam. He was both a political and a religious leader.

- The early leaders of Islam built large empires. Many of the people they conquered became followers of Islam, or **Muslims**.

- Later, through trade, Islam spread into regions that were not ruled by Muslims.

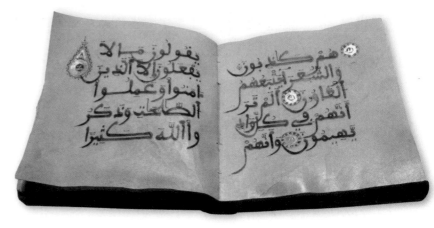

A The **Qur'an** (also spelled *Koran*) is the holy book of Islam. It includes basic religious duties of all Muslims.

more at NWHatlas.com

What's Islam?

Islam is a religion based on the teachings of Muhammad, whom Muslims believe was the messenger of God (called Allah in Arabic). Today Islam is one of the world's most widespread religions.

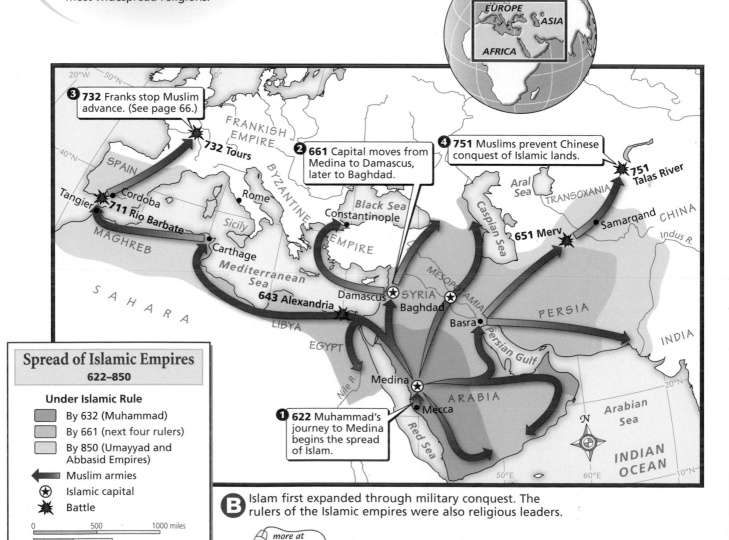

3 732 Franks stop Muslim advance. (See page 66.)

2 661 Capital moves from Medina to Damascus, later to Baghdad.

4 751 Muslims prevent Chinese conquest of Islamic lands.

732 Tours

711 Rio Barbate

643 Alexandria

651 Merv

751 Talas River

1 622 Muhammad's journey to Medina begins the spread of Islam.

Spread of Islamic Empires
622–850

Under Islamic Rule

- By 632 (Muhammad)
- By 661 (next four rulers)
- By 850 (Umayyad and Abbasid Empires)
- Muslim armies
- Islamic capital
- Battle

0   500   1000 miles
0   500   1000 kilometers

B Islam first expanded through military conquest. The rulers of the Islamic empires were also religious leaders.

more at NWHatlas.com

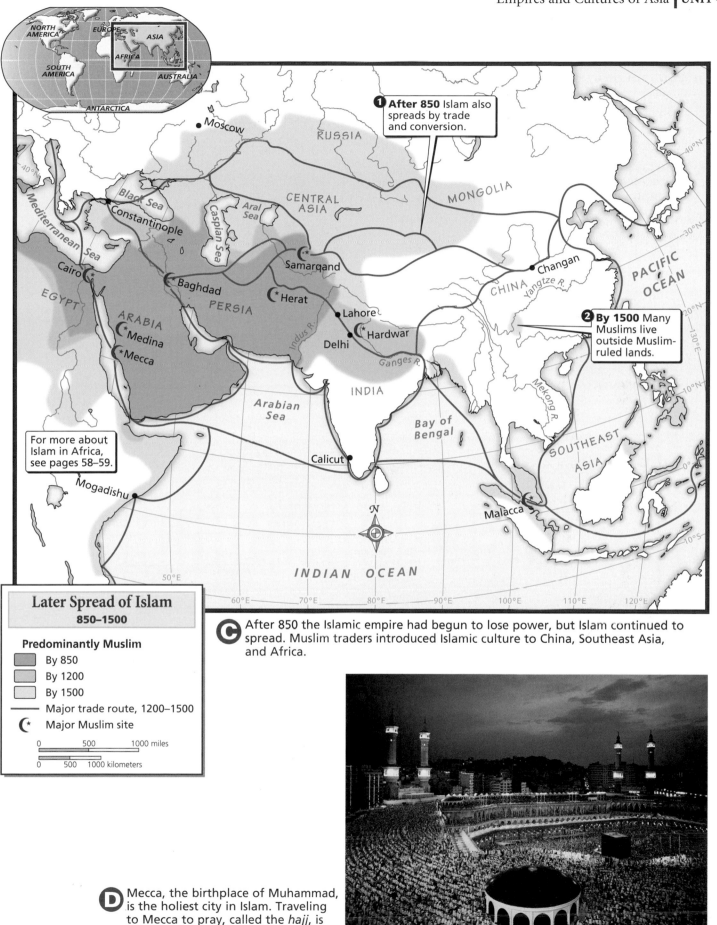

❶ After 850 Islam also spreads by trade and conversion.

❷ By 1500 Many Muslims live outside Muslim-ruled lands.

For more about Islam in Africa, see pages 58–59.

Later Spread of Islam
850–1500

Predominantly Muslim

By 850

By 1200

By 1500

— Major trade route, 1200–1500

☪★ Major Muslim site

0   500   1000 miles

0   500   1000 kilometers

C After 850 the Islamic empire had begun to lose power, but Islam continued to spread. Muslim traders introduced Islamic culture to China, Southeast Asia, and Africa.

D Mecca, the birthplace of Muhammad, is the holiest city in Islam. Traveling to Mecca to pray, called the *hajj*, is one of the five major religious duties of Muslims.

Growth and Decline of the Byzantine Empire

The Eastern Roman Empire became known as the **Byzantine Empire**. It outlasted the Western Empire by nearly 1000 years.

- The Byzantine Empire had many enemies. Islamic empires, led by Arabs and Turks, conquered much of the empire.

- Constantinople, the capital, was a major trade center. Wealth from trade was spent to keep the army strong.

- After 400 years of fighting, Turkish invaders conquered the empire.

A This mosaic, an image made from small bits of tile, shows Mary and the baby Jesus. Emperor Constantine stands to the right, offering them Constantinople.

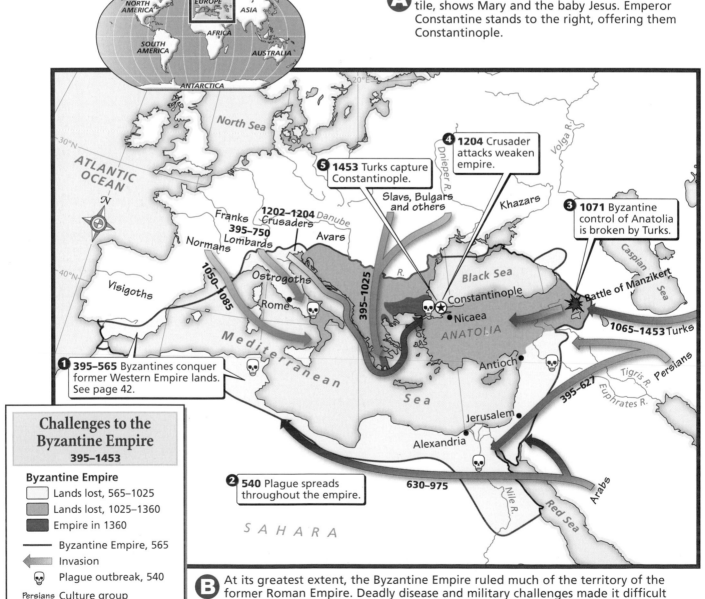

4 **1204** Crusader attacks weaken empire.

5 **1453** Turks capture Constantinople.

3 **1071** Byzantine control of Anatolia is broken by Turks.

1 **395–565** Byzantines conquer former Western Empire lands. See page 42.

2 **540** Plague spreads throughout the empire.

Challenges to the Byzantine Empire
395–1453

Byzantine Empire

- Lands lost, 565–1025
- Lands lost, 1025–1360
- Empire in 1360
- — Byzantine Empire, 565
- ← Invasion
- ☠ Plague outbreak, 540
- Persians Culture group

0   300   600 miles

0   300   600 kilometers

B At its greatest extent, the Byzantine Empire ruled much of the territory of the former Roman Empire. Deadly disease and military challenges made it difficult to hold on to these lands.

Tang and Sung Dynasties of China

During the Tang and Sung dynasties, trade as well as conflict between China and neighboring cultures increased.

- Under the control of the Tang dynasty, trade along the Silk Road flourished.

- Like the Byzantine emperors, Tang and Sung rulers defended their realm against many invasions by neighbors.

- By the end of the Sung dynasty, however, the Mongols had conquered all of China.

C Many Tang dynasty sculptures, such as this one, show horses. The Tang traded with Central Asia for strong, fast horses, which gave them an advantage in war.

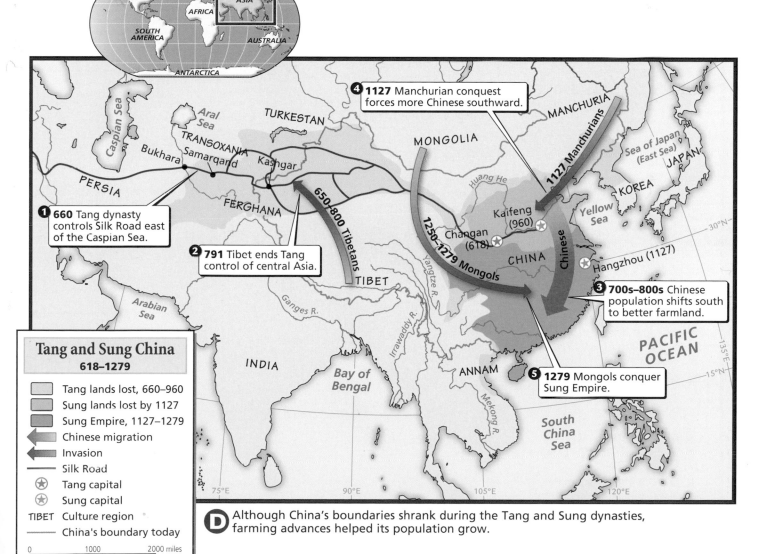

4 1127 Manchurian conquest forces more Chinese southward.

1 660 Tang dynasty controls Silk Road east of the Caspian Sea.

2 791 Tibet ends Tang control of central Asia.

3 700s–800s Chinese population shifts south to better farmland.

5 1279 Mongols conquer Sung Empire.

650–800 Tibetans

1250–1279 Mongols

1127 Manchurians

Changan (618)

Kaifeng (960)

Hangzhou (1127)

Tang and Sung China
618–1279

- Tang lands lost, 660–960
- Sung lands lost by 1127
- Sung Empire, 1127–1279
- ← Chinese migration
- ← Invasion
- — Silk Road
- ⊛ Tang capital
- ⊛ Sung capital
- TIBET Culture region
- — China's boundary today

| 0 | 1000 | 2000 miles |
| 0 | 1000 | 2000 kilometers |

D Although China's boundaries shrank during the Tang and Sung dynasties, farming advances helped its population grow.

The Mongol Empire Spans Eurasia

Mongol tribes swept across Asia and Europe, creating one of the largest empires in world history.

- The Mongols were nomads who originally lived in the dry grasslands of Central Asia. They were excellent horsemen and ruthless warriors.

- The Mongols conquered Islamic and Chinese empires and destroyed major cities along the Silk Road.

- During Mongol rule, trade and cultural exchange in Europe and Asia increased.

- Mongol rulers spread Islamic and Chinese culture throughout their kingdoms.

B This illustration shows a Mongol attack on a neighboring kingdom. Mongol battles often ended in destruction and brutal massacres.

A The Mongols rapidly expanded their territory. Their speed of travel and military skill made them difficult to defeat.

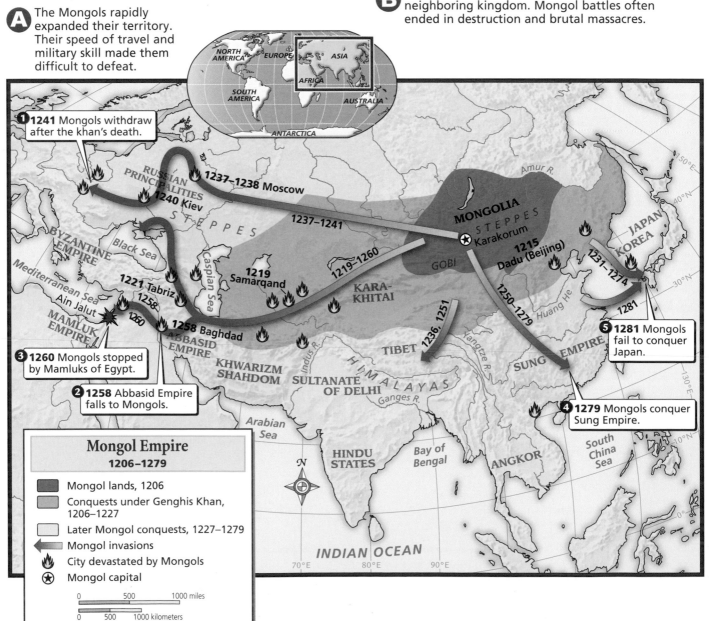

1 **1241** Mongols withdraw after the khan's death.

1237–1238 Moscow

1240 Kiev

1237–1241

1219 Samarqand

1221 Tabriz

1258

1260

1258 Baghdad

1219–1260

1215 Dadu (Beijing)

1231–1274

1281

1250–1279

1236, 1251

3 **1260** Mongols stopped by Mamluks of Egypt.

2 **1258** Abbasid Empire falls to Mongols.

5 **1281** Mongols fail to conquer Japan.

4 **1279** Mongols conquer Sung Empire.

RUSSIAN PRINCIPALITIES
STEPPES
BYZANTINE EMPIRE
Black Sea
Caspian Sea
Mediterranean Sea
Ain Jalut
MAMLUK EMPIRE
ABBASID EMPIRE
KHWARIZM SHAHDOM
SULTANATE OF DELHI
KARA-KHITAI
MONGOLIA
STEPPES
Karakorum
GOBI
Amur R.
Huang He
Yangtze R.
JAPAN
KOREA
SUNG EMPIRE
TIBET
HIMALAYAS
Ganges R.
Indus R.
Arabian Sea
HINDU STATES
Bay of Bengal
ANGKOR
South China Sea
INDIAN OCEAN

NORTH AMERICA
EUROPE
ASIA
AFRICA
SOUTH AMERICA
AUSTRALIA
ANTARCTICA

Mongol Empire
1206–1279

- Mongol lands, 1206
- Conquests under Genghis Khan, 1206–1227
- Later Mongol conquests, 1227–1279
- ⬅ Mongol invasions
- City devastated by Mongols
- ✪ Mongol capital

0   500   1000 miles
0   500   1000 kilometers

How Big Was the Mongol Empire?

more at NWHatlas.com

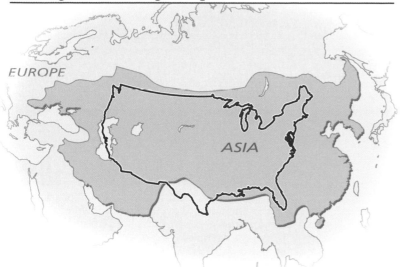

C The Mongol Empire stretched from the Pacific Ocean to Eastern Europe and the Middle East. It was the largest land empire in history. Compare it to the size of the United States.

D Genghis Khan, which roughly means *Universal Ruler*, was born with the name Temujin. He united the Mongol tribes, introduced their first law code, and conquered much of Asia.

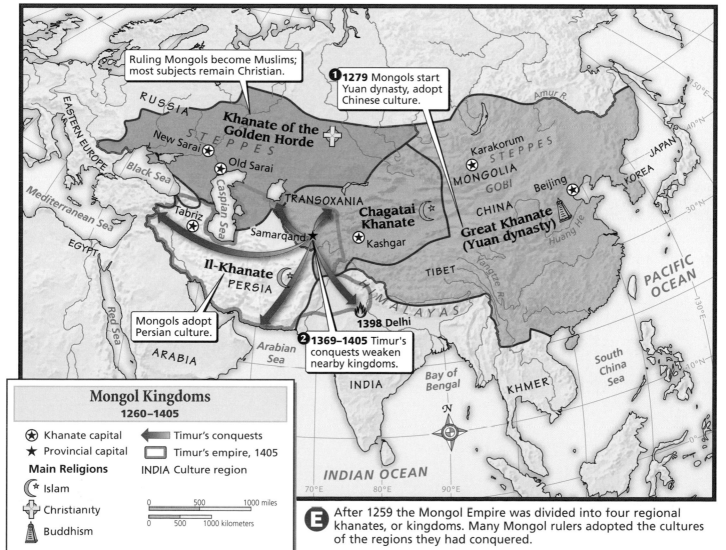

Mongol Kingdoms
1260–1405

⊛ Khanate capital
★ Provincial capital

Main Religions
☪ Islam
✚ Christianity
🏛 Buddhism

⬅ Timur's conquests
▢ Timur's empire, 1405
INDIA Culture region

0   500   1000 miles
0   500   1000 kilometers

Ruling Mongols become Muslims; most subjects remain Christian.

❶ 1279 Mongols start Yuan dynasty, adopt Chinese culture.

Mongols adopt Persian culture.

❷ 1369–1405 Timur's conquests weaken nearby kingdoms.

1398 Delhi

E After 1259 the Mongol Empire was divided into four regional khanates, or kingdoms. Many Mongol rulers adopted the cultures of the regions they had conquered.

51

Kingdoms of Southeast Asia

Unlike its neighbors India and China, Southeast Asia did not develop large empires. The region was ruled by many small kingdoms.

- Many culture groups lived in Southeast Asia. Their kingdoms were often at war.

- Kingdoms were influenced by Indian and Chinese cultures. Hinduism and Buddhism spread through the region.

- The Khmer kingdom of Angkor developed one of the region's longest-lasting civilizations.

A Angkor Wat, built in the 1100s, is located in the ancient city of Angkor. This religious monument is part of the region's largest temple complex.

B Core areas of major kingdoms emerged by the 800s. Surrounding areas were loosely controlled and often had more than one ruler.

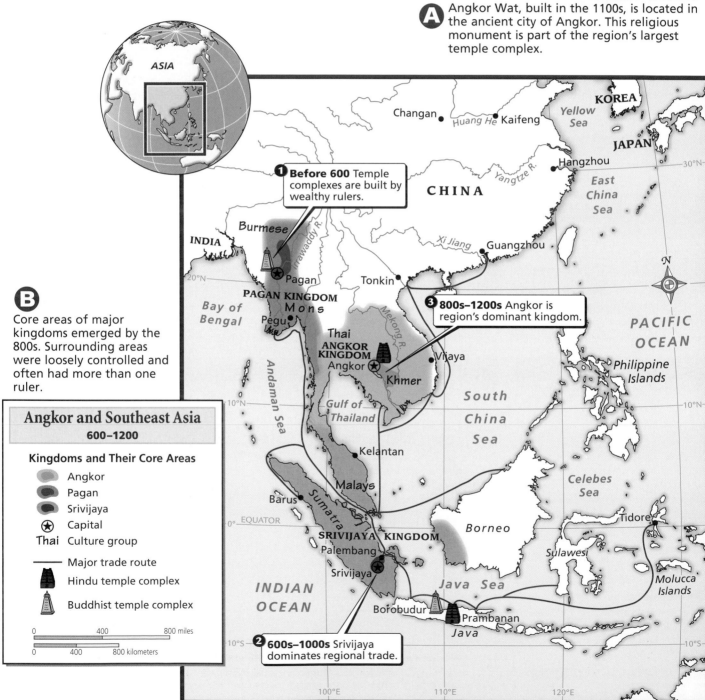

1 Before 600 Temple complexes are built by wealthy rulers.

3 800s–1200s Angkor is region's dominant kingdom.

2 600s–1000s Srivijaya dominates regional trade.

Angkor and Southeast Asia
600–1200

Kingdoms and Their Core Areas

- Angkor
- Pagan
- Srivijaya
- ⭐ Capital
- Thai Culture group
- —— Major trade route
- Hindu temple complex
- Buddhist temple complex

0   400   800 miles

0   400   800 kilometers

ASIA

KOREA
JAPAN
CHINA
Changan
Huang He Kaifeng
Yellow Sea
Hangzhou
East China Sea
Yangtze R.
Xi Jiang Guangzhou
Tonkin
INDIA
Burmese
Pagan
PAGAN KINGDOM
Mons
Bay of Bengal
Pegu
Irrawaddy R.
Mekong R.
Thai
ANGKOR KINGDOM
Angkor
Khmer
Vijaya
PACIFIC OCEAN
Philippine Islands
Andaman Sea
Gulf of Thailand
Kelantan
South China Sea
Celebes Sea
Malays
Barus
Sumatra
EQUATOR
SRIVIJAYA KINGDOM
Palembang
Srivijaya
Borneo
Sulawesi
Tidore
Molucca Islands
INDIAN OCEAN
Java Sea
Borobudur
Prambanan
Java
30°N
20°N
10°N
0°
10°S
100°E 110°E 120°E

Ming Dynasty of China

After almost 100 years of foreign rule in China, the Ming dynasty restored Chinese control. Ming rulers brought political and economic growth to China.

- Ming emperors ended Mongol rule. They rebuilt regions of the empire damaged from years of war.

- To rebuild northern China, Ming rulers moved the capital to Beijing and encouraged people to move back north.

- In the 1600s rebellions and war weakened the Ming dynasty. Northern invaders then conquered China.

C Porcelain, also known as china, was invented during the Tang dynasty. This porcelain vase shows the unique Ming style.

4 **1644** Manchu invasion ends Ming dynasty. Manchu dynasty rules until 1912.

2 **1400s** Mass migration repopulates the North.

1 **1368–1450** Ming dynasty encourages foreign trade.

3 **1557** Macao is first European settlement in China.

MONGOLIA

Beijing (after 1403)

MANCHURIA

JAPAN

KOREA

gold

silver

Nagasaki

30°N

PERSIA

horses

horses

horses

tea, porcelain, silk

TIBET

tea, porcelain, silk

MING EMPIRE

Nanjing (to 1403)

Shanghai

Yangtze R.

Hankou

tea, porcelain, silk

Fuzhou

tea, porcelain, silk

PACIFIC OCEAN

135°E

Ganges R.

BURMA

INDIA

Guangzhou

Macao (Port.)

Philippine Islands

15°N

Arabian Sea

ANNAM

tea, porcelain, silk (to Africa)

ivory (from Africa)

Bay of Bengal

SIAM

Mekong R.

tea, porcelain, silk

spices, silver

15°N

South China Sea

Sumatra

INDIAN OCEAN

Borneo

Sulawesi

Molucca Islands

0°

90°E

120°E

0°

Ming China and Trade
1368–1644

	Ming Empire, 1600
★	Capital
○	Trade center
←	Major import
←	Major export
	Great Wall
BURMA	Culture region
—	China's boundary today

0   500   1000 miles

0   500   1000 kilometers

D Early Ming rulers allowed merchants to trade freely. Later, only the government could legally trade outside China. What were China's main exports?

more at NWHatlas.com

From Imperial to Feudal Japan

Unlike mainland Asian civilizations, Japan was rarely threatened by invaders. However, it was influenced by neighboring cultures.

- Japan's religion, written language, and government were based on ideas from China and Korea.

- Strong emperors ruled early Japan. Over time, civil wars divided Japan into tiny kingdoms with their own rulers.

- As internal conflict decreased, a more unified Japan increased trade with neighboring regions.

A Conflicts between land-owning families weakened the emperor's political power. By 1192 **shoguns** (generals) took over as the true rulers of Japan.

Ruling Families of Japan
552–1300

Main Land-owning Families, 1183

- Fujiwara
- Minamoto
- Taira

- ★ Emperor's capital
- ★ Shogun's capital

0   100   200   300 miles
0   100   200   300 kilometers

Top 10 Cities, 900

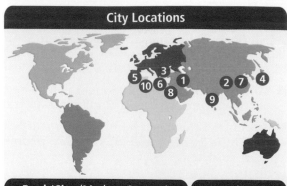

City Locations

Rank/City (Modern Country)	Population
1 Baghdad (Iraq)	900,000
2 Changan (China)	500,000
3 Constantinople (Turkey)	300,000
4 Kyoto (Japan)	200,000
5 Cordoba (Spain)	200,000
6 Alexandria (Egypt)	175,000
7 Luoyang (China)	150,000
8 Fustat (Egypt)	150,000
9 Manyakheta (India)	100,000
10 Kairwan (Tunisia)	100,000

B Kyoto was the imperial, or the emperor's, capital. Strong imperial power made Kyoto one of the world's great cities.

more at NWHatlas.com

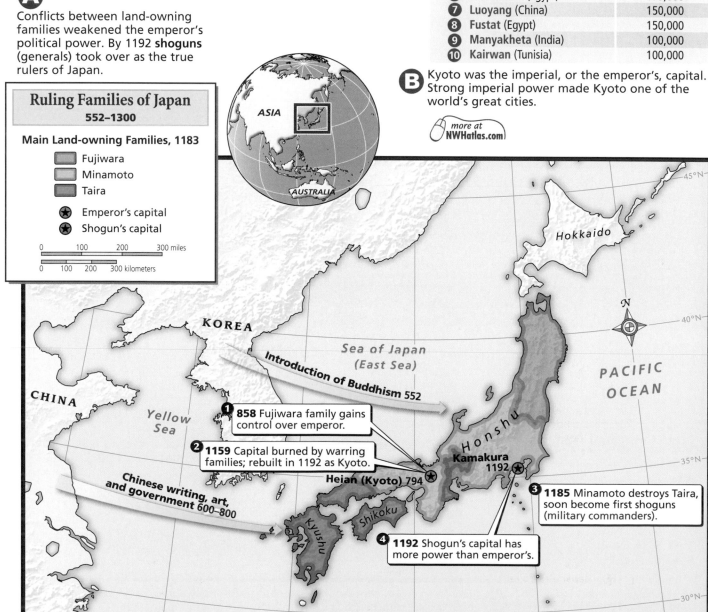

Introduction of Buddhism 552

Chinese writing, art, and government 600–800

❶ 858 Fujiwara family gains control over emperor.

❷ 1159 Capital burned by warring families; rebuilt in 1192 as Kyoto.

❸ 1185 Minamoto destroys Taira, soon become first shoguns (military commanders).

❹ 1192 Shogun's capital has more power than emperor's.

Heian (Kyoto) 794 ★

Kamakura 1192 ★

KOREA

CHINA

Yellow Sea

Sea of Japan (East Sea)

PACIFIC OCEAN

Hokkaido

Honshu

Shikoku

Kyushu

ASIA

AUSTRALIA

SOCIAL STRUCTURE
Japanese Feudal Structure, 1467–1867

C After years of civil war, a new social structure emerged in Japan. Local military leaders, called *daimyo*, challenged the power of the shoguns with armies of paid samurai. Compare this chart with the chart on page 68.

Emperor — Ruler In name only

Shogun — National military leader

Daimyo — Local warlord

Samurai — Warriors serving shogun and daimyo

Merchants and Artisans — Low status, although some were wealthy

Peasants — Largest and poorest group

D Samurai followed a strict honor code called **bushido**, or "way of the warrior." They valued honesty, courage, and fighting skills.

If they fought with swords, why were they called sho-*guns*?

Shogun means *great general* in Japanese. The first shogun, Yoritomo, received his title from the emperor in 1192. Yoritomo established a military government called a *shogunate*.

E In the late 1500s legal and illegal Japanese trade increased in East and Southeast Asia. About ten thousand Japanese lived outside of Japan, some as traders.

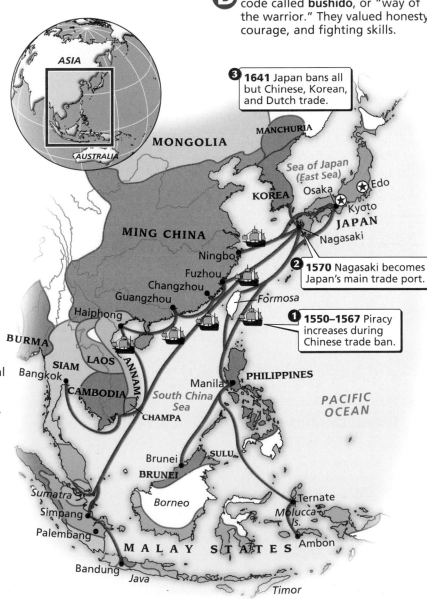

3 1641 Japan bans all but Chinese, Korean, and Dutch trade.

2 1570 Nagasaki becomes Japan's main trade port.

1 1550–1567 Piracy increases during Chinese trade ban.

Japanese Trade
1550–1641

— Major trade route
🚢 Japanese pirate activity, 1550–1567
★ Japanese capital

0 500 1000 miles
0 500 1000 kilometers

55

A.D. 570
Axum loses
control of Yemen.

500 B.C. (B.C.E.)   B.C. (B.C.E.) ◄|► A.D. (C.E.)   A.D. (C.E.) **500**

500 B.C.
Bantu migration begins.

A.D. 321
Christianity is adopted
by king of Axum.

A.D. 639
Muslim Arabs invade
North Africa.

Early Civilizations of Africa

Many different cultures developed in Africa after Egypt and
Kush (see pages 18–19).

- The Bantu people of western Africa spread east and south
  beginning around 500 B.C. They spread ironworking,
  farming, and herding across central and southern Africa.

- In the east, Axum became a strong empire. It defeated
  Kush and controlled trade on the Red Sea.

- Axum kings converted to Christianity, increasing contact
  between eastern Africa and the Mediterranean region.

A

Bantu-speaking farmers and herders migrated for about
1,500 years. They combined with local culture groups
except in areas unsuitable for farming. Today there are
more than 300 different Bantu culture groups.

 more at
NWHatlas.com

SCIENCE & TECHNOLOGY
Bantu Innovations

Iron
Produced iron tools
such as axes, hoes,
knives, and spears.

New Crops
Introduced plantains,
creating a year-round
supply of food.

Pastoralism
Developed the practice
of moving herds to fresh
grazing land.

B Horses and larger breeds of cattle died of
sleeping sickness in central and southern
Africa. As a result, Bantu farmers could not
use plows. They also needed crops that
could survive heat, floods, and drought.

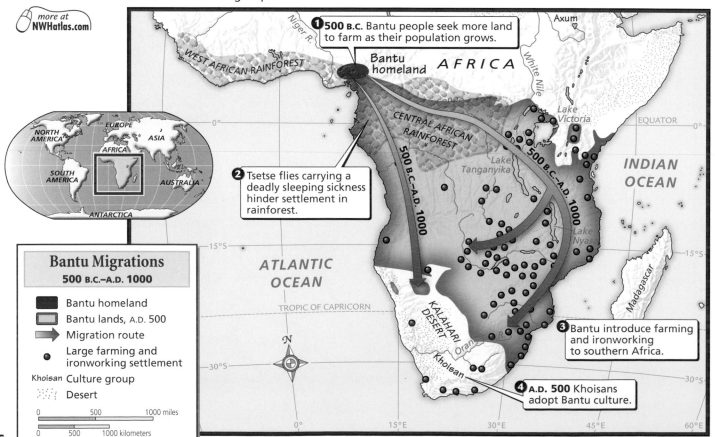

①500 B.C. Bantu people seek more land
to farm as their population grows.

② Tsetse flies carrying a
deadly sleeping sickness
hinder settlement in
rainforest.

③ Bantu introduce farming
and ironworking
to southern Africa.

④ A.D. 500 Khoisans
adopt Bantu culture.

Bantu
homeland

AFRICA

Axum

WEST AFRICAN RAINFOREST

Niger R.

White Nile

CENTRAL AFRICAN RAINFOREST

Lake
Victoria

EQUATOR

500 B.C.–A.D. 1000

500 B.C.–A.D. 1000

INDIAN
OCEAN

Lake
Tanganyika

Lake
Nyasa

ATLANTIC
OCEAN

Madagascar

KALAHARI DESERT

TROPIC OF CAPRICORN

Orange R.

Khoisan

Bantu Migrations
500 B.C.–A.D. 1000

- Bantu homeland
- Bantu lands, A.D. 500
- → Migration route
- • Large farming and
  ironworking settlement
- *Khoisan* Culture group
- Desert

0   500   1000 miles
0   500   1000 kilometers

NORTH
AMERICA

EUROPE

ASIA

AFRICA

SOUTH
AMERICA

AUSTRALIA

ANTARCTICA

0°

15°S

30°S

15°S

30°S

0°   15°E   30°E   45°E   60°E

A.D. 700 Ghana becomes the first empire in West Africa.	A.D. 919 Fatamids take over Tunisia.	A.D. 1187 Ayyubid sultan Saladin captures Jerusalem.	A.D. 1240 Mali Empire is established.	A.D. 1355 Ibn Battuta finishes his book *Travels*.	A.D. 1500 Swahili city-states thrive on trade.

A.D. (C.E.) 1000   **A.D. (C.E.) 1500**

A.D. 850 Kilwa is one of the earliest Swahili cities.	A.D. 1076 Almoravids conquer Ghana.	A.D. 1100 Great Zimbabwe controls southern trade routes.	A.D. 1335 Songhai Empire is established.	A.D. 1400 Timbuktu is the center of Mali culture.	A.D. 1591 Songhai falls.

C

The royal tombs of Axum have large steles, or stone monuments, carved with false doors and windows. This stele is for the tomb of King Ezana, the first Christian king.

Where does it come from?

Both the Axum and Bantu cultures are **indigenous** to Africa, meaning they originally developed there. Christianity is not indigenous to Africa but was introduced to the continent by travelers.

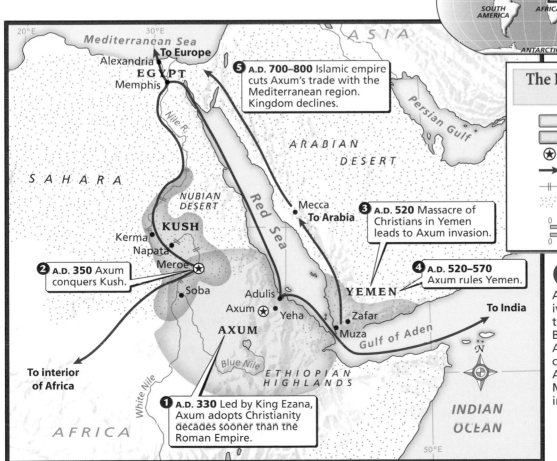

The Kingdom of Axum
A.D. 100–800

- Kingdom of Axum
- Kingdom of Kush
- ★ Capital
- → Flow of trade
- Cataract (waterfall)
- Desert

0   200   400 miles
0   200   400 kilometers

❺ A.D. 700–800 Islamic empire cuts Axum's trade with the Mediterranean region. Kingdom declines.

❸ A.D. 520 Massacre of Christians in Yemen leads to Axum invasion.

❹ A.D. 520–570 Axum rules Yemen.

❷ A.D. 350 Axum conquers Kush.

❶ A.D. 330 Led by King Ezana, Axum adopts Christianity decades sooner than the Roman Empire.

D

Axum controlled the ivory and incense trade to India and the Byzantine Empire. Axum fought Persia for control of Yemen and Arabia just before Muhammad was born in Mecca (see page 46).

57

Islamic Kingdoms of North Africa

Muslims began conquering the Byzantines and Vandals in North Africa in 639 (see page 46). However, Muslim North Africans soon gained independence from the Islamic empires further east.

- Arab migrants and the indigenous Berber people formed new kingdoms. These kingdoms expanded into sub-Saharan Africa, Europe, and southwest Asia.

- North Africa grew as a center of learning. Muslim and Jewish scholars wrote books on mathematics, science, and philosophy (see page 66). These books later influenced Western European thought.

- North Africa also became a major center of trade. North African goods and merchants moved across Europe, Asia, and Africa.

more at NWHatlas.com

A This illustration shows warriors from the Fatimid Caliphate. The Fatimids conquered Egypt and later founded Cairo.

B Anger against the greed of Muslim rulers in Spain and Arabia led the Fatimids and Almoravids to power. Their kingdoms faced continuous threats from Christians, other Muslims, and each other.

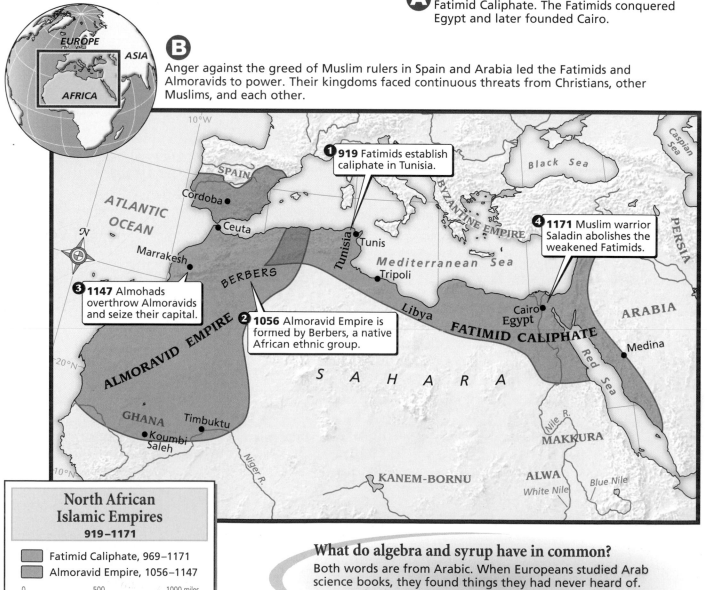

1 919 Fatimids establish caliphate in Tunisia.

4 1171 Muslim warrior Saladin abolishes the weakened Fatimids.

3 1147 Almohads overthrow Almoravids and seize their capital.

2 1056 Almoravid Empire is formed by Berbers, a native African ethnic group.

North African Islamic Empires
919–1171

Fatimid Caliphate, 969–1171
Almoravid Empire, 1056–1147

0   500   1000 miles
0   500   1000 kilometers

What do algebra and syrup have in common?

Both words are from Arabic. When Europeans studied Arab science books, they found things they had never heard of. As a result, they incorporated Arabic words including *al-jabr* and *sarab* into their vocabulary.

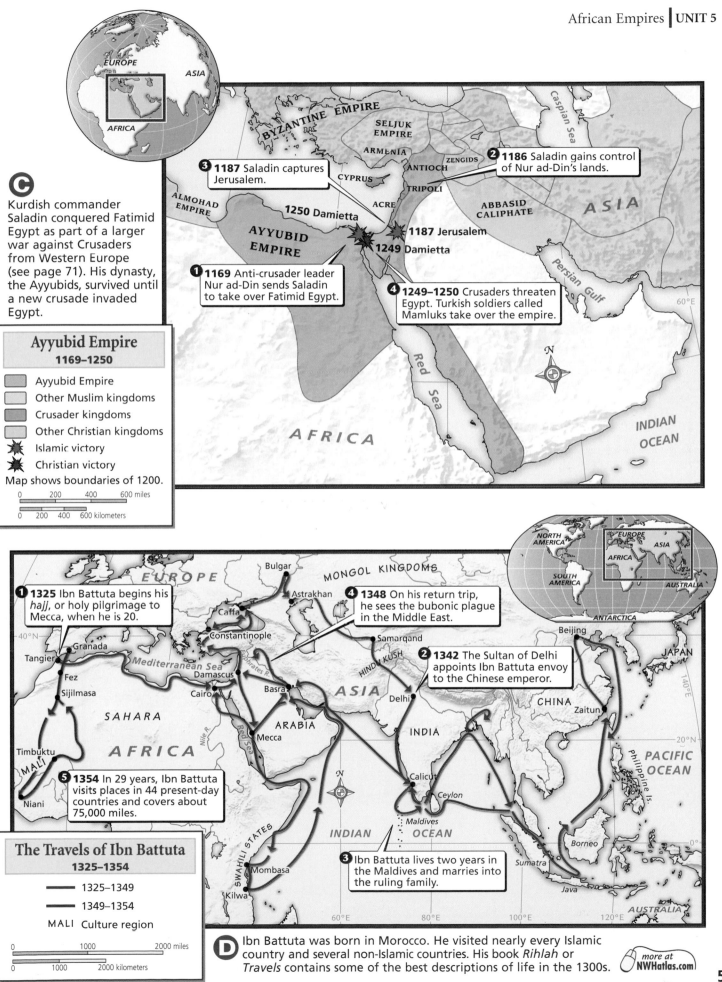

C Kurdish commander Saladin conquered Fatimid Egypt as part of a larger war against Crusaders from Western Europe (see page 71). His dynasty, the Ayyubids, survived until a new crusade invaded Egypt.

EUROPE
ASIA
AFRICA

3 **1187** Saladin captures Jerusalem.

2 **1186** Saladin gains control of Nur ad-Din's lands.

BYZANTINE EMPIRE
SELJUK EMPIRE
ARMENIA
ANTIOCH
ZENGIDS
CYPRUS
TRIPOLI
ACRE
ABBASID CALIPHATE
ASIA

ALMOHAD EMPIRE

1250 Damietta
AYYUBID EMPIRE

1 **1169** Anti-crusader leader Nur ad-Din sends Saladin to take over Fatimid Egypt.

1187 Jerusalem
1249 Damietta

4 **1249–1250** Crusaders threaten Egypt. Turkish soldiers called Mamluks take over the empire.

Persian Gulf

60°E

N

Red Sea

AFRICA

INDIAN OCEAN

Ayyubid Empire
1169–1250

- Ayyubid Empire
- Other Muslim kingdoms
- Crusader kingdoms
- Other Christian kingdoms
- Islamic victory
- Christian victory

Map shows boundaries of 1200.

0   200   400   600 miles
0   200   400   600 kilometers

NORTH AMERICA
EUROPE
ASIA
AFRICA
SOUTH AMERICA
AUSTRALIA
ANTARCTICA

1 **1325** Ibn Battuta begins his *hajj*, or holy pilgrimage to Mecca, when he is 20.

Bulgar
MONGOL KINGDOMS
Astrakhan
Caffa

4 **1348** On his return trip, he sees the bubonic plague in the Middle East.

Beijing

EUROPE

40°N
Granada
Tangier
Fez
Sijilmasa

Constantinople
Mediterranean Sea
Damascus
Cairo
Euphrates R.
Basra

Samarqand
HINDU KUSH

2 **1342** The Sultan of Delhi appoints Ibn Battuta envoy to the Chinese emperor.

JAPAN
140°E

ASIA
Delhi
CHINA
Zaitun

SAHARA
Nile R.
Red Sea
Mecca
ARABIA
INDIA

PACIFIC OCEAN

Timbuktu
MALI

5 **1354** In 29 years, Ibn Battuta visits places in 44 present-day countries and covers about 75,000 miles.

Niani

Calicut
Ceylon
20°N

Philippine Is.

SWAHILI STATES
INDIAN OCEAN
Maldives

3 Ibn Battuta lives two years in the Maldives and marries into the ruling family.

Borneo
Sumatra
Java

Mombasa
Kilwa

0°

AUSTRALIA

60°E   80°E   100°E   120°E

The Travels of Ibn Battuta
1325–1354

—— 1325–1349
—— 1349–1354

MALI   Culture region

0   1000   2000 miles
0   1000   2000 kilometers

D Ibn Battuta was born in Morocco. He visited nearly every Islamic country and several non-Islamic countries. His book *Rihlah* or *Travels* contains some of the best descriptions of life in the 1300s.

more at NWHatlas.com

Empires of West Africa

Western African empires developed south of the Sahara, in the Sahel region. These kingdoms became wealthy through trade.

■ Ghana first controlled the crucial gold-producing areas and the southern end of the Saharan trade routes.

■ After Ghana fell, new Islamic empires grew in the same area. First Mali then Songhai controlled the gold and the southern trade route.

■ Trade cities such as Jenne and Timbuktu were centers of West African learning for centuries.

A Western African cities developed along trade routes to the Mediterranean. The city of Jenne, in the modern country of Mali, remains a trading center.

1 **Ghana** grows strong trading salt and gold.

2 **1076** Almoravids gain control of Ghana's capital, and the empire loses its power.

Empire of Ghana
700–1076

☐ Ghana Empire
⊛ Capital
EGYPT Culture region
⋯⋯ Desert
— Trade route

0   400   800 miles
0 400 800 kilometers

B No one is sure exactly when the Ghana Empire was established. By 700 Ghana was the most powerful kingdom in West Africa. The Almoravids (see page 58) probably weakened or destroyed the empire.

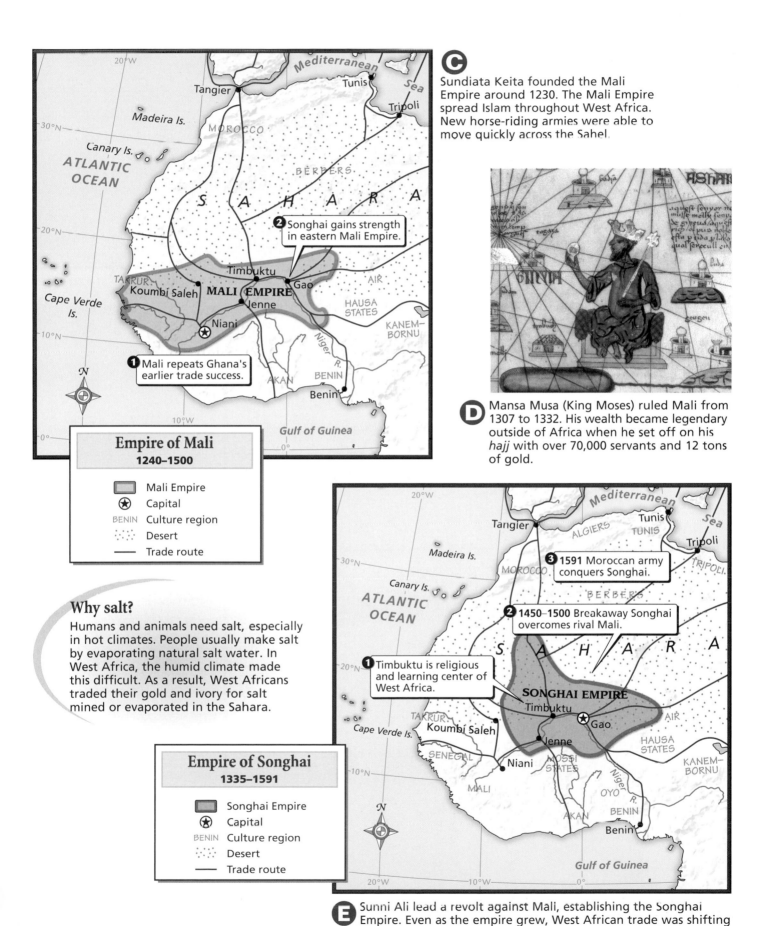

Empire of Mali
1240–1500

Mali Empire
⭐ Capital
BENIN Culture region
Desert
Trade route

❷ Songhai gains strength in eastern Mali Empire.

❶ Mali repeats Ghana's earlier trade success.

⊂ Sundiata Keita founded the Mali Empire around 1230. The Mali Empire spread Islam throughout West Africa. New horse-riding armies were able to move quickly across the Sahel.

⊃ Mansa Musa (King Moses) ruled Mali from 1307 to 1332. His wealth became legendary outside of Africa when he set off on his *hajj* with over 70,000 servants and 12 tons of gold.

Why salt?

Humans and animals need salt, especially in hot climates. People usually make salt by evaporating natural salt water. In West Africa, the humid climate made this difficult. As a result, West Africans traded their gold and ivory for salt mined or evaporated in the Sahara.

Empire of Songhai
1335–1591

Songhai Empire
⭐ Capital
BENIN Culture region
Desert
Trade route

❸ 1591 Moroccan army conquers Songhai.

❷ 1450–1500 Breakaway Songhai overcomes rival Mali.

❶ Timbuktu is religious and learning center of West Africa.

⊂ Sunni Ali lead a revolt against Mali, establishing the Songhai Empire. Even as the empire grew, West African trade was shifting from the Sahara to the Atlantic Ocean.

African States and Trade

Trade strengthened African states and empires as it linked the economies of Africa, Asia, and Europe.

- In East Africa, Islamic and indigenous African cultures mixed to form a new culture called Swahili. Swahili city-states developed along the coast.

- Bantu farming villages grew into many different states throughout central and southern Africa.

- Before 1500 most African trade went across the Sahara or to the Indian Ocean.

- Salt and gold were the most important goods within Africa. Gold and ivory were valuable for trade with the rest of the world.

A The Shona of southeastern Africa built Great Zimbabwe as a trade center and capital. This walled area was designed to look like a cattle pen, probably as a sign of the king's wealth. Locate Great Zimbabwe on map B.

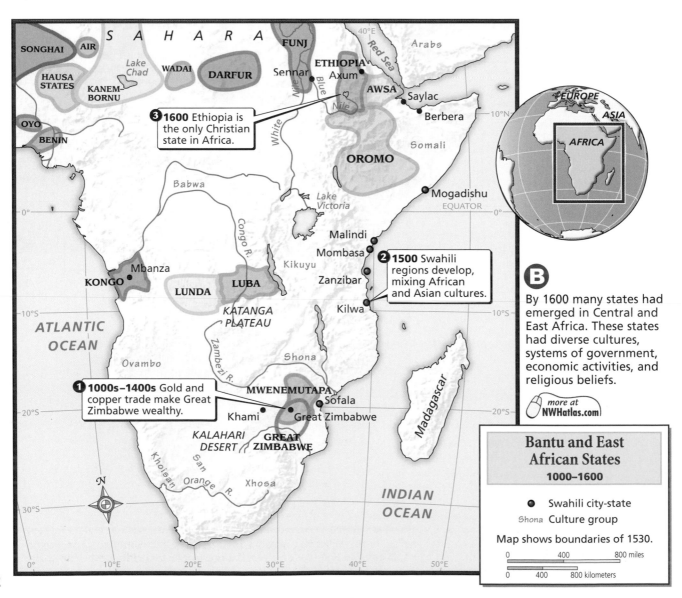

3 **1600** Ethiopia is the only Christian state in Africa.

2 **1500** Swahili regions develop, mixing African and Asian cultures.

1 **1000s–1400s** Gold and copper trade make Great Zimbabwe wealthy.

B By 1600 many states had emerged in Central and East Africa. These states had diverse cultures, systems of government, economic activities, and religious beliefs.

more at NWHatlas.com

Bantu and East African States
1000–1600

- ● Swahili city-state
- *Shona* Culture group

Map shows boundaries of 1530.

| 0 | 400 | 800 miles |
| 0 | 400 | 800 kilometers |

Top 10 Cities, 1200

City Locations	Rank/City (Modern Country)	Population
	❶ Hangzhou (China)	255,000
	❷ Fez (Morocco)	200,000
	❸ Cairo (Egypt)	200,000
	❹ Pagan (Myanmar [Burma])	180,000
	❺ Kamakura (Japan)	175,000
	❻ Angkor (Cambodia)	150,000
	❼ Constantinople (Turkey)	150,000
	❽ Palermo (Italy)	150,000
	❾ Marrakech (Morocco)	150,000
	❿ Seville (Spain)	150,000

C In 1200 most of the largest cities were in East Asia and Africa. Where in Africa were the continent's largest cities?

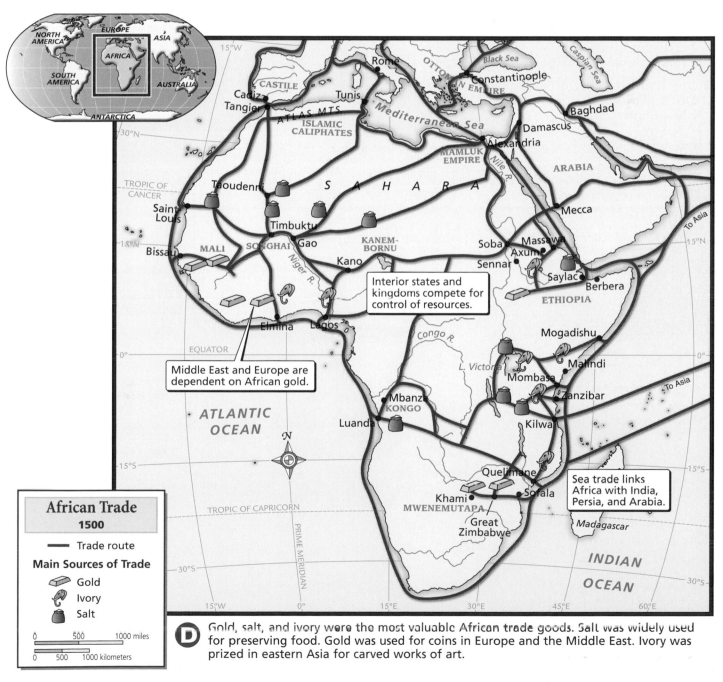

African Trade
1500

— Trade route

Main Sources of Trade

🪙 Gold

🦷 Ivory

🧂 Salt

0 500 1000 miles
0 500 1000 kilometers

Interior states and kingdoms compete for control of resources.

Middle East and Europe are dependent on African gold.

Sea trade links Africa with India, Persia, and Arabia.

D Gold, salt, and ivory were the most valuable African trade goods. Salt was widely used for preserving food. Gold was used for coins in Europe and the Middle East. Ivory was prized in eastern Asia for carved works of art.

Europe in the Middle Ages

418 to 1492

711–1492
Moors rule Spain.

400   600   800

418
Visigoths start a
kingdom in Spain.

432
St. Patrick introduces
Christianity to Ireland.

789
Vikings' first raid strikes
Portland, England.

800
Charlemagne is
crowned "Emperor
of the West."

Early Kingdoms of Medieval Europe

During the Middle Ages or medieval era, many Europeans were poor, uneducated, and violent.

- Early in the Middle Ages, barbarian tribes settled in Western Europe and established their own kingdoms.

- Barbarian kings, wanting to be as civilized as the Romans, became Roman Catholic.

- One Frankish king, Charlemagne, conquered much of Western Europe and launched education reforms.

B Charlemagne, a Frank, conquered the Bavarians, Lombards, and Avars. He hoped to restore the Roman Empire in the West. Here his army battles the Saxons.

A Compare the barbarian invasions on page 43 with the kingdoms on this map.

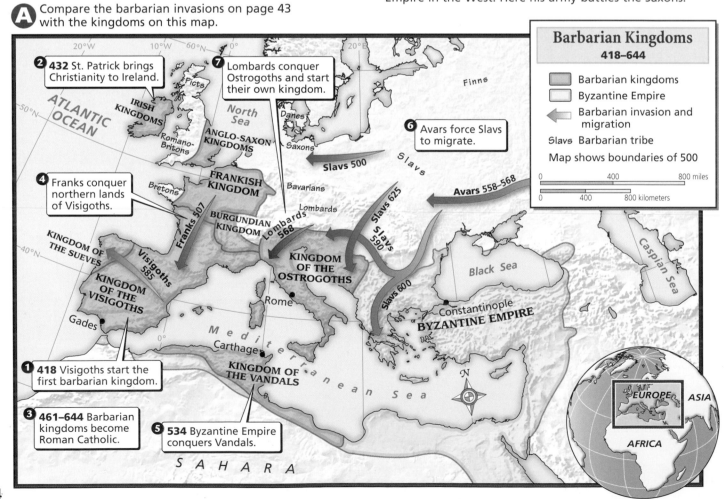

2 432 St. Patrick brings Christianity to Ireland.

7 Lombards conquer Ostrogoths and start their own kingdom.

4 Franks conquer northern lands of Visigoths.

6 Avars force Slavs to migrate.

1 418 Visigoths start the first barbarian kingdom.

3 461–644 Barbarian kingdoms become Roman Catholic.

5 534 Byzantine Empire conquers Vandals.

Barbarian Kingdoms
418–644

Barbarian kingdoms
Byzantine Empire
Barbarian invasion and migration
Slavs Barbarian tribe
Map shows boundaries of 500

0   400   800 miles
0   400   800 kilometers

ATLANTIC OCEAN
IRISH KINGDOMS
Picts
Romano-Britons
ANGLO-SAXON KINGDOMS
North Sea
Danes
Saxons
Finns
Slavs
FRANKISH KINGDOM
Bretons
Bavarians
Slavs 500
Franks 507
BURGUNDIAN KINGDOM
Lombards
Lombards 568
Avars 558–568
Slavs 625
Slavs 590
KINGDOM OF THE SUEVES
Visigoths 585
KINGDOM OF THE VISIGOTHS
KINGDOM OF THE OSTROGOTHS
Rome
Black Sea
Caspian Sea
Gades
Mediterranean Sea
Carthage
Slavs 600
Constantinople
BYZANTINE EMPIRE
KINGDOM OF THE VANDALS
SAHARA

EUROPE
ASIA
AFRICA

| 1066 | 1095 | 1347 | 1453 |
| Normans take control of England. | First Crusade is called by Pope Urban II. | Plague-infected rats arrive in Sicily. | Ottomans conquer Constantinople. |

| 1000 | 1200 | 1400 | 1600 |

| 936 | 1215 | 1337–1453 |
| Otto I creates what will be the Holy Roman Empire. | Magna Carta gives rights to free men in England. | Hundred Years' War fought between England and France. |

more at NWHatlas.com

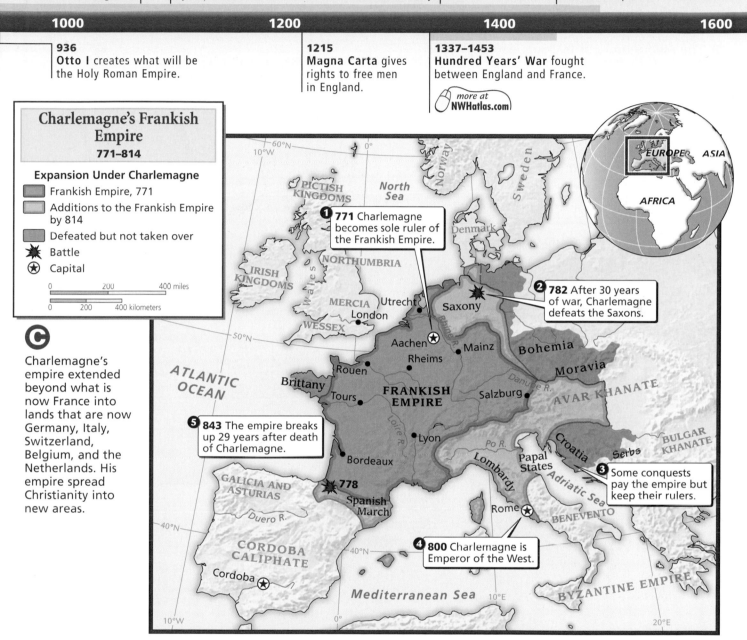

Charlemagne's Frankish Empire
771–814

Expansion Under Charlemagne

- Frankish Empire, 771
- Additions to the Frankish Empire by 814
- Defeated but not taken over
- ✴ Battle
- ★ Capital

0   200   400 miles
0 200 400 kilometers

C Charlemagne's empire extended beyond what is now France into lands that are now Germany, Italy, Switzerland, Belgium, and the Netherlands. His empire spread Christianity into new areas.

1 771 Charlemagne becomes sole ruler of the Frankish Empire.

2 782 After 30 years of war, Charlemagne defeats the Saxons.

3 Some conquests pay the empire but keep their rulers.

4 800 Charlemagne is Emperor of the West.

5 843 The empire breaks up 29 years after death of Charlemagne.

778

EUROPE   ASIA   AFRICA

PICTISH KINGDOMS, North Sea, Norway, Sweden, Denmark, NORTHUMBRIA, IRISH KINGDOMS, Wales, MERCIA, Utrecht, London, WESSEX, Saxony, Aachen, Rheims, Mainz, Bohemia, Moravia, ATLANTIC OCEAN, Brittany, Rouen, Tours, FRANKISH EMPIRE, Salzburg, Danube R., AVAR KHANATE, Rhine R., Lyon, Loire R., Po R., Croatia, Serbs, BULGAR KHANATE, Bordeaux, Lombardy, Papal States, Adriatic Sea, BENEVENTO, GALICIA AND ASTURIAS, Duero R., Spanish March, Rome, CORDOBA CALIPHATE, Cordoba, Mediterranean Sea, BYZANTINE EMPIRE

CULTURE
Education in the Frankish Empire

Who can read?

After the fall of Rome, education in most of Western Europe collapsed. Monks saved and copied books and taught a few students to read. Monasteries remained the center of European learning for almost 1000 years.

Before Charlemagne		Charlemagne's Education Reform
Boys studying to be clergy Some children of aristocrats	**Students**	All boys
Grammar, Rhetoric*	**Subjects taught**	Grammar, Rhetoric, Logic, Geometry, Arithmetic, Astronomy, Music
Monasteries Schools founded by bishops	**Location of schools**	Palace School in Aachen Primary schools in every city and village

*involved reading, rereading, commenting on, and imitating the classics

D At that time, lessons were taught in Latin. Charlemagne brought in teachers from England, Ireland, Spain, and Italy. But, without money or enough teachers, Charlemagne's education reform was largely a dream.

Moorish Spain

In 711 the Moors, Muslims from northwestern Africa, invaded Spain. Their Islamic kingdoms survived in Spain and Portugal for 800 years.

- The Moors brought learning back to Spain with ancient Greek and new Arab books on science, math, and philosophy.

- Many Moorish kingdoms were tolerant of Christians and Jews.

- Over the centuries, Christians from northern Spain, France, and England fought to push the Moors out of Europe.

②732 Frankish army defeats Moorish invaders.

732 Tours

Paris

Sens

Poitiers

FRANKISH KINGDOM

Lyon

ATLANTIC OCEAN

Toulouse

718 Covadonga

ASTURIAS

PYRENEES

719 Narbonne

713 Segoyuela

713 Zaragoza

Mediterranean Sea

CORDOBA CALIPHATE

712 Toledo

714 Valencia

Balearic Islands

716 Lisbon

711 Ecija

711 Cordoba

③756 Moorish Spain becomes the Cordoba Caliphate.

711 Jerez de la Frontera

Str. of Gibraltar

①711–719 Moors conquer Visigoths.

Fez

MIDRARID DYNASTY

EUROPE

ASIA

AFRICA

Moorish Conquest

- ➤ Moorish army invasion
- ▨ Moorish control, 710
- ▨ Moorish gains, 711–719
- ▨ Christian control, 719
- ✸ Moorish victory
- ✸ Christian victory

0   100   200   300 miles

0   100   200   300 kilometers

A The Moors quickly fought their way across Spain and Portugal. Christian forces retreated and held out in Asturias.

B This mosque in Cordoba, the Mezquita, was once a Visigoth Christian church. The Moors started rebuilding it in 784, using materials from an old Roman temple on the site. Today the building is used as a Roman Catholic cathedral.

SCIENCE & TECHNOLOGY
Islamic Contributions

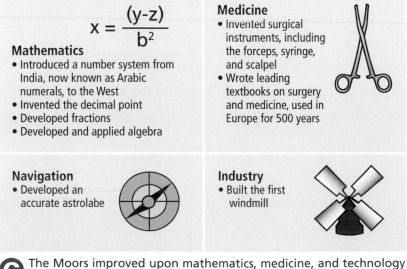

$$x = \frac{(y-z)}{b^2}$$

Mathematics
- Introduced a number system from India, now known as Arabic numerals, to the West
- Invented the decimal point
- Developed fractions
- Developed and applied algebra

Medicine
- Invented surgical instruments, including the forceps, syringe, and scalpel
- Wrote leading textbooks on surgery and medicine, used in Europe for 500 years

Navigation
- Developed an accurate astrolabe

Industry
- Built the first windmill

C The Moors improved upon mathematics, medicine, and technology from the East (see pages 44–45). The rest of Western Europe was significantly behind Spain in these areas.

Viking Impact on Europe

Vikings came from Scandinavia—Denmark, Sweden, and Norway. They were fierce warriors and superb sailors.

- Vikings terrorized towns along the coasts and rivers of Europe. They murdered villagers and looted and burned their towns.

- Vikings also built settlements in Europe as well as in Iceland and Greenland.

- Viking sailors reached North America, becoming the first Europeans to see the Americas.

D Viking ships used sails and oars to cross open water and move up rivers. Vikings landed quickly and left before defenders could gather.

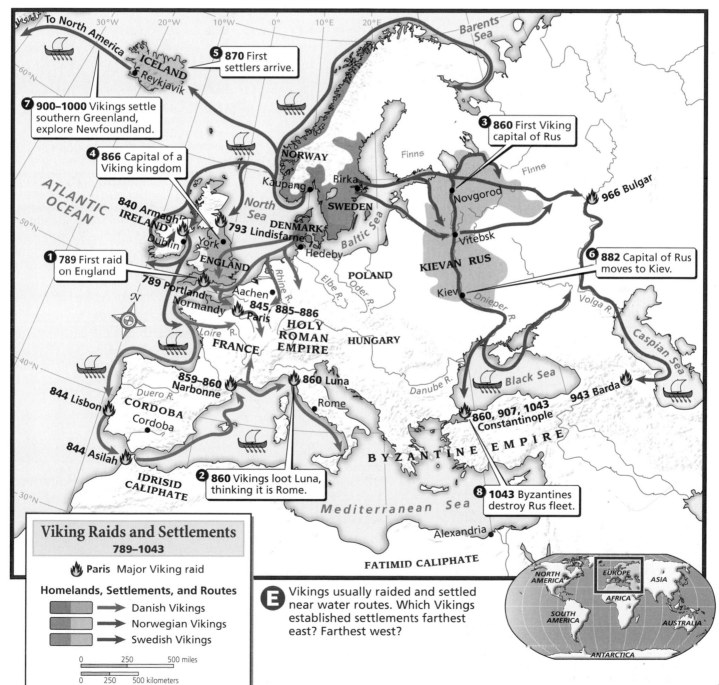

5 870 First settlers arrive.

7 900–1000 Vikings settle southern Greenland, explore Newfoundland.

4 866 Capital of a Viking kingdom

3 860 First Viking capital of Rus

966 Bulgar

6 882 Capital of Rus moves to Kiev.

1 789 First raid on England

840 Armagh
IRELAND
Dublin
York
793 Lindisfarne
789 Portland
Normandy
845 Paris
885–886
HOLY ROMAN EMPIRE
HUNGARY
943 Barda

859–860 Narbonne
860 Luna
Rome

2 860 Vikings loot Luna, thinking it is Rome.

860, 907, 1043 Constantinople

8 1043 Byzantines destroy Rus fleet.

844 Lisbon
CORDOBA
Cordoba
844 Asilah
IDRISID CALIPHATE

To North America
ICELAND
Reykjavik
ATLANTIC OCEAN
NORWAY
Kaupang
Birka
SWEDEN
North Sea
DENMARK
Hedeby
Baltic Sea
POLAND
KIEVAN RUS
Kiev
Novgorod
Vitebsk
Finns
Finns
Barents Sea
ENGLAND
FRANCE
Rhine R.
Aachen
Elbe R.
Oder R.
Loire R.
Duero R.
Dnieper R.
Volga R.
Caspian Sea
Danube R.
Black Sea
BYZANTINE EMPIRE
Mediterranean Sea
Alexandria
FATIMID CALIPHATE

Viking Raids and Settlements
789–1043

🔥 **Paris** Major Viking raid

Homelands, Settlements, and Routes

→ Danish Vikings
→ Norwegian Vikings
→ Swedish Vikings

| 0 | 250 | 500 miles |
| 0 | 250 | 500 kilometers |

E Vikings usually raided and settled near water routes. Which Vikings established settlements farthest east? Farthest west?

NORTH AMERICA
EUROPE
ASIA
AFRICA
SOUTH AMERICA
AUSTRALIA
ANTARCTICA

Feudalism and the Holy Roman Empire

Although there were kings during the Middle Ages, power was held by local leaders.

- To govern his land and protect it from invaders, each local leader—usually a noble—needed his own soldiers, supplies, and fortified castles. The result was a system known as **feudalism**.

- One leader, Otto I, created a feudal empire later called the Holy Roman Empire. In the empire, local leaders held the real power.

- The Holy Roman Empire survived for over 800 years.

SOCIAL STRUCTURE
Feudalism in the Middle Ages

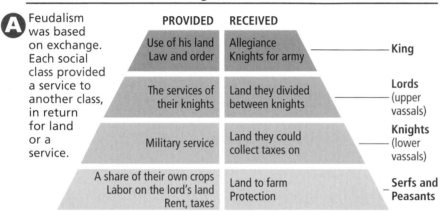

A Feudalism was based on exchange. Each social class provided a service to another class, in return for land or a service.

	PROVIDED	RECEIVED	
	Use of his land, Law and order	Allegiance, Knights for army	King
	The services of their knights	Land they divided between knights	Lords (upper vassals)
	Military service	Land they could collect taxes on	Knights (lower vassals)
	A share of their own crops, Labor on the lord's land, Rent, taxes	Land to farm, Protection	Serfs and Peasants

B In 1215 English barons (lords) forced King John to sign the Magna Carta or Great Charter. This document limited the power of the king and is still considered part of the English constitution.

more at NWHatlas.com

Medieval Manor and Village
1100

1. Manor (lord's home)
2. Church
3. Mill
4. Mill pond
5. Village
6. Community pasture
7. Wood lot
8. Lands for lord's personal use

C In much of Europe, lords owned manors like this one. Peasants who were the property of their lords were called **serfs**. Serfs farmed land both for their lords, who were usually nobles, and for themselves.

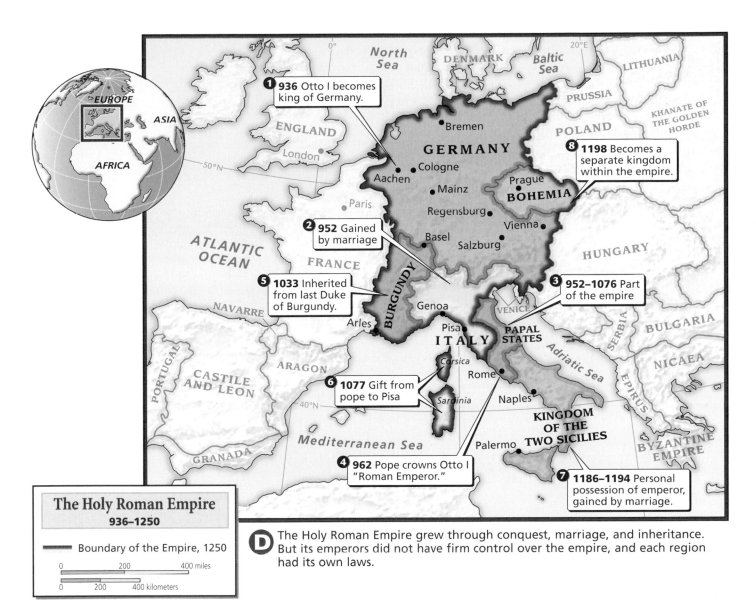

1 936 Otto I becomes king of Germany.

8 1198 Becomes a separate kingdom within the empire.

2 952 Gained by marriage

5 1033 Inherited from last Duke of Burgundy.

3 952–1076 Part of the empire

6 1077 Gift from pope to Pisa

4 962 Pope crowns Otto I "Roman Emperor."

7 1186–1194 Personal possession of emperor, gained by marriage.

The Holy Roman Empire
936–1250

—— Boundary of the Empire, 1250

0   200   400 miles

0   200   400 kilometers

D The Holy Roman Empire grew through conquest, marriage, and inheritance. But its emperors did not have firm control over the empire, and each region had its own laws.

Holy? Roman? Empire?

Otto I united northern Europe with the Roman Catholic Church. Later emperors named this territory the Holy Roman Empire. Like Otto, they were violent, German, and did not have much real power.

How Big Was the Holy Roman Empire?

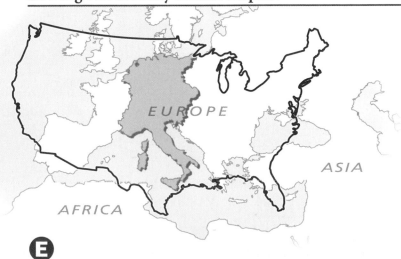

E

The Holy Roman Empire included almost all of central Europe. Compare this empire with the original Roman Empire on page 39. Also compare it to the size of the United States.

Crusades to the Holy Land

In 1095 the Byzantine emperor asked the pope for help in defending his empire from Muslim attacks. The pope agreed and called on European Catholics to join in a crusade against the Muslims.

- It was the first of eight crusades in which Europe sent huge armies to drive Muslims from the Holy Land, especially from Jerusalem.

- Thousands of Muslims, Jews, pagans, and Christians died in the brutal fighting.

- The crusades did not win permanent Christian control over the Holy Land. But they had the accidental benefit of increasing trade and knowledge of other cultures.

B When the First Crusaders captured Jerusalem, they massacred 40,000 Muslims and Jews.

A Disease, hunger, and war along the way killed as many Crusaders as battles with Muslims did. Three of the eight crusades are shown below.

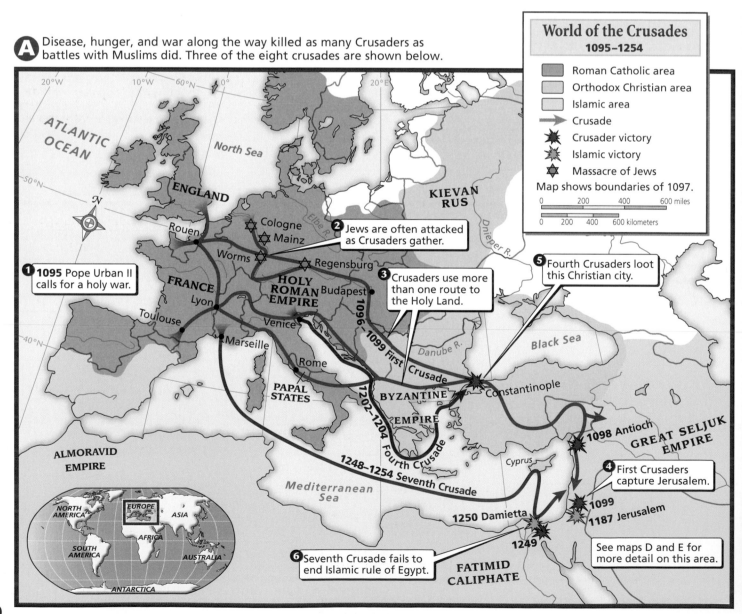

World of the Crusades
1095–1254

- Roman Catholic area
- Orthodox Christian area
- Islamic area
- → Crusade
- ✸ Crusader victory
- ✸ Islamic victory
- ✡ Massacre of Jews

Map shows boundaries of 1097.

0   200   400   600 miles
0   200   400   600 kilometers

ATLANTIC OCEAN

North Sea

ENGLAND

KIEVAN RUS

Rouen

Cologne

Mainz

Worms

2 Jews are often attacked as Crusaders gather.

Regensburg

1 **1095** Pope Urban II calls for a holy war.

FRANCE

HOLY ROMAN EMPIRE

Budapest

3 Crusaders use more than one route to the Holy Land.

5 Fourth Crusaders loot this Christian city.

Lyon

Toulouse

Venice

Marseille

Rome

PAPAL STATES

1096–1099 First Crusade

1202–1204 Fourth Crusade

BYZANTINE EMPIRE

Danube R.

Dnieper R.

Black Sea

Constantinople

1098 Antioch

GREAT SELJUK EMPIRE

4 First Crusaders capture Jerusalem.

Cyprus

ALMORAVID EMPIRE

1248–1254 Seventh Crusade

Mediterranean Sea

1250 Damietta

1099

1187 Jerusalem

1249

See maps D and E for more detail on this area.

6 Seventh Crusade fails to end Islamic rule of Egypt.

FATIMID CALIPHATE

NORTH AMERICA   EUROPE   ASIA   AFRICA   SOUTH AMERICA   AUSTRALIA   ANTARCTICA

The Crusades, 1092–1291

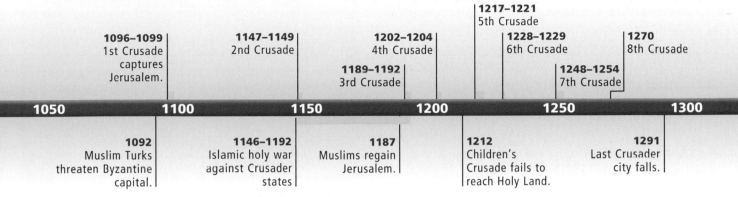

	1096–1099 1st Crusade captures Jerusalem.		1147–1149 2nd Crusade		1202–1204 4th Crusade	1189–1192 3rd Crusade	1217–1221 5th Crusade 1228–1229 6th Crusade 1248–1254 7th Crusade	1270 8th Crusade	
1050		**1100**		**1150**		**1200**		**1250**	**1300**
	1092 Muslim Turks threaten Byzantine capital.		1146–1192 Islamic holy war against Crusader states		1187 Muslims regain Jerusalem.		1212 Children's Crusade fails to reach Holy Land.		1291 Last Crusader city falls.

C Over a span of two centuries, Crusaders left for the Holy Land eight times. Which crusade was the longest?

D The First Crusaders divided the land they captured in the Middle East into four states. They also built castles to protect these states.

The Crusader States
1099–1140

- ▨ Roman Catholic area
- ▢ Orthodox Christian area
- ▢ Islamic area
- — Crusader States, 1140

Crusade or jihad?

Christians viewed crusades as armed pilgrimages—wars for a religious cause. Muslims viewed these wars as **jihads** or armed struggles against enemies of Islam. Both Christians and Muslims believed dying in these wars would get them directly into heaven.

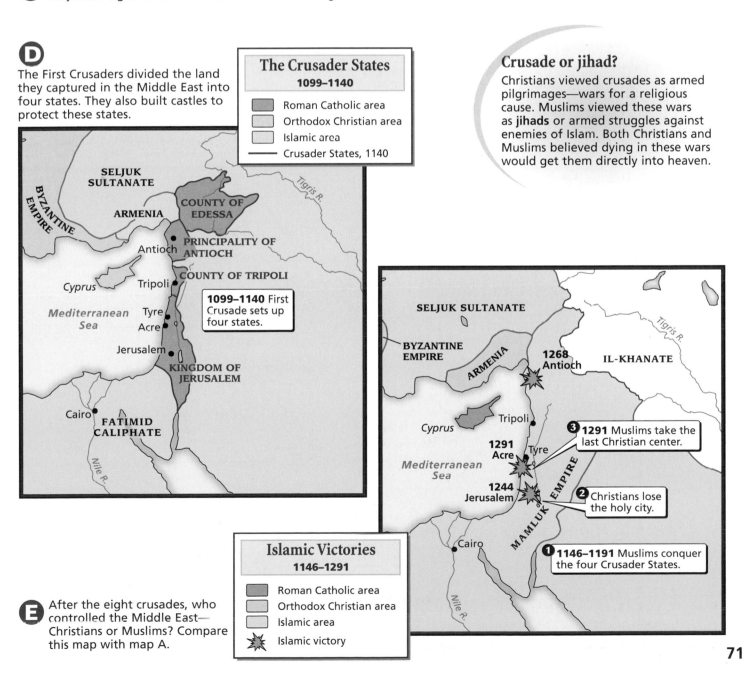

1099–1140 First Crusade sets up four states.

1146–1192 Muslims conquer the four Crusader States.

❷ Christians lose the holy city.

❸ 1291 Muslims take the last Christian center.

Islamic Victories
1146–1291

- ▨ Roman Catholic area
- ▢ Orthodox Christian area
- ▢ Islamic area
- ✸ Islamic victory

E After the eight crusades, who controlled the Middle East—Christians or Muslims? Compare this map with map A.

Trade Routes and Plague

Increased trade spread new goods across Europe. However, it also spread the worst disease in European history—the bubonic plague.

- Northern Europeans traded wool cloth, grain, wine, and silver for silk, perfume, and spices from Asia.

- Goods from Asia passed through the Mediterranean, and so did the bubonic plague. Rats, fleas, and people spread the plague along trade routes.

- In five years the bubonic plague killed a quarter of the people in Europe.

B Trade from the eastern Mediterranean made Venice rich. But it also brought the plague. Worsened by overcrowding and poor sanitation, the plague devastated the city.

A As trade increased, European cities grew. To protect their trade routes, a number of northern cities formed an alliance called the Hanseatic League.

European Trade
1200–1360

Main Trade Routes

—— By land and river

—— By sea

● City in Hanseatic League

• Other city

Map shows boundaries of 1360.

0   250   500 miles
0   250   500 kilometers

Hanseatic League controls trade in Baltic and North Seas.

Venice controls trade between Asia and Europe.

Genoa controls trade in western Mediterranean.

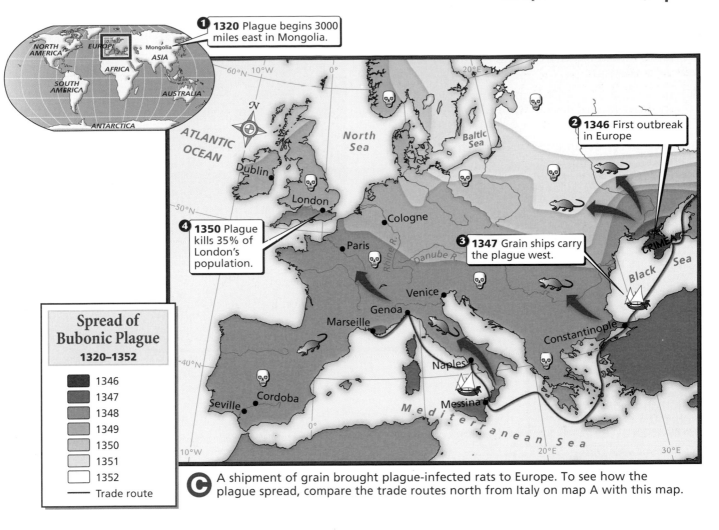

1 **1320** Plague begins 3000 miles east in Mongolia.

2 **1346** First outbreak in Europe

4 **1350** Plague kills 35% of London's population.

3 **1347** Grain ships carry the plague west.

Spread of Bubonic Plague
1320–1352

- 1346
- 1347
- 1348
- 1349
- 1350
- 1351
- 1352
— Trade route

C A shipment of grain brought plague-infected rats to Europe. To see how the plague spread, compare the trade routes north from Italy on map A with this map.

How did the plague change Europe?

The bubonic plague altered European society. After the plague, surviving peasants demanded higher wages and lower taxes. Nobles had to accept their demands because so few workers were left.

D Relatively peaceful times allowed Europe's population to rise—until the plague struck. How many years did it take for the population of Europe to recover?

more at NWHatlas.com

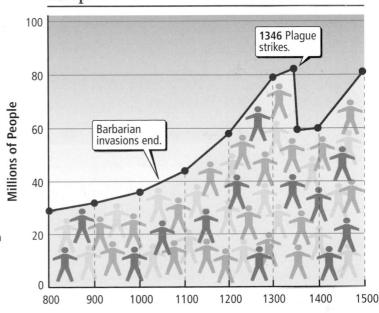

POPULATION
Europe 800–1500

1346 Plague strikes.

Barbarian invasions end.

Millions of People

Year

Reconquest of Spain

For almost 800 years, Christians fought to regain Spain and Portugal.

- Far northern Spain was the only region that remained independent throughout Moorish rule.

- From there, Christian kingdoms gradually fought their way south.

- In 1469 the marriage of Ferdinand of Aragon and Isabella of Castile united most of Spain. They completed the reconquest in 1492.

- These rulers began the Spanish Inquisition in 1480 to imprison, expel, or kill Jews and Muslims left in Spain.

B Boabdil (left), the last Moorish king in Spain, surrendered Granada to Ferdinand and Isabella in 1492. This ended almost 800 years of Moorish rule.

A Although this map shows only a few major battles, nearly continuous war slowly pushed the Moors back to North Africa.

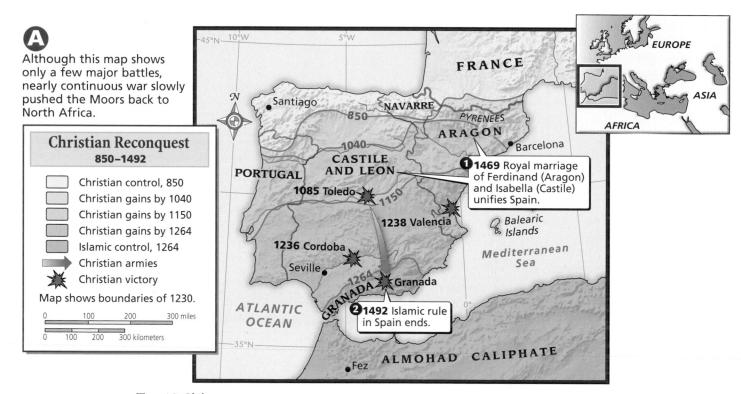

Christian Reconquest
850–1492

- Christian control, 850
- Christian gains by 1040
- Christian gains by 1150
- Christian gains by 1264
- Islamic control, 1264
- Christian armies
- Christian victory

Map shows boundaries of 1230.

0   100   200   300 miles
0   100   200   300 kilometers

1 **1469** Royal marriage of Ferdinand (Aragon) and Isabella (Castile) unifies Spain.

2 **1492** Islamic rule in Spain ends.

1085 Toledo
1238 Valencia
1236 Cordoba
1264 GRANADA / Granada

Top 10 Cities, 1400

City Locations	Rank/City (Modern Country)	Population
	1 Nanjing (China)	487,000
	2 Vijayanagar (India)	400,000
	3 Cairo (Egypt)	360,000
	4 Paris (France)	280,000
	5 Hangzhou (China)	235,000
	6 Tabriz (Iran)	150,000
	7 Guangzhou (China)	150,000
	8 Kyoto (Japan)	150,000
	9 Beijing (China)	150,000
	10 Samarqand (Uzbekistan)	130,000

C In 1400 most of the largest cities in the world were in Asia. Why do you think only one was in Europe? (Look again at page 73.)

Rise of the Ottoman Empire

The Ottoman Empire began as a small kingdom in the region known as Anatolia, near the Black Sea.

- The Ottomans were Muslim Turks who warred with neighboring Islamic kingdoms and European Christians.

- In the 1300s, the Ottomans organized the Janissaries. These were slaves, prisoners of war, and children trained as professional soldiers.

- Under Sultan Mehmet II, the Ottomans conquered Constantinople.

- After conquering the Byzantine Empire, the Ottomans gained power and wealth by controlling important trade routes.

D This illustration from an old text shows a European army battling Ottoman invaders. Europeans feared that the invaders would conquer all of Europe and put an end to Christianity.

Who were the Ottomans?

Groups of Turkish nomads migrated from Central Asia to Anatolia. In 1300 one of these groups began to expand its territory and build an empire. Its leader was named **Osman**, and his followers and successors came to be known as **Ottomans**.

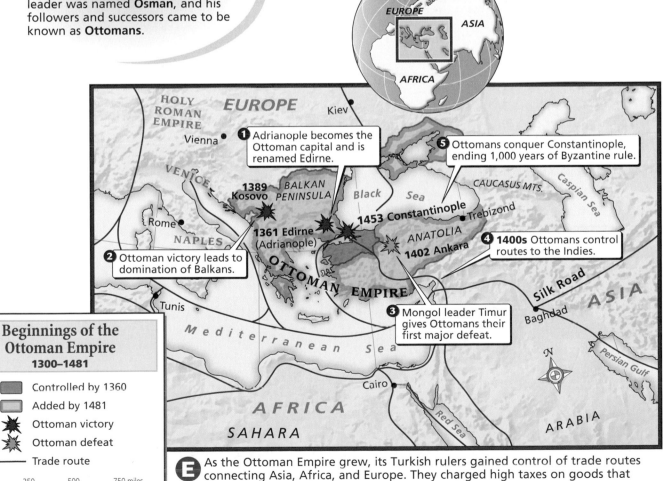

1 Adrianople becomes the Ottoman capital and is renamed Edirne.

5 Ottomans conquer Constantinople, ending 1,000 years of Byzantine rule.

2 Ottoman victory leads to domination of Balkans.

3 Mongol leader Timur gives Ottomans their first major defeat.

4 1400s Ottomans control routes to the Indies.

1389 Kosovo

1361 Edirne (Adrianople)

1453 Constantinople

1402 Ankara

Beginnings of the Ottoman Empire
1300–1481

- Controlled by 1360
- Added by 1481
- Ottoman victory
- Ottoman defeat
- Trade route

0   250   500   750 miles

0   250   500   750 kilometers

E As the Ottoman Empire grew, its Turkish rulers gained control of trade routes connecting Asia, Africa, and Europe. They charged high taxes on goods that were carried through their territory.

1521
Cortés conquers **Aztecs**.

1500
Cabral claims **Brazil** for Portugal.

1420
Portuguese begin exploring western Africa.

1492
Columbus reaches the Americas.

1300	1400	1500

1275
Marco Polo leaves Venice for China.

1325
Aztec people settle at Tenochtitlan.

1405
Zheng He begins his first voyage.

1438–1471
Inca Empire rises to power in South America.

1505
First slaves arrive at Hispaniola.

Trade in the Indies

Exotic trade goods from southeast Asia—the **Indies**—and from East Asia were highly desired by Western Europeans. These goods were extremely expensive.

- Travelers from Europe brought back stories of wealth and technology from the East.

- Travel on the Silk Road became dangerous as the Mongol Empire fell apart (see page 51). People began to look for another route.

- Middlemen in Central Asia and the Mediterranean region marked up the price of goods, making them too expensive for all but the richest people.

- Zheng He, a Chinese captain, lead seven voyages to expand Chinese power and find a replacement trade route for the Silk Road.

A Marco Polo travelled the Silk Road and across the Indian Ocean. His stories excited European interest in Asia. This illustration from his *Book of Marvels* shows him in India with pepper farmers.

more at **NWHatlas.com**

B

Merchants in Central Asia and the Middle East controlled trade between the Indies and Europe (see pages 44–45 and 75). Merchants and rulers in China and Western Europe wanted to by-pass them and increase their own profits.

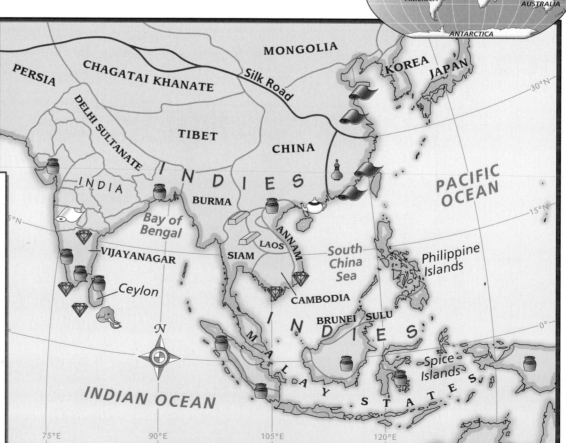

The Riches of the Indies
1400–1500

 Gold

 Silver

 Precious stones

Ivory

 Porcelain

Perfume

 Spices

Cotton

 Silk

 — Trade route

| 1535 New Spain extends from Mexico to Chile. | 1600 Horses from Spain are first raised by Native Americans. | 1667 French Guiana becomes a French colony. | 1721 Recolonization of Greenland begins. | 1788 Australia is colonized by the British. |

1600 — **1700** — **1800**

| 1550 Taino Indians of Hispaniola die out. | 1607 Jamestown is established by the English. | 1750 European powers claim most lands in the Americas. | 1763 France loses its largest colonies in North America. |

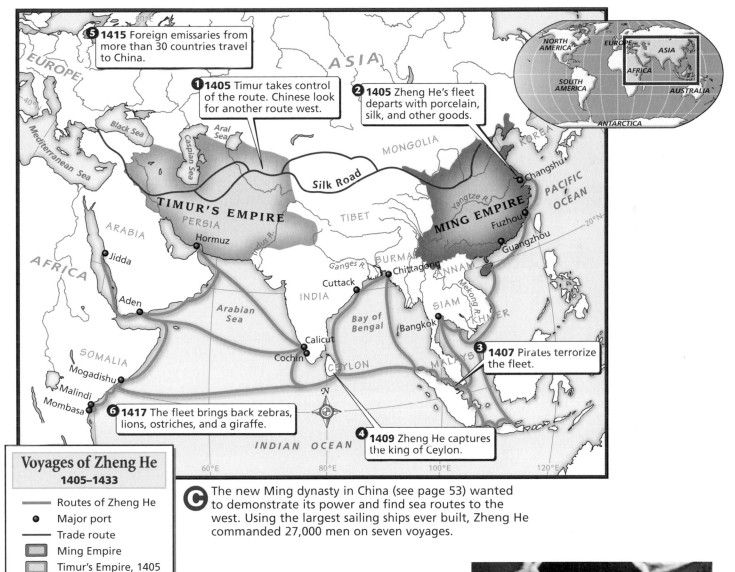

5 1415 Foreign emissaries from more than 30 countries travel to China.

1 1405 Timur takes control of the route. Chinese look for another route west.

2 1405 Zheng He's fleet departs with porcelain, silk, and other goods.

Silk Road

TIMUR'S EMPIRE

MING EMPIRE

3 1407 Pirates terrorize the fleet.

6 1417 The fleet brings back zebras, lions, ostriches, and a giraffe.

4 1409 Zheng He captures the king of Ceylon.

Voyages of Zheng He
1405–1433

—— Routes of Zheng He

● Major port

—— Trade route

▭ Ming Empire

▭ Timur's Empire, 1405

INDIA Culture region

0   500   1000 miles
0 500 1000 kilometers

C The new Ming dynasty in China (see page 53) wanted to demonstrate its power and find sea routes to the west. Using the largest sailing ships ever built, Zheng He commanded 27,000 men on seven voyages.

Why stop?

After several of Zheng He's expeditions, many officials felt they cost too much and produced too little. As a result, the ships were left to rot and Zheng's journals were burned.

D Spices from the Indies, such as cloves, cinnamon, and pepper, were worth as much as gold to Western Europeans. Kings sponsored explorations to win control of the spice trade.

77

Age of European Exploration

Beginning in 1420, Europeans began to explore the lands around the Atlantic Ocean. They hoped to find new sources of wealth including a route to the Indies.

- Competing European powers developed new technologies in shipbuilding and navigation that allowed them to explore new routes to the Indies.

- Europeans encountered American, African, and Asian cultures they had never known before.

- Often the European power that first explored an area later returned to conquer it.

NORTH AMERICA

30°N

PACIFIC OCEAN

7 See page 82 for more about the Americas.

0°   EQUATOR

30°S

1519–1522 Magellan

5 **1519** Rejected by Portugal, Magellan seeks Spice Islands for Spain.

60°S

A New ships such as the caravel were faster and safer than earlier ships. This Japanese screen shows a Portuguese trading caravel. By the 1500s more goods were being moved by sea than by land.

Where are we?

Inventions from Asia allowed Europeans to sail farther than ever before. The **compass**, from China, showed direction and the **astrolabe**, from the Middle East, showed latitude. The triangular **lanteen sail**, also from the Middle East, allowed ships to sail almost straight into the wind.

B

From 1420 on, Prince Henry of Portugal (in black) sponsored expeditions along the African coast, urging his captains to "go back and go still further." Although he never sailed a ship, he is called "Henry the Navigator."

more at NWHatlas.com

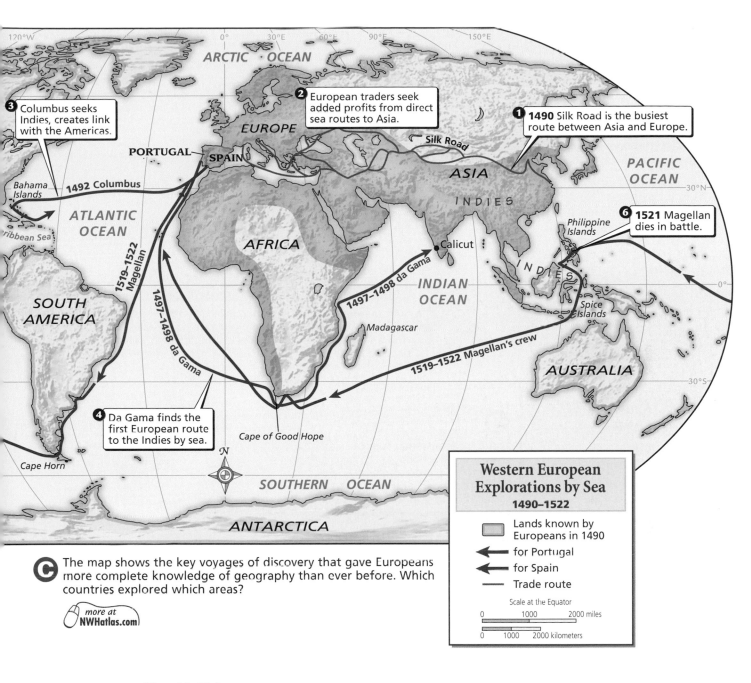

❸ Columbus seeks Indies, creates link with the Americas.

❷ European traders seek added profits from direct sea routes to Asia.

❶ 1490 Silk Road is the busiest route between Asia and Europe.

❻ 1521 Magellan dies in battle.

❹ Da Gama finds the first European route to the Indies by sea.

120°W 0° 30°E 60°E 90°E 150°E

ARCTIC · OCEAN

EUROPE

PORTUGAL

SPAIN

Silk Road

ASIA

INDIES

PACIFIC OCEAN

30°N

Bahama Islands

1492 Columbus

ATLANTIC OCEAN

Caribbean Sea

AFRICA

Calicut

Philippine Islands

INDIES

1519–1522 Magellan

1497–1498 da Gama

INDIAN OCEAN

Spice Islands

0°

SOUTH AMERICA

Madagascar

AUSTRALIA

30°S

1519–1522 Magellan's crew

Cape of Good Hope

Cape Horn

N

SOUTHERN OCEAN

ANTARCTICA

Western European Explorations by Sea
1490–1522

Lands known by Europeans in 1490

⬅ for Portugal

⬅ for Spain

— Trade route

Scale at the Equator

0 1000 2000 miles

0 1000 2000 kilometers

C The map shows the key voyages of discovery that gave Europeans more complete knowledge of geography than ever before. Which countries explored which areas?

more at NWHatlas.com

Top 10 Cities, 1600

City Locations	Rank/City (Modern Country)	Population
	❶ Beijing (China)	706,000
	❷ Constantinople (Turkey)	700,000
	❸ Agra (India)	500,000
	❹ Osaka (Japan)	360,000
	❺ Kyoto (Japan)	300,000
	❻ Hangzhou (China)	270,000
	❼ Paris (France)	245,000
	❽ Naples (Italy)	224,000
	❾ Cairo (Egypt)	200,000
	❿ Bijapur (India)	200,000

D Most of the largest cities in 1600 were still in the Mediterranean, India, and East Asia. Western European cities remained smaller, but trade and colonies increased their wealth.

Aztec Empire

The Aztec migrated from the north to a small island in the Valley of Mexico. They built one of the largest empires of Middle America.

- Religion dominated every part of Aztec life. The Aztec worshipped hundreds of gods and performed many kinds of religious ceremonies.

- The Aztec were fierce warriors. They waged war to expand their empire.

- The Spanish came to Mexico in 1519. They conquered the Aztec Empire in 1521 and destroyed its capital.

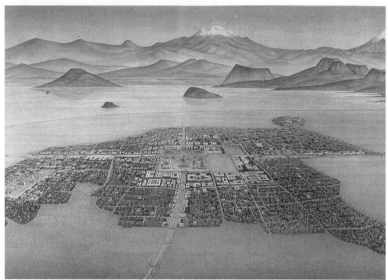

A Built on a lake, Tenochtitlan was larger than most cities in Europe. Its palaces, markets, and temple pyramids amazed the Spanish. Hernan Cortés, the commander of the Spanish, said, "It is hardly possible to describe their beauty."

more at NWHatlas.com

B The Aztec constantly fought with their neighbors in order to gain more territory and capture more people to sacrifice to their gods.

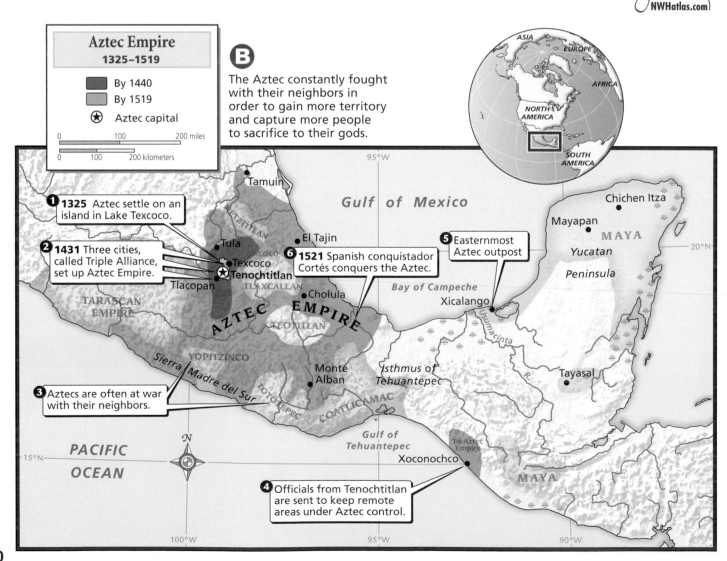

Aztec Empire
1325–1519

- By 1440
- By 1519
- ★ Aztec capital

| 0   100   200 miles |
| 0   100   200 kilometers |

1 **1325** Aztec settle on an island in Lake Texcoco.

2 **1431** Three cities, called Triple Alliance, set up Aztec Empire.

3 Aztecs are often at war with their neighbors.

4 Officials from Tenochtitlan are sent to keep remote areas under Aztec control.

5 Easternmost Aztec outpost

6 **1521** Spanish conquistador Cortés conquers the Aztec.

Tamuin

Gulf of Mexico

Chichen Itza

Mayapan

MAYA

Yucatan

Peninsula

METZTITLAN

Tula

El Tajin

Texcoco

Tenochtitlan

Tlacopan

TLAXCALLAN

Cholula

Bay of Campeche

Xicalango

TARASCAN EMPIRE

AZTEC EMPIRE

TEOTITLAN

Usumacinta

YOPITZINCO

Sierra Madre del Sur

TOTOTEPEC

Monte Alban

Isthmus of Tehuantepec

Tayasal

COATLICAMAC

PACIFIC OCEAN

Gulf of Tehuantepec

To Aztec Empire

Xoconochco

MAYA

ASIA

EUROPE

AFRICA

NORTH AMERICA

SOUTH AMERICA

95°W

20°N

15°N

100°W

95°W

90°W

Inca Empire

Around the same time the Aztec were building their empire, the Inca developed a large empire in South America.

- The Inca built an empire that extended through the Andes Mountains and along the west coast.

- They were excellent architects and engineers and built a vast network of roads and bridges. These helped their strong central government control even the most remote parts of the empire.

- The Spanish came to South America in 1532. They killed the Inca emperor and took over the empire.

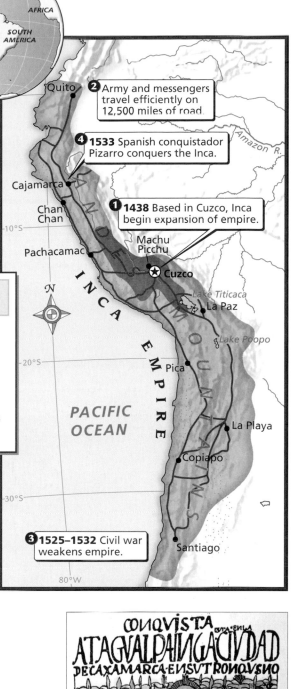

2 Army and messengers travel efficiently on 12,500 miles of road.

4 1533 Spanish conquistador Pizarro conquers the Inca.

1 1438 Based in Cuzco, Inca begin expansion of empire.

3 1525–1532 Civil war weakens empire.

Inca Empire
1438–1533

- ◼ By 1463
- ◻ By 1525
- ★ Inca capital
- — Main road
- ⋯ Desert

0   250   500 miles
0   250   500 kilometers

C Powerful emperors greatly expanded Inca territory in less than 100 years. By 1525 the empire stretched 2,600 miles.

more at NWHatlas.com

SCIENCE & TECHNOLOGY
Aztec and Inca Contributions

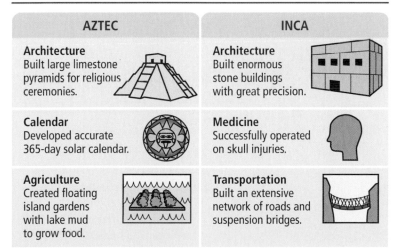

AZTEC	INCA
Architecture Built large limestone pyramids for religious ceremonies.	**Architecture** Built enormous stone buildings with great precision.
Calendar Developed accurate 365-day solar calendar.	**Medicine** Successfully operated on skull injuries.
Agriculture Created floating island gardens with lake mud to grow food.	**Transportation** Built an extensive network of roads and suspension bridges.

D Use this chart and the one on page 29 to compare and contrast Aztec, Inca, and Maya contributions.

E Francisco Pizarro, a Spanish conquistador, captured Atahualpa, the Inca emperor, and held him for ransom. When the ransom was paid, Pizarro had Atahualpa killed anyway. This was drawn by a native Peruvian in 1615.

Europeans Explore and Settle the Americas

Early European explorers searching for the Indies found unexpected opportunities in the Americas. By 1750 Europeans controlled most of the Americas.

- Europeans established colonies in the Americas and looked for ways to make a profit from the land and its resources.

- European colonization led to the conquest of Native American peoples, including the Aztec and Inca Empires.

- As European land claims expanded, Native Americans lost control of their traditional lands.

What about Australia?

Australia wasn't settled by Europeans until the late 1700s. At the time, **transportation** (deportation) was a common punishment for crimes. Between 1787 and 1868, about 162,000 convicts were shipped from Great Britain to Australia.

more at NWHatlas.com

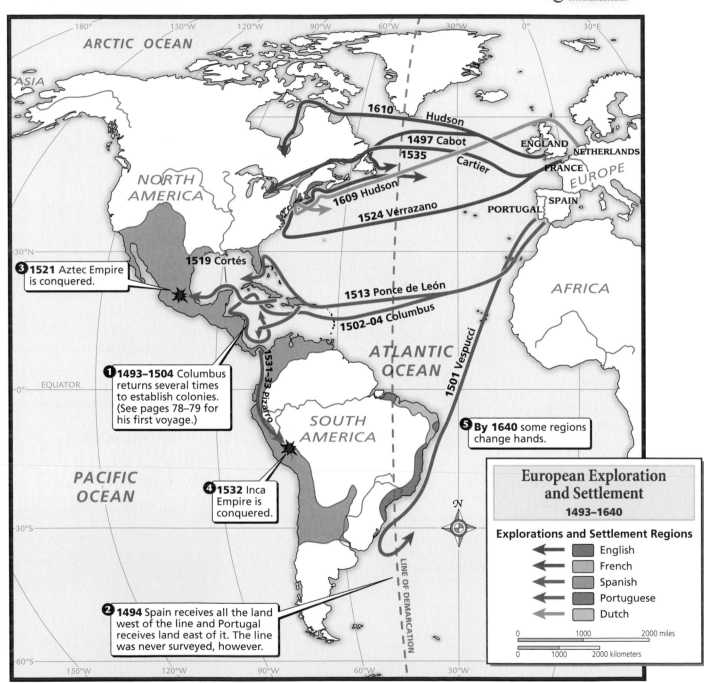

1610 Hudson
1497 Cabot
1535 Cartier
1609 Hudson
1524 Verrazano
1519 Cortés
1513 Ponce de León
1502–04 Columbus
1501 Vespucci
1531–33 Pizarro

❸ **1521** Aztec Empire is conquered.

❶ **1493–1504** Columbus returns several times to establish colonies. (See pages 78–79 for his first voyage.)

❹ **1532** Inca Empire is conquered.

❺ **By 1640** some regions change hands.

❷ **1494** Spain receives all the land west of the line and Portugal receives land east of it. The line was never surveyed, however.

LINE OF DEMARCATION

European Exploration and Settlement
1493–1640

Explorations and Settlement Regions

←	English
←	French
←	Spanish
←	Portuguese
←	Dutch

0   1000   2000 miles
0   1000   2000 kilometers

Ⓐ Exploration of the Americas led to the establishment of European land claims and settlement regions. By 1640 which European country had the largest settlement regions?

more at NWHatlas.com

82

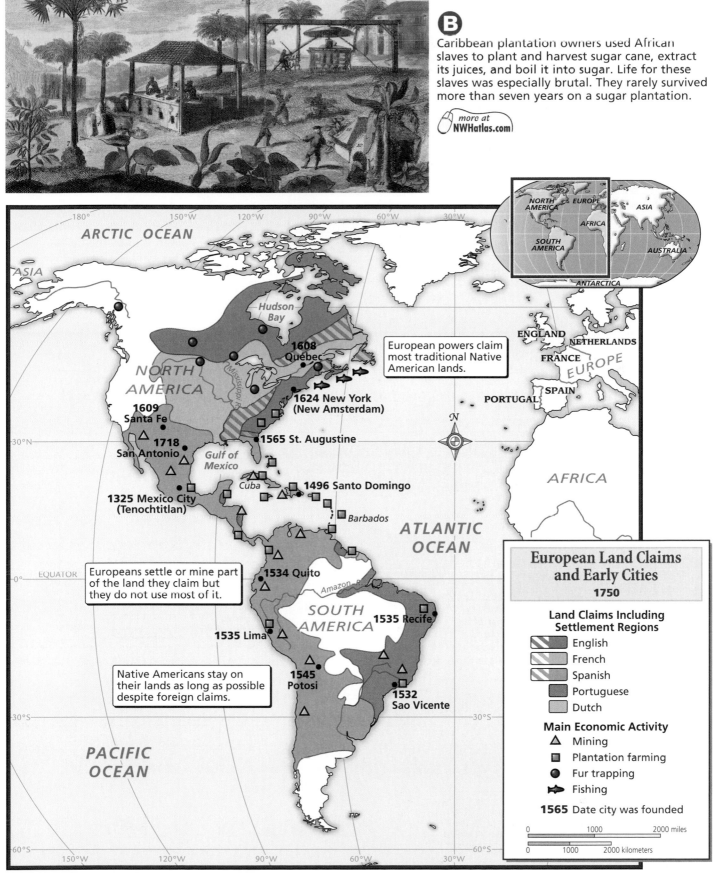

B Caribbean plantation owners used African slaves to plant and harvest sugar cane, extract its juices, and boil it into sugar. Life for these slaves was especially brutal. They rarely survived more than seven years on a sugar plantation.

more at NWHatlas.com

ARCTIC OCEAN

NORTH AMERICA EUROPE
AFRICA
SOUTH AMERICA
ANTARCTICA

ASIA
AUSTRALIA

ASIA

Hudson Bay

1608 Québec

European powers claim most traditional Native American lands.

ENGLAND NETHERLANDS
FRANCE
SPAIN
PORTUGAL

EUROPE

NORTH AMERICA

Mississippi R.

1624 New York (New Amsterdam)

1609 Santa Fe

1718 San Antonio

1565 St. Augustine

Gulf of Mexico

AFRICA

Cuba

1496 Santo Domingo

1325 Mexico City (Tenochtitlan)

Barbados

ATLANTIC OCEAN

Europeans settle or mine part of the land they claim but they do not use most of it.

EQUATOR

1534 Quito

Amazon R.

SOUTH AMERICA

1535 Recife

1535 Lima

Native Americans stay on their lands as long as possible despite foreign claims.

1545 Potosí

1532 Sao Vicente

PACIFIC OCEAN

European Land Claims and Early Cities
1750

Land Claims Including Settlement Regions

- English
- French
- Spanish
- Portuguese
- Dutch

Main Economic Activity

- △ Mining
- ◻ Plantation farming
- ● Fur trapping
- ⤞ Fishing

1565 Date city was founded

0   1000   2000 miles
0   1000   2000 kilometers

C Europeans in Middle and South America made money through activities such as sugar production and silver mining. An estimated one third of Europe's economy came from sugar.

more at NWHatlas.com

Impact of Colonization

European colonization of the Americas changed millions of lives throughout the world. When Europeans and Africans came to the Americas, three cultures were brought together.

- European ships carried plants and animals across the Atlantic Ocean in both directions. People on both sides of the Atlantic encountered goods that they had never seen before.

- As Europeans settled in the Americas, they often forced Native Americans to work for them. Millions of Native Americans died from overwork or disease.

- As the Native American population declined, Europeans began capturing, enslaving, and bringing Africans to the Americas to work as slaves.

A Native Americans were impressed by the horses Spanish soldiers rode. After 1690 Native Americans began raising horses themselves. Horses eventually changed the lives of the Plains Indians.

more at NWHatlas.com

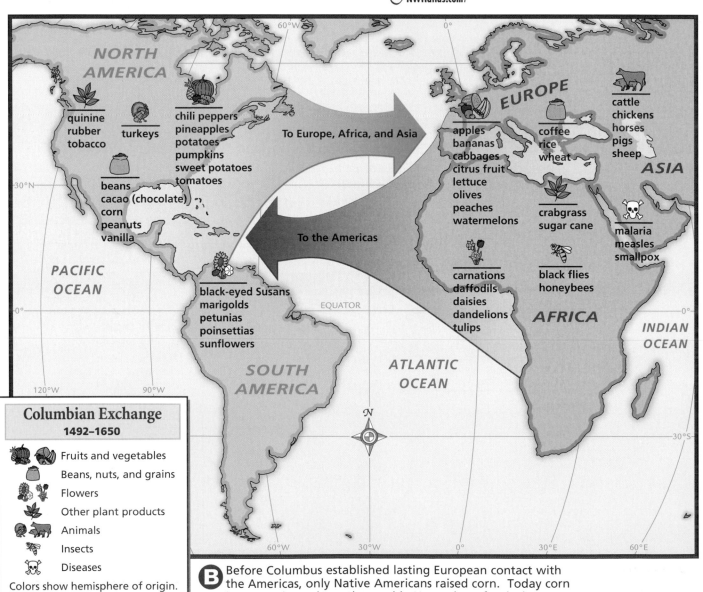

NORTH AMERICA

quinine
rubber
tobacco

turkeys

chili peppers
pineapples
potatoes
pumpkins
sweet potatoes
tomatoes

beans
cacao (chocolate)
corn
peanuts
vanilla

To Europe, Africa, and Asia

EUROPE

apples
bananas
cabbages
citrus fruit
lettuce
olives
peaches
watermelons

coffee
rice
wheat

cattle
chickens
horses
pigs
sheep

ASIA

crabgrass
sugar cane

malaria
measles
smallpox

To the Americas

carnations
daffodils
daisies
dandelions
tulips

black flies
honeybees

PACIFIC OCEAN

black-eyed Susans
marigolds
petunias
poinsettias
sunflowers

EQUATOR

AFRICA

INDIAN OCEAN

SOUTH AMERICA

ATLANTIC OCEAN

Columbian Exchange
1492–1650

- Fruits and vegetables
- Beans, nuts, and grains
- Flowers
- Other plant products
- Animals
- Insects
- Diseases

Colors show hemisphere of origin.

B Before Columbus established lasting European contact with the Americas, only Native Americans raised corn. Today corn is grown throughout the world. Name three foods that are not originally from the Americas.

84

POPULATION
Destination of Slaves, 1400s to 1800s

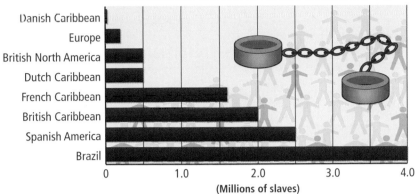

Danish Caribbean	
Europe	
British North America	
Dutch Caribbean	
French Caribbean	
British Caribbean	
Spanish America	
Brazil	

0   1.0   2.0   3.0   4.0
(Millions of slaves)

C Nearly 12 million Africans were enslaved and brought to the Americas. They worked mainly on plantations producing sugar, tobacco, and later cotton. No one can be sure how many slaves were sent to the Middle East.

more at NWHatlas.com

What happened to the original Americans?

Diseases from Africa and Europe, such as smallpox and measles, killed millions of Native Americans, who had no resistance to them. Whole civilizations were destroyed.

more at NWHatlas.com

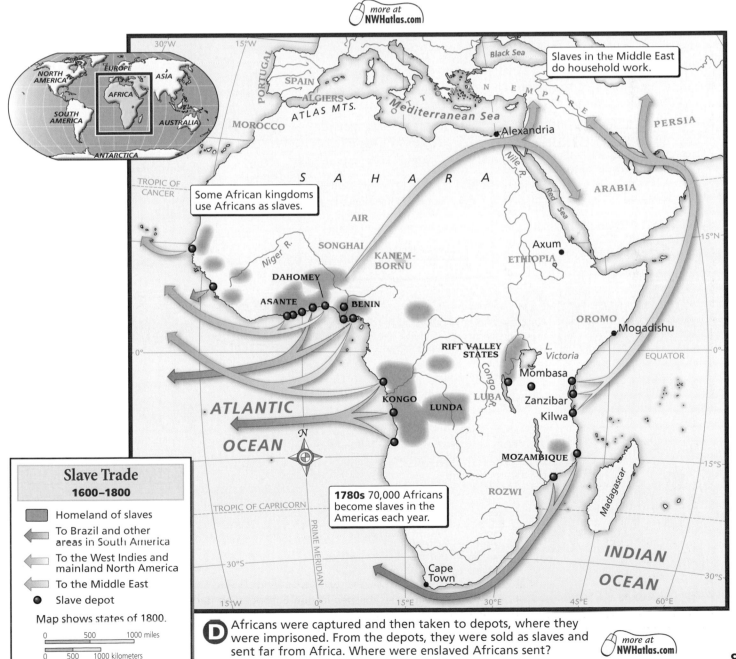

Slaves in the Middle East do household work.

Some African kingdoms use Africans as slaves.

1780s 70,000 Africans become slaves in the Americas each year.

Slave Trade
1600–1800

- Homeland of slaves
- To Brazil and other areas in South America
- To the West Indies and mainland North America
- To the Middle East
- ● Slave depot

Map shows states of 1800.

0   500   1000 miles
0   500   1000 kilometers

D Africans were captured and then taken to depots, where they were imprisoned. From the depots, they were sold as slaves and sent far from Africa. Where were enslaved Africans sent?

more at NWHatlas.com

1450
Gutenberg perfects the printing press.

1517
Martin Luther begins the Reformation.

1300	1400	1500

1350–1600
Renaissance flourishes in Western Europe.

1420
Work begins on **Brunelleschi's** dome in Florence.

1503
Leonardo da Vinci paints the *Mona Lisa*.

1543
Copernicus publishes theory on planets.

Europe During the Renaissance

Near the end of the Middle Ages, the **Renaissance**, a "rebirth" of European learning and art, transformed Western Europe.

- The Renaissance began in Italy. Scholars there rediscovered Greek and Roman art, science, and philosophy.

- The great works of the past inspired new artistic styles.

- Wealthy Italian city-states gave money to support new works of art based on Renaissance ideas.

more at NWHatlas.com

Scholars, merchants, and bankers spread Renaissance ideas across Europe.

The Renaissance Spreads Across Europe
1350–1600

⬅ Flow of Renaissance ideas

Ⓐ Home of Renaissance artist

Map shows boundaries of 1470.

0 — 250 — 500 miles
0 — 250 — 500 kilometers

SCOTLAND
IRELAND
ENGLAND
London Ⓐ
North Sea
NETHERLANDS
Paris
Ⓑ Mainz
ATLANTIC OCEAN
FRANCE
ARAGON
PORTUGAL
Madrid Ⓒ
CASTILE AND LEON
Lisbon
Seville

Soldiers returning home spread Renaissance ideas from Italy to France, Castile and Leon, and the Holy Roman Empire.

Ⓐ Plays by William Shakespeare are still performed around the world today. Other Renaissance playwrights included Marlowe, Moliere, and Vega.

more at NWHatlas.com

Ⓑ Johannes Gutenberg invented uniform movable metal type. His improvements to the printing press made books and pamphlets less expensive and helped ideas spread.

Ⓒ Miguel de Cervantes' *Don Quixote* was the first western novel. It was written in the **vernacular**, or language of the people, not in Latin, and in prose, not poetry. Other Renaissance novelists included More and Rabelais.

more at NWHatlas.com

EL INGENIOSO
HIDALGO DON QVI-
xote de la Mancha.
Compuesto por Miguel de Ceruantes
Saauedra.
DIRIGIDO AL DVQVE DE
Beiar, Marques de Gibraleon, Conde de Benalcaçar, y
Bañares, Vizconde dela Puebla de Alcozer, Señor
de las villas de Capilla, Curiel, y
Burguillos.

Impreſſo con licencia, en Valencia, en caſa de
Pedro Patricio Mey. 1605.
A costa de Iuſepe Ferrer mercader de libros,
delante la Diputacion.

1618–1648 Thirty Years' War is fought by religious rivals.	1683 Ottomans defeated at Vienna.	1784 Russia starts building trading forts in North America.

1600   **1700**   **1800**

1605 Cervantes publishes *Don Quixote*.	1650 Dutch control most European trade in Asia.	1762 Rousseau publishes *The Social Contract*.	1770 Colonial powers control most of the Americas.

D Balance, harmony, and perspective were key elements of Renaissance paintings. Compare Leonardo da Vinci's *Mona Lisa* with the medieval painting on page 70. Other Renaissance painters included Raphael, Van Eyck, Durer, and Brueghel.

E Renaissance architects admired the symmetry, proportion, columns, domes, and round arches of buildings from ancient Greece and Rome. This dome was designed by Filippo Brunelleschi. Other Renaissance architects included Palladio and Alberti.

F Renaissance sculptors were influenced by the realistic works of ancient Greece and Rome. Compare Michelangelo's *La Pieta* here with the Greek carvings on pages 33–34. Other Renaissance sculptors included Donatello, Cellini, and Verrocchio.

87

Reformation and Counter Reformation

During the Reformation, Western Christianity split into two groups: Roman Catholics and Protestants.

- In 1517 Martin Luther, a Catholic monk, began the **Reformation**, a movement to reform the Roman Catholic Church.

- Luther disapproved of the Church's practice of indulgences, the pardoning of sins for money. This and other criticisms led to the creation of separate **Protestant** churches.

- Conflicts between Catholics and Protestants caused wars throughout Europe.

Why are they called Protestants?

Protestants got their name from protesting, or speaking out against, the authority of the Catholic Church. Protestantism is the name for most non-Catholic and non-Orthodox Christian churches.

A Martin Luther, shown preaching here, thought sermons should be given in the congregation's native language, rather than Latin. He also wrote and translated hymns and the Christian Bible into his native language, German.

more at NWHatlas.com

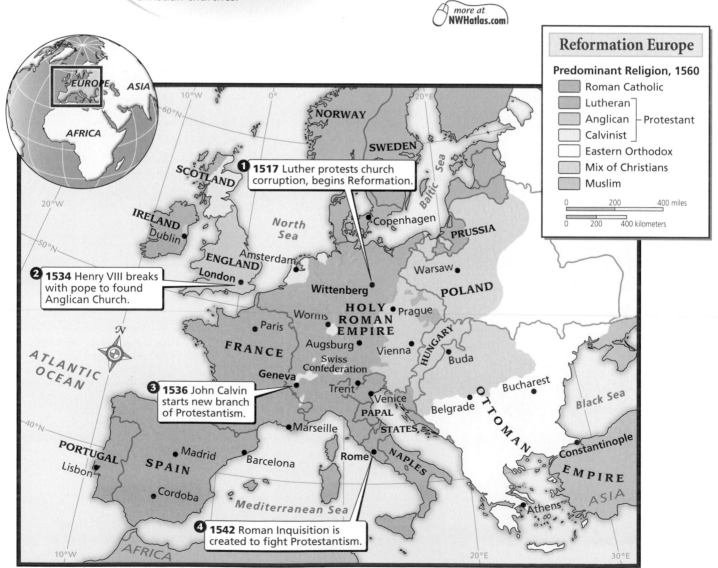

Reformation Europe

Predominant Religion, 1560
- Roman Catholic
- Lutheran ⎤
- Anglican ⎬ Protestant
- Calvinist ⎦
- Eastern Orthodox
- Mix of Christians
- Muslim

0   200   400 miles
0   200   400 kilometers

1 1517 Luther protests church corruption, begins Reformation.

2 1534 Henry VIII breaks with pope to found Anglican Church.

3 1536 John Calvin starts new branch of Protestantism.

4 1542 Roman Inquisition is created to fight Protestantism.

B Lutheran, Calvinist, Anglican, and other Protestant churches rapidly gained followers. Which regions had become mostly Protestant by 1560?

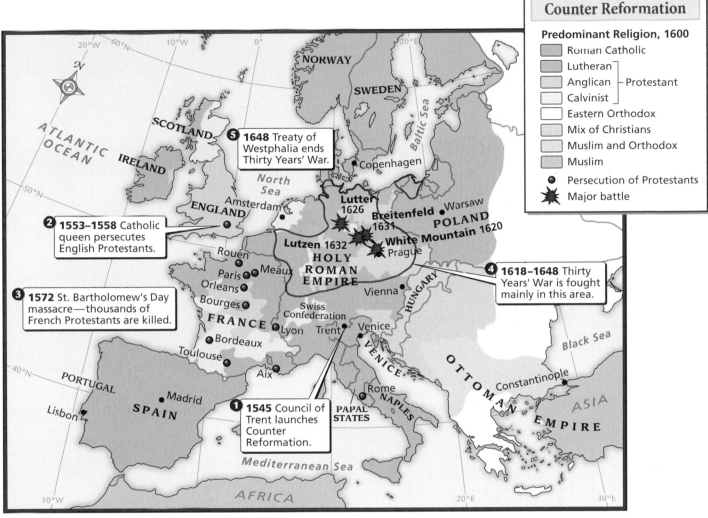

Counter Reformation

Predominant Religion, 1600

- Roman Catholic
- Lutheran ⎤
- Anglican ⎬ Protestant
- Calvinist ⎦
- Eastern Orthodox
- Mix of Christians
- Muslim and Orthodox
- Muslim
- ● Persecution of Protestants
- ✹ Major battle

5 1648 Treaty of Westphalia ends Thirty Years' War.

2 1553–1558 Catholic queen persecutes English Protestants.

3 1572 St. Bartholomew's Day massacre—thousands of French Protestants are killed.

4 1618–1648 Thirty Years' War is fought mainly in this area.

1 1545 Council of Trent launches Counter Reformation.

C Catholic efforts to stop the spread of Protestantism became known as the Counter Reformation. Religious conflicts and land disputes erupted into the Thirty Years' War.

D Catholic leaders made it a crime to print or read Protestant books. Forbidden books were burned in public.

CULTURE
Major Christian Churches, 1600

	Church	Began	Key Figure	Leadership
	Roman Catholic	1st century*	Peter	Pope, Cardinals, Bishops
	Eastern Orthodox	1st century*	Peter	Patriarchs and Bishops
PROTESTANT	Lutheran	1530	Martin Luther	Pastors
	Anglican	1534	Henry VIII	King of England
	Calvinist	1536	John Calvin	Elected councils

*1054 Christianity splits into two churches: Eastern Orthodox and Roman Catholic.

E The major Christian churches survived the Reformation and Counter Reformation. They still exist today, either with the same names or as the foundations of more recent churches.

89

Growth of Eastern Empires

In the 1600s the Ottoman Empire was the world's strongest and wealthiest empire. Around that same time Russia was growing into the world's largest country.

- Under Ottoman rule, Islam spread into Eastern Europe. However, the Ottomans allowed their non-Muslim subjects to practice other religions.

- In 1547 Ivan the Terrible became the first czar of Russia. The czars would remain in power until 1917.

- Under the rule of Peter the Great and then Catherine the Great, Russia grew in power and adopted many customs of Western Europe.

A The Suleimaniye Mosque was built to honor the great Ottoman ruler Suleiman the Magnificent. Today it is one of the largest mosques in Istanbul, the Turkish name for Constantinople.

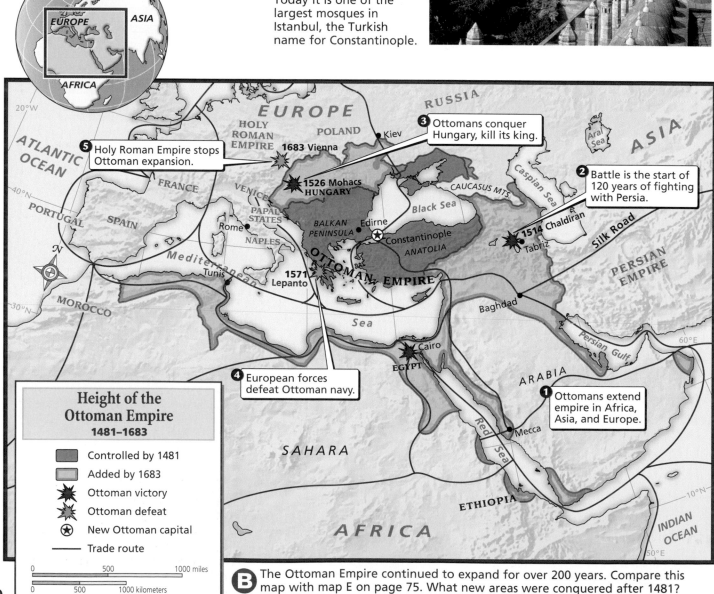

5 Holy Roman Empire stops Ottoman expansion.

3 Ottomans conquer Hungary, kill its king.

2 Battle is the start of 120 years of fighting with Persia.

1683 Vienna

1526 Mohacs HUNGARY

1514 Chaldiran

1571 Lepanto

4 European forces defeat Ottoman navy.

1 Ottomans extend empire in Africa, Asia, and Europe.

Height of the Ottoman Empire
1481–1683

- Controlled by 1481
- Added by 1683
- ✹ Ottoman victory
- ✹ Ottoman defeat
- ⊛ New Ottoman capital
- — Trade route

0   500   1000 miles
0   500   1000 kilometers

B The Ottoman Empire continued to expand for over 200 years. Compare this map with map E on page 75. What new areas were conquered after 1481?

4 **1784** Russians establish their first trading forts in North America.

2 **1721** Capital moves to a new city built by Peter the Great.

3 **1740** Russians finally gain an ice-free port.

1 **1585** Russians start building fortified towns east of the Urals.

Expansion of Russia
1533–1796

▓	In 1533
▓	Added by 1613
▓	Added by 1725
▓	Added by 1796
✪	Russian capital
1652	Date Russian colony founded
—	Russia's boundary today

0   200   400   600 miles
0   200   400   600 kilometers

C Once a country of modest size, Russia grew into the world's largest country. The greatest expansion took place under Peter the Great, whose reign ended in 1725.

GOVERNMENT
Types of Monarchies

LIMITED		ABSOLUTE
• Have a constitution • Have laws written by parliament	**Limits on Monarch's Power**	• None Have no constitution Have no working parliament Have laws created by monarch alone
• Have legal rights and privileges • Are members of parliament	**Aristocrats**	• Are controlled by monarch
• Henry IV, France, 1589–1610 • William and Mary, England, 1689–1702 • Maria Theresa, Austria 1740–1780	**Examples of Monarchies**	• Suleiman I, Ottoman Empire, 1522–1566 • Louis XIV, France, 1654–1715 • Peter the Great, Russia 1689–1725

D In the Ottoman Empire and Russia, many sultans and czars were absolute monarchs. Over generations, many absolute monarchies became limited monarchies.

E Catherine the Great was not Russian, yet she ruled Russia for over 30 years. During her reign she promoted religious tolerance, improved medical care, and promoted the arts.

Dawn of the Global Economy

As Europeans formed colonies overseas, most of the world became linked through trade.

- Based on the voyages of early explorers, Europeans claimed land in Asia, Africa, and the Americas.

- These regions were sources of valuable trade goods. European countries competed for access to these goods.

- As European trade expanded, more and more goods were exchanged among different regions of the world. A world economy began to form.

 more at NWHatlas.com

ECONOMICS
Mercantilism and Free Trade

Mercantilism		Free Trade
• Gold and silver for government • More exports than imports (favorable balance of trade)	**Goals**	• Easy access to goods and services • High standard of living
• Government monopolies on trade • Colonies to provide raw materials and a market for goods • High taxes on imports (tariffs)	**Methods**	• Little or no government involvement in the economy • Raw materials from cheapest source • Colonies unimportant economically • Competitive prices force efficient production and cheap goods
• Thomas Mun • Jean-Baptiste Colbert	**Advocates**	• Adam Smith

 Trade was an important issue for both colonists and colonial powers. While colonists preferred free trade, colonial powers benefitted from the control that mercantilism offered.

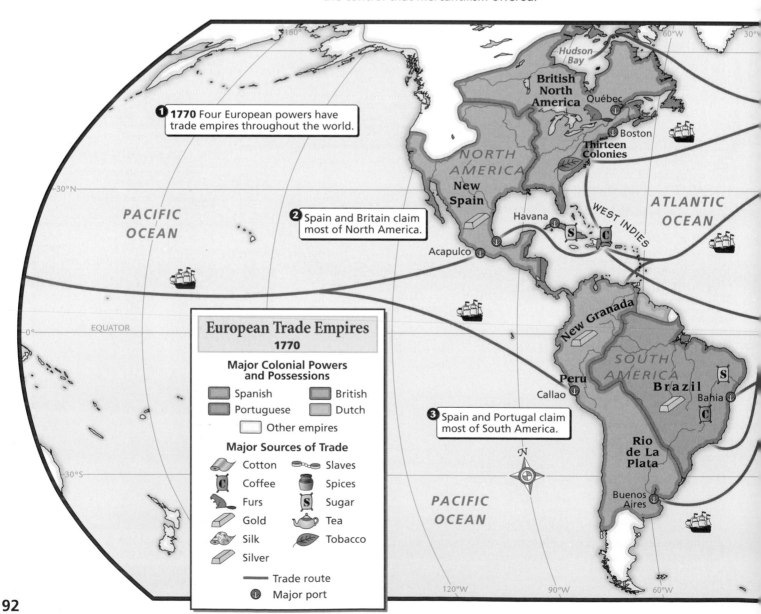

❶ 1770 Four European powers have trade empires throughout the world.

❷ Spain and Britain claim most of North America.

❸ Spain and Portugal claim most of South America.

Hudson Bay

British North America

Québec

Boston

Thirteen Colonies

NORTH AMERICA

New Spain

Havana

Acapulco

WEST INDIES

ATLANTIC OCEAN

PACIFIC OCEAN

New Granada

SOUTH AMERICA

Peru

Callao

Brazil

Bahia

Rio de La Plata

Buenos Aires

PACIFIC OCEAN

EQUATOR

30°N

0°

30°S

180°

60°W

30°W

120°W

90°W

60°W

European Trade Empires
1770

Major Colonial Powers and Possessions

- Spanish
- Portuguese
- Other empires
- British
- Dutch

Major Sources of Trade

- Cotton
- Coffee
- Furs
- Gold
- Silk
- Silver
- Slaves
- Spices
- Sugar
- Tea
- Tobacco

― Trade route
⊕ Major port

Top 10 Cities, 1800

City Locations	Rank/City (Modern Country)	Population
	① Beijing (China)	1,100,000
	② London (United Kingdom)	861,000
	③ Canton (China)	800,000
	④ Edo (Japan)	685,000
	⑤ Constantinople (Turkey)	570,000
	⑥ Paris (France)	547,000
	⑦ Naples (Italy)	430,000
	⑧ Hangzhou (China)	387,000
	⑨ Osaka (Japan)	383,000
	⑩ Kyoto (Japan)	377,000

C Most of the largest cities in 1800 were trade centers. As the global trade network grew, the world became more interconnected.

B Europeans traded in goods, such as coffee and silk, as well as in slaves. Usually European trading powers controlled the ports near the sources of trade.

more at NWHatlas.com

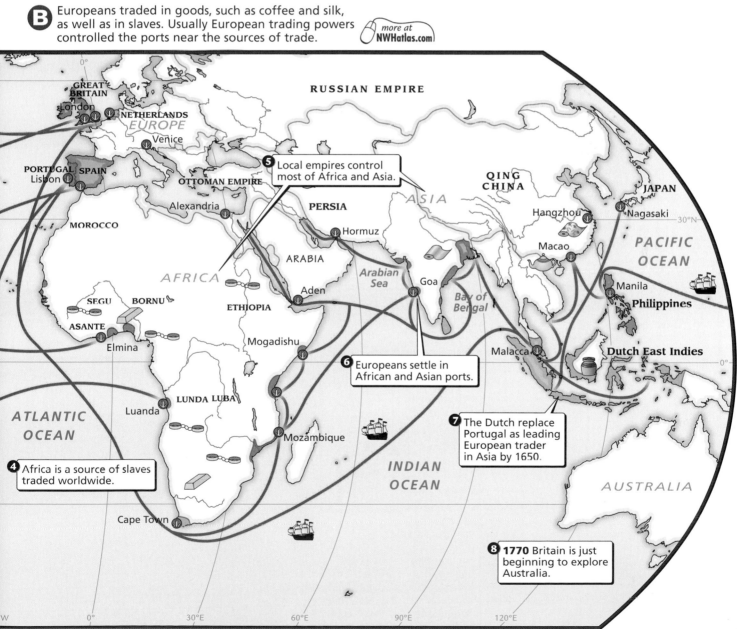

5 Local empires control most of Africa and Asia.

6 Europeans settle in African and Asian ports.

7 The Dutch replace Portugal as leading European trader in Asia by 1650.

4 Africa is a source of slaves traded worldwide.

8 1770 Britain is just beginning to explore Australia.

Scientific Revolution and Enlightenment

The 17th and 18th centuries have been called the **Age of Reason**. People began to question religion, science, and government.

- Scientists developed the scientific method, testing old ideas against new observations made with more precise instruments.

- The resulting **Scientific Revolution** completely changed how people saw the world.

- Philosophers and governments hoped to replace older ideas of government and society with new ones that worked better. This movement was called the **Enlightenment**.

- Enlightenment philosophers concluded that society was a voluntary group of free and equal people. This encouraged people to fight for freedom and equality.

B Marie Anne and Antoine Lavoisier conducted experiments together. She recorded the results, translated them into English, and drew illustrations of the equipment used.

SCIENCE & TECHNOLOGY
Scientific Revolution, 1543–1800

A Some of these scientists, particularly Copernicus and Galileo, were denounced by religious authorities. Their discoveries contradicted the Bible.

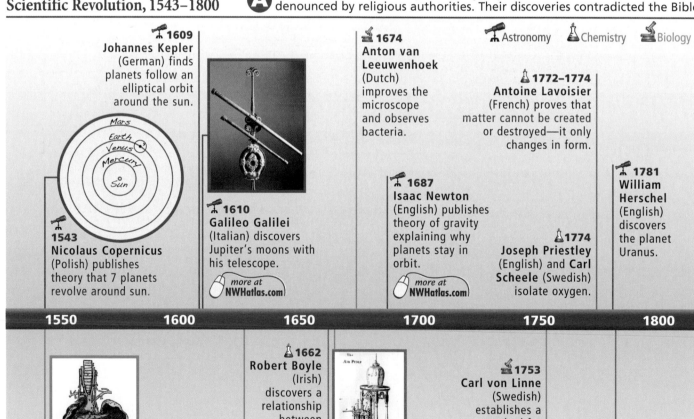

🔭 Astronomy   ⚗ Chemistry   🔬 Biology

🔭 **1609**
Johannes Kepler (German) finds planets follow an elliptical orbit around the sun.

🔭 **1610**
Galileo Galilei (Italian) discovers Jupiter's moons with his telescope.
more at NWHatlas.com

🔭 **1543**
Nicolaus Copernicus (Polish) publishes theory that 7 planets revolve around sun.

🔬 **1674**
Anton van Leeuwenhoek (Dutch) improves the microscope and observes bacteria.

🔭 **1687**
Isaac Newton (English) publishes theory of gravity explaining why planets stay in orbit.
more at NWHatlas.com

⚗ **1772–1774**
Antoine Lavoisier (French) proves that matter cannot be created or destroyed—it only changes in form.

⚗ **1774**
Joseph Priestley (English) and **Carl Scheele** (Swedish) isolate oxygen.

🔭 **1781**
William Herschel (English) discovers the planet Uranus.

1550   1600   1650   1700   1750   1800

🔬 **1543**
Andreas Vesalius (Flemish) publishes the first illustrated manual of human anatomy.

🔬 **1628**
William Harvey (English) publishes his findings on how blood circulates through the body.

⚗ **1662**
Robert Boyle (Irish) discovers a relationship between pressure and volume of a gas.

🔬 **1665**
Robert Hooke (English) studies plants under a microscope and discovers cells.

🔬 **1753**
Carl von Linne (Swedish) establishes a method for naming and classifying plants.

⚗ **1782**
James Watt (Scottish) invents a new steam engine.

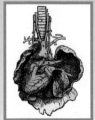

94

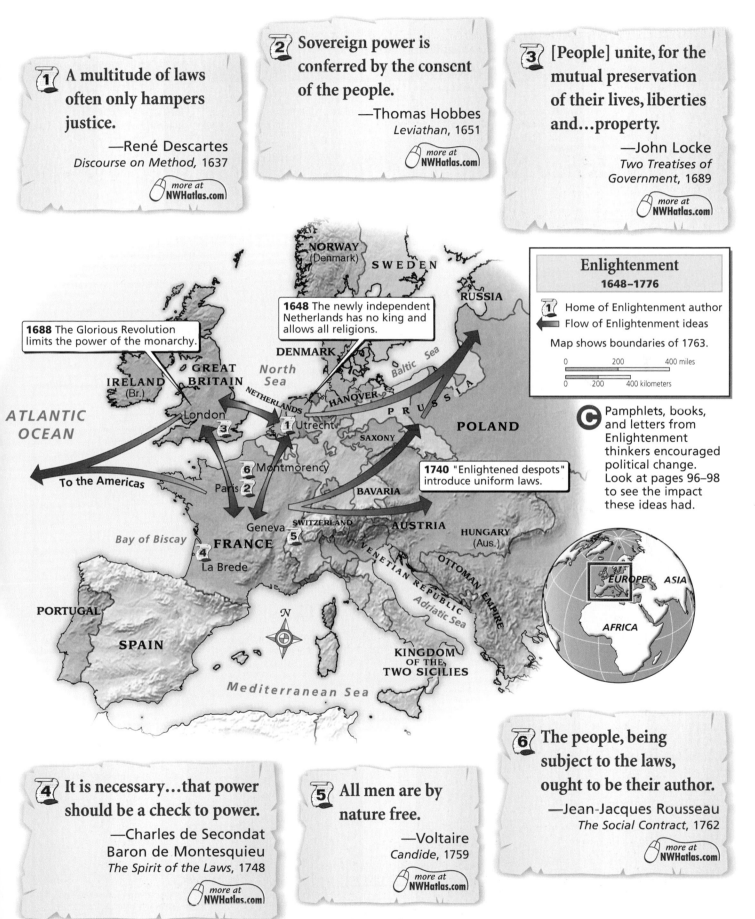

1. A multitude of laws often only hampers justice.

—René Descartes
Discourse on Method, 1637

more at NWHatlas.com

2. Sovereign power is conferred by the consent of the people.

—Thomas Hobbes
Leviathan, 1651

more at NWHatlas.com

3. [People] unite, for the mutual preservation of their lives, liberties and...property.

—John Locke
Two Treatises of Government, 1689

more at NWHatlas.com

Enlightenment
1648–1776

1. Home of Enlightenment author
Flow of Enlightenment ideas

Map shows boundaries of 1763.

0   200   400 miles
0   200   400 kilometers

1648 The newly independent Netherlands has no king and allows all religions.

1688 The Glorious Revolution limits the power of the monarchy.

1740 "Enlightened despots" introduce uniform laws.

NORWAY (Denmark)
SWEDEN
RUSSIA
DENMARK
North Sea
Baltic Sea
GREAT BRITAIN
IRELAND (Br.)
London
NETHERLANDS
HANOVER
PRUSSIA
POLAND
Utrecht
SAXONY
Montmorency
Paris
BAVARIA
ATLANTIC OCEAN
To the Americas
Geneva
SWITZERLAND
AUSTRIA
HUNGARY (Aus.)
Bay of Biscay
FRANCE
La Brede
VENETIAN REPUBLIC
OTTOMAN EMPIRE
Adriatic Sea
PORTUGAL
SPAIN
KINGDOM OF THE TWO SICILIES
Mediterranean Sea

EUROPE   ASIA
AFRICA

C Pamphlets, books, and letters from Enlightenment thinkers encouraged political change. Look at pages 96–98 to see the impact these ideas had.

4. It is necessary...that power should be a check to power.

—Charles de Secondat
Baron de Montesquieu
The Spirit of the Laws, 1748

more at NWHatlas.com

5. All men are by nature free.

—Voltaire
Candide, 1759

more at NWHatlas.com

6. The people, being subject to the laws, ought to be their author.

—Jean-Jacques Rousseau
The Social Contract, 1762

more at NWHatlas.com

1785
Steam-powered loom is invented.

1815
Napoleon is defeated at Waterloo.

1821
Mexico wins independence from Spain.

| 1775 | 1800 | 1825 |

1775–1781
American Revolution frees United States from Britain.

1789
French Revolution begins.

1819
Bolívar becomes first president of Gran Colombia.

Independence in the Americas

Most colonies in the Americas—British, French, Spanish, and Portuguese—won their independence over a period of just 50 years.

- Colonists throughout the Americas resented European rule. They could not govern themselves. Their businesses were hurt by taxes and trade limits. Their protests were ignored by European governments.

- In 1776 colonists in 13 British colonies rebelled. Their struggle encouraged colonists in other parts of the Americas to fight for independence.

How does a revolution turn things around?

When King George III of England took away some of his colonists' rights, they declared a **revolution** (a circular movement) to get them back. The result was American independence. Now a "revolution" means an extraordinary change.

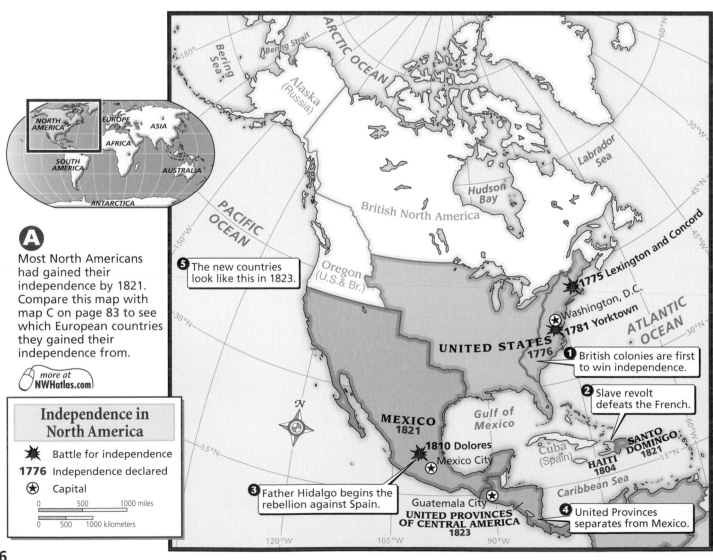

A

Most North Americans had gained their independence by 1821. Compare this map with map C on page 83 to see which European countries they gained their independence from.

more at NWHatlas.com

Independence in North America

✸ Battle for independence

1776 Independence declared

✪ Capital

0   500   1000 miles
0 500 1000 kilometers

5 The new countries look like this in 1823.

Oregon (U.S.& Br.)

Alaska (Russia)

British North America

Hudson Bay

Labrador Sea

1775 Lexington and Concord

Washington, D.C.
1781 Yorktown

UNITED STATES
1776

1 British colonies are first to win independence.

2 Slave revolt defeats the French.

MEXICO
1821

Gulf of Mexico

Cuba (Spain)

SANTO DOMINGO **1821**

HAITI **1804**

1810 Dolores
Mexico City

3 Father Hidalgo begins the rebellion against Spain.

Guatemala City
UNITED PROVINCES OF CENTRAL AMERICA
1823

Caribbean Sea

4 United Provinces separates from Mexico.

1848	1857			1895	1898	
Revolutions erupt throughout Europe.	**Indian troops** mutiny against British commanders.	**1869** **Suez Canal** links Red and Mediterranean Seas.		**Sino-Japanese War** ends.	**Spanish-American War** **1900** **Boxer Rebellion** pits Chinese against foreigners.	

1850	**1875**	**1900**	**1925**

	1853	1867	1884–1914	1910
	Perry's fleet opens the way to U.S.-Japanese trade.	**Japanese emperor** regains power from shoguns.	**Control of Africa** is seized by European powers.	**Japan** annexes Korea.

B Simón Bolívar, the "George Washington of South America," fought the Spanish for six years. He succeeded in gaining independence for South American countries, but his plan for a United States of South America failed.

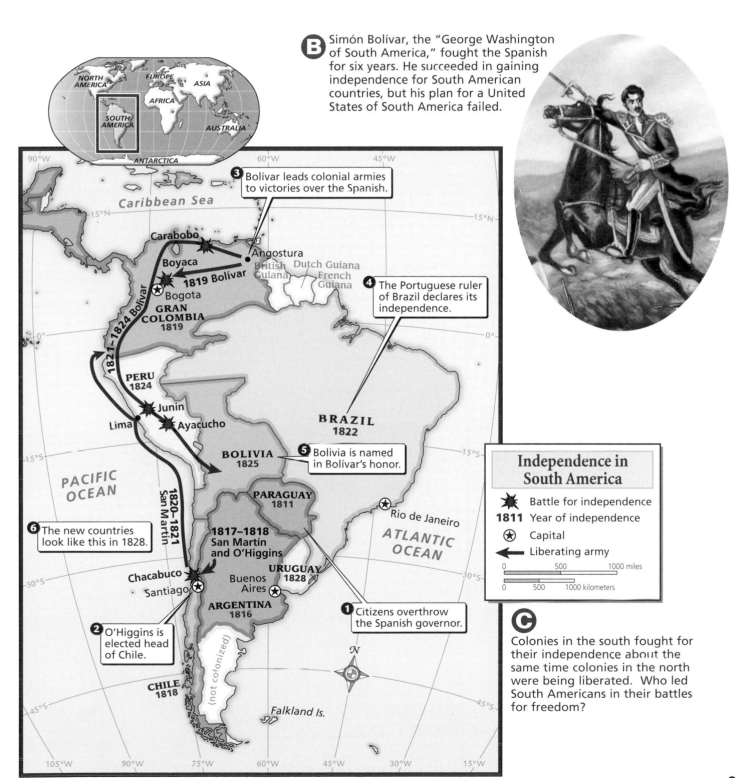

3 Bolívar leads colonial armies to victories over the Spanish.

4 The Portuguese ruler of Brazil declares its independence.

5 Bolivia is named in Bolívar's honor.

6 The new countries look like this in 1828.

1 Citizens overthrow the Spanish governor.

2 O'Higgins is elected head of Chile.

Independence in South America

- ✹ Battle for independence
- **1811** Year of independence
- ✪ Capital
- ⬅ Liberating army

| 0 | 500 | 1000 miles |
| 0 | 500 | 1000 kilometers |

C Colonies in the south fought for their independence about the same time colonies in the north were being liberated. Who led South Americans in their battles for freedom?

French Revolution

French kings had complete power. By 1789, however, France was bankrupt and the French people wanted a new government.

- The people of Paris revolted and formed a new revolutionary government that took power away from the king.

- The new government promised freedom and equality to all people in France. By 1791 France was a republic.

- King Louis XVI plotted to overthrow the new government. Instead, the government overthrew the king, tried him for treason, and had him beheaded.

SOCIAL STRUCTURE
Three Estates, 1789

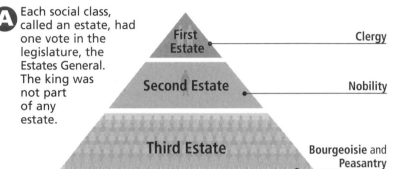

A Each social class, called an estate, had one vote in the legislature, the Estates General. The king was not part of any estate.

First Estate — Clergy

Second Estate — Nobility

Third Estate — Bourgeoisie and Peasantry

B The people of Paris were determined to protect their new government. Mobs seized weapons to prevent royal troops from arresting the revolutionaries.

C The French Revolution began with the capture of the Bastille, a prison in Paris. Four years later the revolutionary government executed its enemies, including the king, queen, and nobles. This violent time is known as the "Reign of Terror."

more at NWHatlas.com

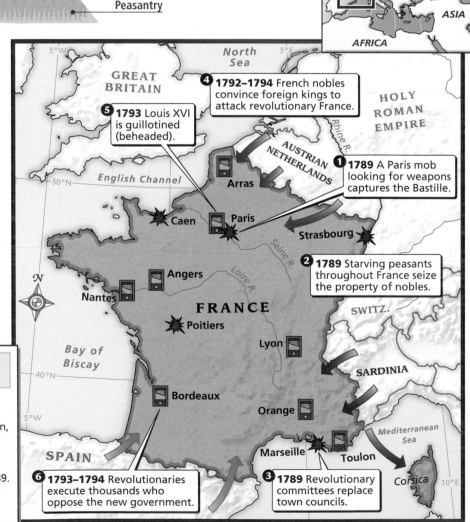

4 **1792–1794** French nobles convince foreign kings to attack revolutionary France.

5 **1793** Louis XVI is guillotined (beheaded).

1 **1789** A Paris mob looking for weapons captures the Bastille.

2 **1789** Starving peasants throughout France seize the property of nobles.

6 **1793–1794** Revolutionaries execute thousands who oppose the new government.

3 **1789** Revolutionary committees replace town councils.

French Revolution
1789–1794

- ✸ Urban uprising
- ▯ Reign of Terror execution, 1793–1794
- ➡ Foreign invasion

Map shows boundaries of 1789.

0   100   200 miles
0   100   200 kilometers

Empire of Napoleon

Napoleon Bonaparte was a young, popular, and very successful general during the French Revolution.

- In 1799 Napoleon seized power from the French government. Five years later, he crowned himself emperor.

- Napoleon expanded the French Empire with conquests across Europe. He placed his relatives and friends on thrones in Italy, Spain, Holland, Germany, and Poland.

- After terrible losses in Russia and again at Waterloo, Napoleon's enemies removed him from power and sent him into exile.

D Napoleon invaded Russia with 600,000 men. They reached Moscow, but winter forced them to retreat. Disease, cold, hunger, and Russian attacks nearly destroyed Napoleon's army.

E Napoleon defeated most of the major nations of Europe, forcing them to become his allies. Only Britain and Russia were able to resist him. Compare the size of France in 1799 when Napoleon took power with the areas under French control by 1812.

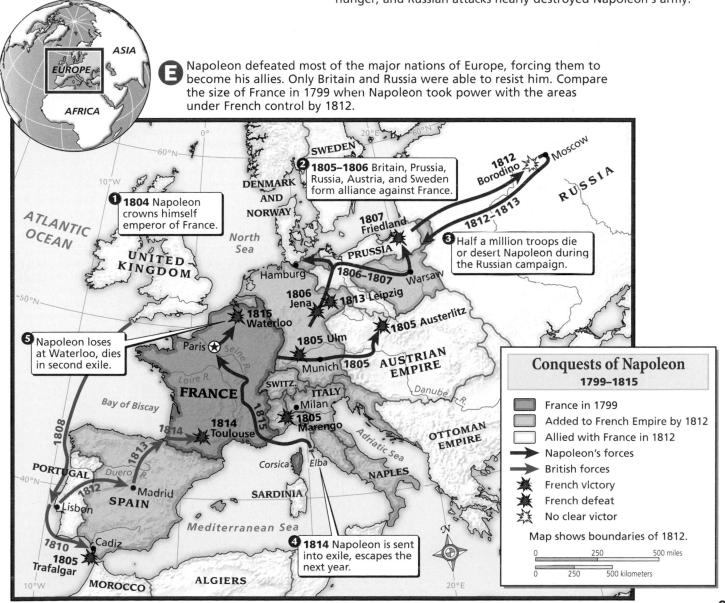

1 **1804** Napoleon crowns himself emperor of France.

2 **1805–1806** Britain, Prussia, Russia, Austria, and Sweden form alliance against France.

3 Half a million troops die or desert Napoleon during the Russian campaign.

4 **1814** Napoleon is sent into exile, escapes the next year.

5 Napoleon loses at Waterloo, dies in second exile.

Conquests of Napoleon
1799–1815

- France in 1799
- Added to French Empire by 1812
- Allied with France in 1812
- → Napoleon's forces
- → British forces
- ✳ French victory
- ✳ French defeat
- ✳ No clear victor

Map shows boundaries of 1812.

0   250   500 miles
0   250   500 kilometers

Industrial Revolution Changes Europe

The Industrial Revolution changed the way goods were produced, which changed the way people lived and worked. These changes are known as **industrialization**.

- Machines were developed to produce goods faster and in greater quantities. Coal powered these machines.

- Factories were built near coal deposits. Cities near the new industrial areas grew larger and larger.

- The Industrial Revolution began in Great Britain. But industrialization quickly spread to other parts of Europe and to North America.

How did industrialization affect people's lives?

The use of machines to manufacture goods changed where people worked, in factories rather than at home. It also changed where they lived, in cities rather than on farms.

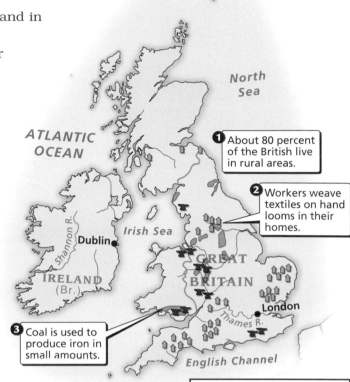

1 About 80 percent of the British live in rural areas.

2 Workers weave textiles on hand looms in their homes.

3 Coal is used to produce iron in small amounts.

A In 1750 most British products were still made by hand. A few years later, most textiles were machine-made in factories.

Industry in Great Britain
1750

- Coal mining
- Iron workshops
- Cloth-making in homes
- City with over 100,000 people

```
0          100        200 miles
0     100    200 kilometers
```

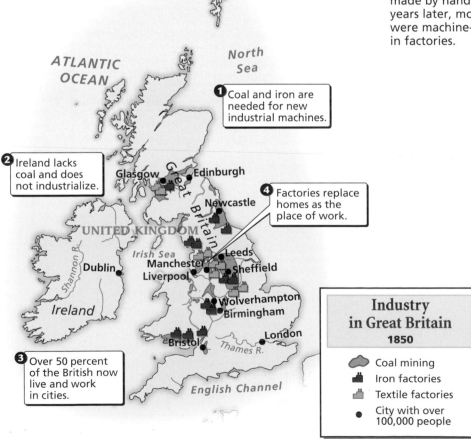

1 Coal and iron are needed for new industrial machines.

2 Ireland lacks coal and does not industrialize.

4 Factories replace homes as the place of work.

3 Over 50 percent of the British now live and work in cities.

Industry in Great Britain
1850

- Coal mining
- Iron factories
- Textile factories
- City with over 100,000 people

B As Britain became industrialized, cities grew larger. Compare map B with map A. How many more cities with over 100,000 people were there in Britain (now the United Kingdom) by 1850?

Economics
Quality of Life Changes

C The Industrial Revolution began in Great Britain, but it soon spread throughout the world. This political cartoon from the United States shows heads of industry benefiting from their workers, while offering little in return.

more at
NWHatlas.com

	1760	1850
Average annual earnings (in present-day dollars)	$2,900	$3,200
Life expectancy	34.2 years	39.5 years
Average schooling	1.4 years	2.7 years

D The quality of workers' lives improved in some ways during the Industrial Revolution, even though industrial jobs were often menial and dangerous.

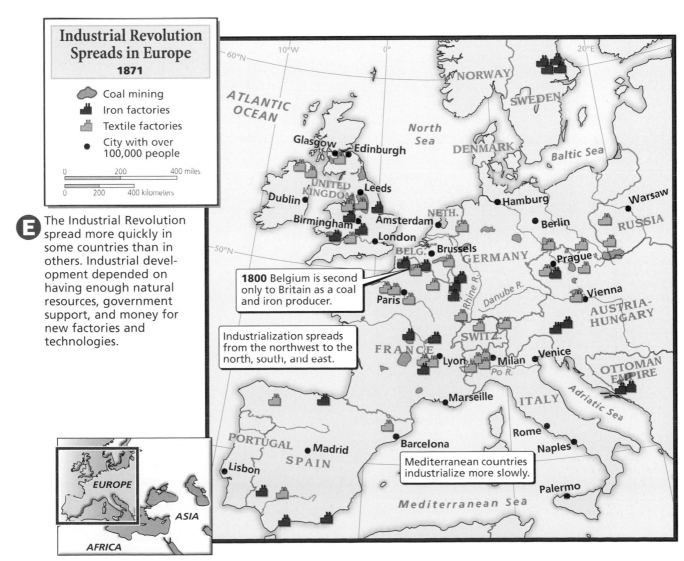

Industrial Revolution Spreads in Europe
1871

- Coal mining
- Iron factories
- Textile factories
- City with over 100,000 people

0   200   400 miles
0   200   400 kilometers

E The Industrial Revolution spread more quickly in some countries than in others. Industrial development depended on having enough natural resources, government support, and money for new factories and technologies.

1800 Belgium is second only to Britain as a coal and iron producer.

Industrialization spreads from the northwest to the north, south, and east.

Mediterranean countries industrialize more slowly.

101

Nationalism Sweeps Europe

After the fall of Napoleon, kings tried to return Europe to its condition before the French Revolution.

- In 1815 many kings and princes of Europe met at the Congress of Vienna. They returned power to kings who had been removed by Napoleon.

- In 1848 uprisings erupted across Europe. Many people were unhappy with their rulers and governments.

- By 1878 the map of Europe had changed again. New countries and boundaries were created.

Whose country is this?

The Austrian Empire ruled Hungarians, Italians, Czechs, and others. Supporters of **nationalism** argued that their own groups should have their own countries with democratic constitutions.

B Revolution swept Europe in 1848. German workers, such as those pictured here in Berlin, fought for social reform, democracy, and nationalism.

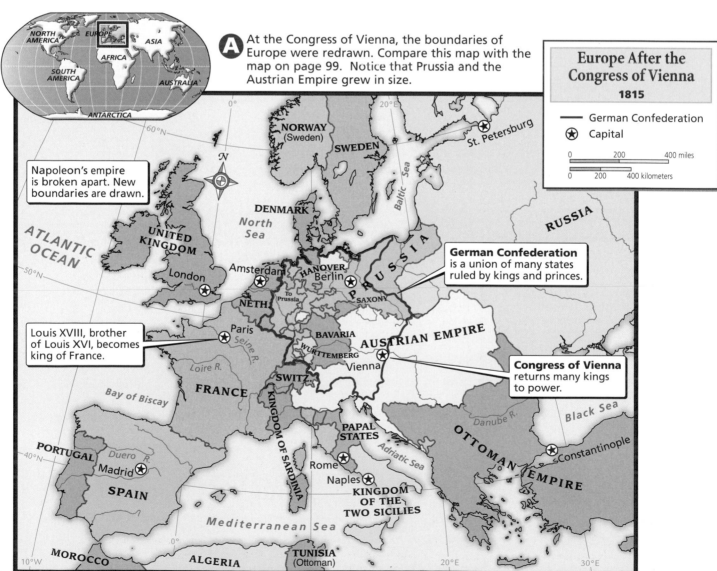

A At the Congress of Vienna, the boundaries of Europe were redrawn. Compare this map with the map on page 99. Notice that Prussia and the Austrian Empire grew in size.

Europe After the Congress of Vienna
1815

—— German Confederation
⊛ Capital

0   200   400 miles
0   200   400 kilometers

Napoleon's empire is broken apart. New boundaries are drawn.

Louis XVIII, brother of Louis XVI, becomes king of France.

German Confederation is a union of many states ruled by kings and princes.

Congress of Vienna returns many kings to power.

NORWAY (Sweden)
SWEDEN
St. Petersburg
RUSSIA
DENMARK
North Sea
Baltic Sea
UNITED KINGDOM
ATLANTIC OCEAN
London
Amsterdam
HANOVER
Berlin
To Prussia
PRUSSIA
SAXONY
NETH.
Paris
Seine R.
Loire R.
BAVARIA
WÜRTTEMBERG
SWITZ.
Vienna
AUSTRIAN EMPIRE
FRANCE
Bay of Biscay
KINGDOM OF SARDINIA
PAPAL STATES
Rome
Naples
KINGDOM OF THE TWO SICILIES
Danube R.
Adriatic Sea
OTTOMAN EMPIRE
Black Sea
Constantinople
PORTUGAL
Duero R.
Madrid
SPAIN
Mediterranean Sea
MOROCCO
ALGERIA
TUNISIA (Ottoman)

60°N
50°N
40°N
0°
10°W
20°E
30°E

Revolutions in Europe, 1815–1850

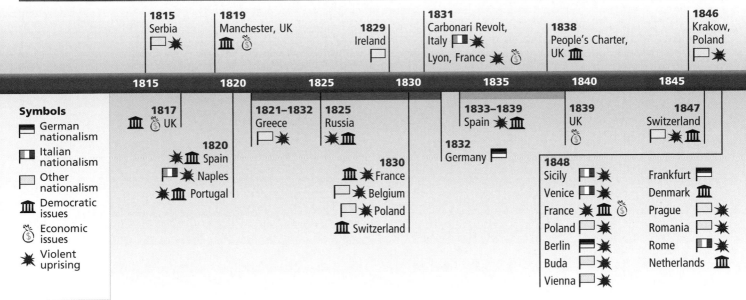

Symbols

- German nationalism
- Italian nationalism
- Other nationalism
- Democratic issues
- Economic issues
- Violent uprising

1815 Serbia

1819 Manchester, UK

1829 Ireland

1831 Carbonari Revolt, Italy
Lyon, France

1838 People's Charter, UK

1846 Krakow, Poland

1815 1820 1825 1830 1835 1840 1845

1817 UK

1820 Spain / Naples / Portugal

1821–1832 Greece

1825 Russia

1830 France / Belgium / Poland / Switzerland

1832 Germany

1833–1839 Spain

1839 UK

1847 Switzerland

1848
- Sicily
- Venice
- France
- Poland
- Berlin
- Buda
- Vienna
- Frankfurt
- Denmark
- Prague
- Romania
- Rome
- Netherlands

C The early 1800s was a time of great social unrest in Europe. There were many causes for upheaval, and it was clear to many that the time for change had arrived. *more at NWHatlas.com*

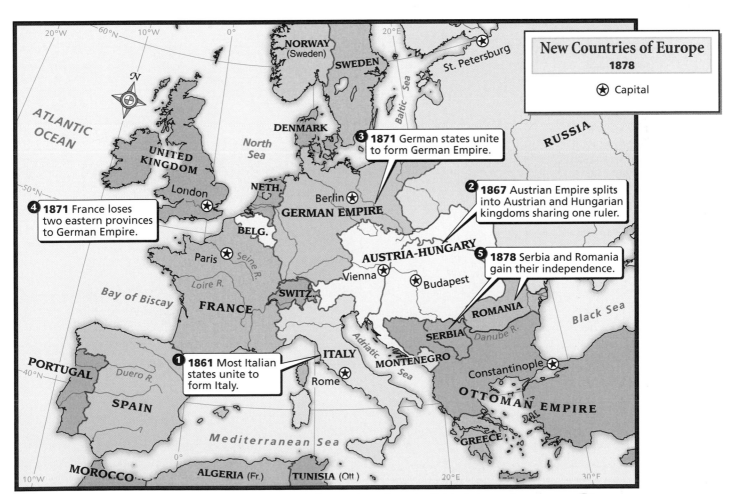

New Countries of Europe 1878
⊛ Capital

3 **1871** German states unite to form German Empire.

2 **1867** Austrian Empire splits into Austrian and Hungarian kingdoms sharing one ruler.

4 **1871** France loses two eastern provinces to German Empire.

5 **1878** Serbia and Romania gain their independence.

1 **1861** Most Italian states unite to form Italy.

D In some places nationalism united countries, while in other places it divided them. Compare this map with map A. Where did the revolutions in the timeline lead to new nations? *more at NWHatlas.com*

Imperialism in Asia and the Pacific

For centuries European imperialists had claimed land in Asia and the Pacific for the purpose of controlling trade.

- Asian products such as tea, porcelain, and silk were very popular and valuable in Europe and the Americas.

- Most of Japan's and China's ports, however, were closed to European ships and goods. By 1860 American and British troops had forced them to open.

- Rebel lords overthrew Japan's ruling shogun for not protecting the country from foreigners.

B Commodore Matthew Perry of the United States (center) threatened to attack Edo, the capital of Japan, unless government officials agreed to meet with him. Perry forced them to sign a treaty opening Japan to trade with the United States.

A

European countries controlled vast territories from northern Asia to the South Pacific. Which countries in eastern Asia were not under European control?

more at NWHatlas.com

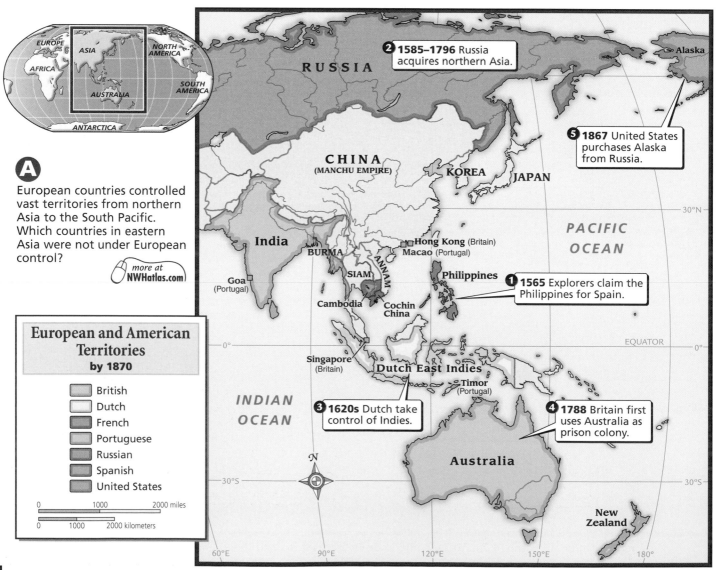

2 1585–1796 Russia acquires northern Asia.

5 1867 United States purchases Alaska from Russia.

1 1565 Explorers claim the Philippines for Spain.

3 1620s Dutch take control of Indies.

4 1788 Britain first uses Australia as prison colony.

RUSSIA

CHINA (MANCHU EMPIRE)

KOREA

JAPAN

India

BURMA

Hong Kong (Britain)
Macao (Portugal)

SIAM

ANNAM

Goa (Portugal)

Philippines

Cambodia

Cochin China

Singapore (Britain)

Dutch East Indies

Timor (Portugal)

Australia

New Zealand

PACIFIC OCEAN

INDIAN OCEAN

EQUATOR

Alaska

European and American Territories
by 1870

- British
- Dutch
- French
- Portuguese
- Russian
- Spanish
- United States

```
0        1000       2000 miles
0     1000    2000 kilometers
```

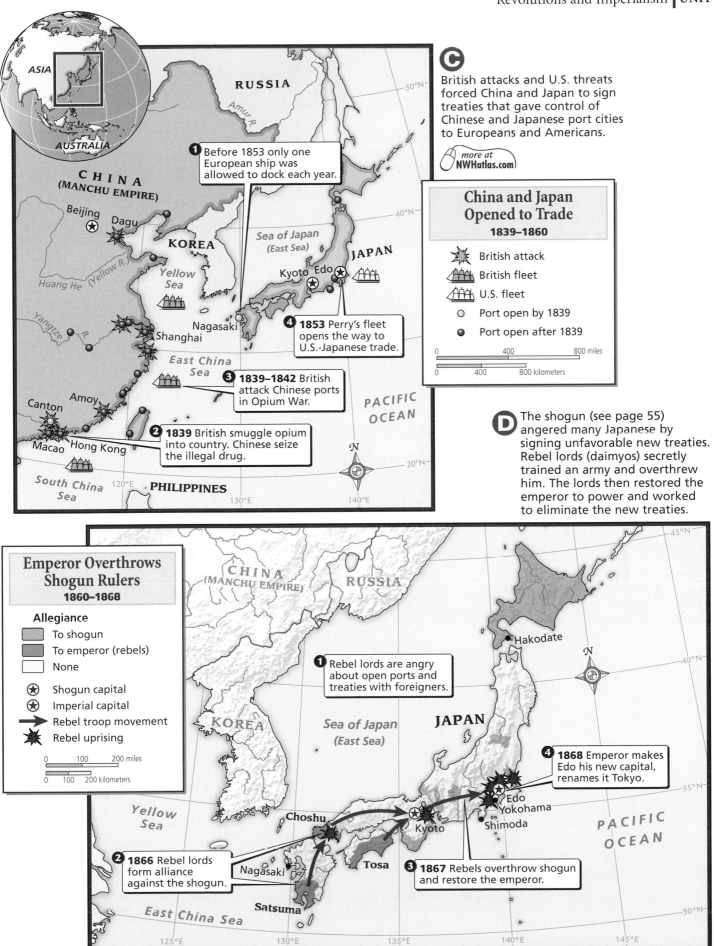

ASIA
AUSTRALIA

C British attacks and U.S. threats forced China and Japan to sign treaties that gave control of Chinese and Japanese port cities to Europeans and Americans.

more at NWHatlas.com

RUSSIA

CHINA (MANCHU EMPIRE)

Beijing
Dagu
KOREA
Sea of Japan (East Sea)
JAPAN
Kyoto Edo
Yellow Sea
Nagasaki
Shanghai
Huang He (Yellow R.)
Yangtze R.
East China Sea
Amoy
Canton
Macao Hong Kong
South China Sea
PHILIPPINES

1 Before 1853 only one European ship was allowed to dock each year.

4 1853 Perry's fleet opens the way to U.S.-Japanese trade.

3 1839–1842 British attack Chinese ports in Opium War.

2 1839 British smuggle opium into country. Chinese seize the illegal drug.

PACIFIC OCEAN

China and Japan Opened to Trade
1839–1860

✴ British attack
🛥 British fleet
🛥 U.S. fleet
○ Port open by 1839
● Port open after 1839

| 0 | 400 | 800 miles |
| 0 | 400 | 800 kilometers |

D The shogun (see page 55) angered many Japanese by signing unfavorable new treaties. Rebel lords (daimyos) secretly trained an army and overthrew him. The lords then restored the emperor to power and worked to eliminate the new treaties.

Emperor Overthrows Shogun Rulers
1860–1868

Allegiance
▨ To shogun
▩ To emperor (rebels)
☐ None
⊛ Shogun capital
⊛ Imperial capital
➜ Rebel troop movement
✴ Rebel uprising

| 0 | 100 | 200 miles |
| 0 | 100 | 200 kilometers |

CHINA (MANCHU EMPIRE)
RUSSIA
Hakodate
KOREA
Sea of Japan (East Sea)
JAPAN
Yellow Sea
Choshu
Nagasaki
Tosa
Satsuma
Kyoto
Edo
Yokohama
Shimoda
PACIFIC OCEAN
East China Sea

1 Rebel lords are angry about open ports and treaties with foreigners.

4 1868 Emperor makes Edo his new capital, renames it Tokyo.

2 1866 Rebel lords form alliance against the shogun.

3 1867 Rebels overthrow shogun and restore the emperor.

Imperialism Continues in Asia

As European countries and the United States expanded their empires in Asia and the Pacific, Asian resistance increased.

- In European and American territories, Asians rebelled against imperialist control without success.

- The Chinese royal family tried to protect ancient traditions. They supported an uprising, the Boxer Rebellion, to force foreigners out. The revolt failed.

- Japan's emperor decided his country needed to change. Japan developed a western army and an economy. Soon Japan, too, became powerful and imperialistic, and it quickly won two wars.

A Many Chinese resented foreign interference. One group called "Boxers" killed thousands of foreigners, including the German ambassador.

more at NWHatlas.com

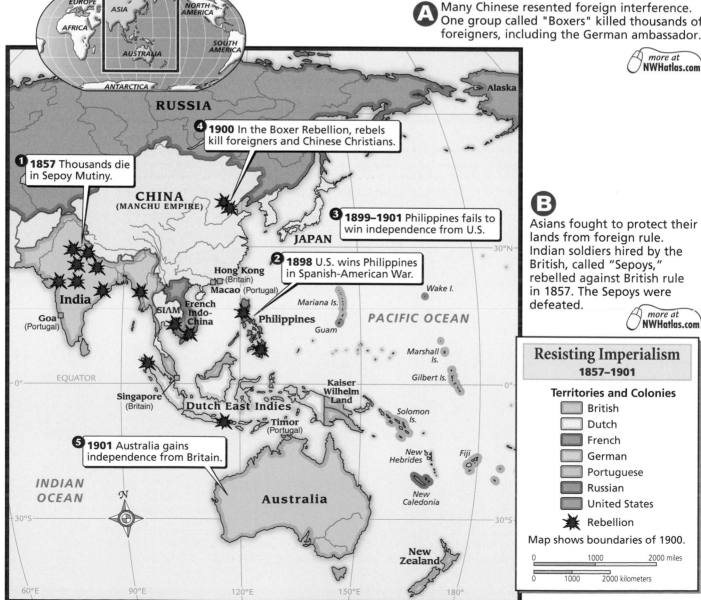

1 **1857** Thousands die in Sepoy Mutiny.

4 **1900** In the Boxer Rebellion, rebels kill foreigners and Chinese Christians.

3 **1899–1901** Philippines fails to win independence from U.S.

2 **1898** U.S. wins Philippines in Spanish-American War.

5 **1901** Australia gains independence from Britain.

RUSSIA

Alaska

CHINA (MANCHU EMPIRE)

JAPAN

Hong Kong (Britain)

Macao (Portugal)

India

Goa (Portugal)

SIAM

French Indo-China

Philippines

Wake I.

Mariana Is.

Guam

PACIFIC OCEAN

Marshall Is.

Gilbert Is.

Singapore (Britain)

Dutch East Indies

Kaiser Wilhelm Land

Timor (Portugal)

Solomon Is.

New Hebrides

Fiji

New Caledonia

INDIAN OCEAN

Australia

New Zealand

EQUATOR

EUROPE

ASIA

NORTH AMERICA

AFRICA

SOUTH AMERICA

AUSTRALIA

ANTARCTICA

B Asians fought to protect their lands from foreign rule. Indian soldiers hired by the British, called "Sepoys," rebelled against British rule in 1857. The Sepoys were defeated.

more at NWHatlas.com

Resisting Imperialism
1857–1901

Territories and Colonies

- British
- Dutch
- French
- German
- Portuguese
- Russian
- United States
- ✹ Rebellion

Map shows boundaries of 1900.

0   1000   2000 miles
0   1000   2000 kilometers

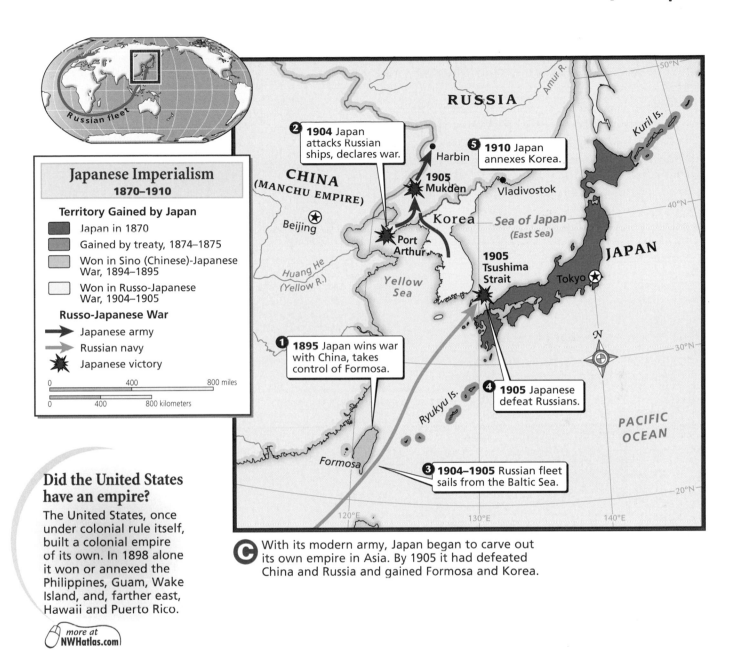

Japanese Imperialism
1870–1910

Territory Gained by Japan

- Japan in 1870
- Gained by treaty, 1874–1875
- Won in Sino (Chinese)-Japanese War, 1894–1895
- Won in Russo-Japanese War, 1904–1905

Russo-Japanese War

- → Japanese army
- → Russian navy
- ✸ Japanese victory

0   400   800 miles
0   400   800 kilometers

2 **1904** Japan attacks Russian ships, declares war.

5 **1910** Japan annexes Korea.

1895 Japan wins war with China, takes control of Formosa.

4 **1905** Japanese defeat Russians.

3 **1904–1905** Russian fleet sails from the Baltic Sea.

C With its modern army, Japan began to carve out its own empire in Asia. By 1905 it had defeated China and Russia and gained Formosa and Korea.

Did the United States have an empire?

The United States, once under colonial rule itself, built a colonial empire of its own. In 1898 alone it won or annexed the Philippines, Guam, Wake Island, and, farther east, Hawaii and Puerto Rico.

more at NWHatlas.com

Top 10 Cities, 1900

City Locations	Rank/City (Modern Country)	Population
	❶ **London** (United Kingdom)	6,480,000
	❷ **New York** (United States)	4,242,000
	❸ **Paris** (France)	3,330,000
	❹ **Berlin** (Germany)	2,707,000
	❺ **Chicago** (United States)	1,717,000
	❻ **Vienna** (Austria)	1,698,000
	❼ **Tokyo** (Japan)	1,497,000
	❽ **St. Petersburg** (Russia)	1,439,000
	❾ **Manchester** (United Kingdom)	1,435,000
	❿ **Philadelphia** (United States)	1,418,000

D In 1900, the largest cities were in countries that had experienced an industrial revolution (see pages 100–101). Where were most of these countries located? Which Asian country had an industrial revolution?

more at NWHatlas.com

Imperialism in Africa

After the slave trade was abolished, Europeans looked for new sources of wealth in Africa. In less than 50 years, Europeans took over almost all of Africa.

- European countries claimed land in Africa to make a profit from resources, expand territory, and gain power.

- The European competition to claim African land became known as "The Scramble for Africa."

- Africans often tried resisting European imperialism, but only two African states remained independent.

How Big Was Britain's Empire in Africa?

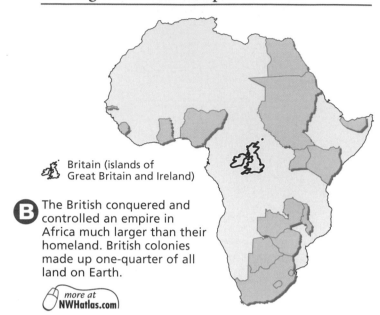

Britain (islands of Great Britain and Ireland)

B The British conquered and controlled an empire in Africa much larger than their homeland. British colonies made up one-quarter of all land on Earth.

more at NWHatlas.com

A Until the late 1800s, there were many independent African states and most European colonies in Africa were along the coast. Compare this map with map E.

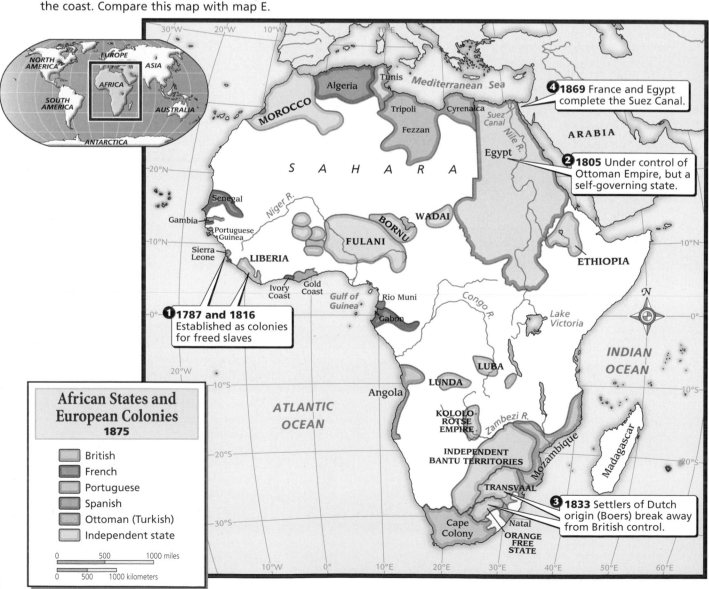

④ 1869 France and Egypt complete the Suez Canal.

② 1805 Under control of Ottoman Empire, but a self-governing state.

① 1787 and 1816 Established as colonies for freed slaves

③ 1833 Settlers of Dutch origin (Boers) break away from British control.

African States and European Colonies
1875

- British
- French
- Portuguese
- Spanish
- Ottoman (Turkish)
- Independent state

0   500   1000 miles
0   500   1000 kilometers

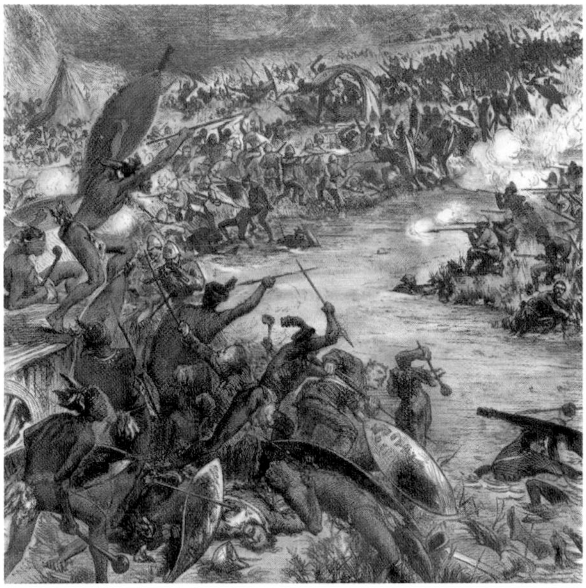

C Rifles and cannon were faster and deadlier than the weapons of Africans. Despite a remarkable early victory, the Zulus, above, were conquered by the British in six months.

WARFARE
Battle Casualties

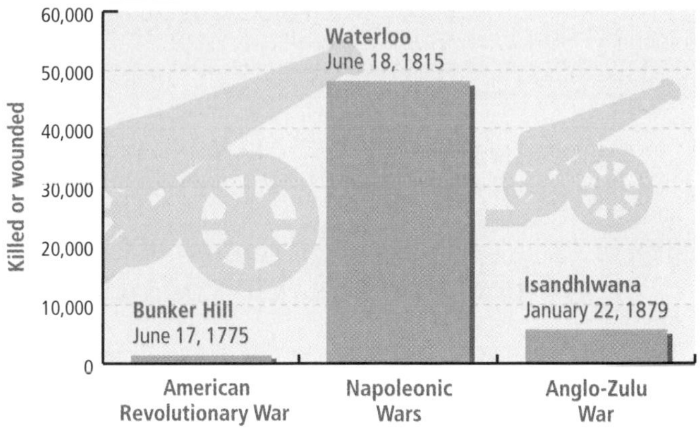

Killed or wounded
60,000
50,000
40,000
30,000
20,000
10,000
0
Bunker Hill
June 17, 1775
Waterloo
June 18, 1815
Isandhlwana
January 22, 1879
American Revolutionary War
Napoleonic Wars
Anglo-Zulu War

D Revolutionary France organized huge conscripted armies, leading to very high casualties. By contrast small, professional armies fought colonial wars with fewer losses.

E European leaders met in 1884 to peacefully divide claims on African lands. Africans had no say in this agreement. By 1914 European colonies had been set up in nearly every part of Africa.

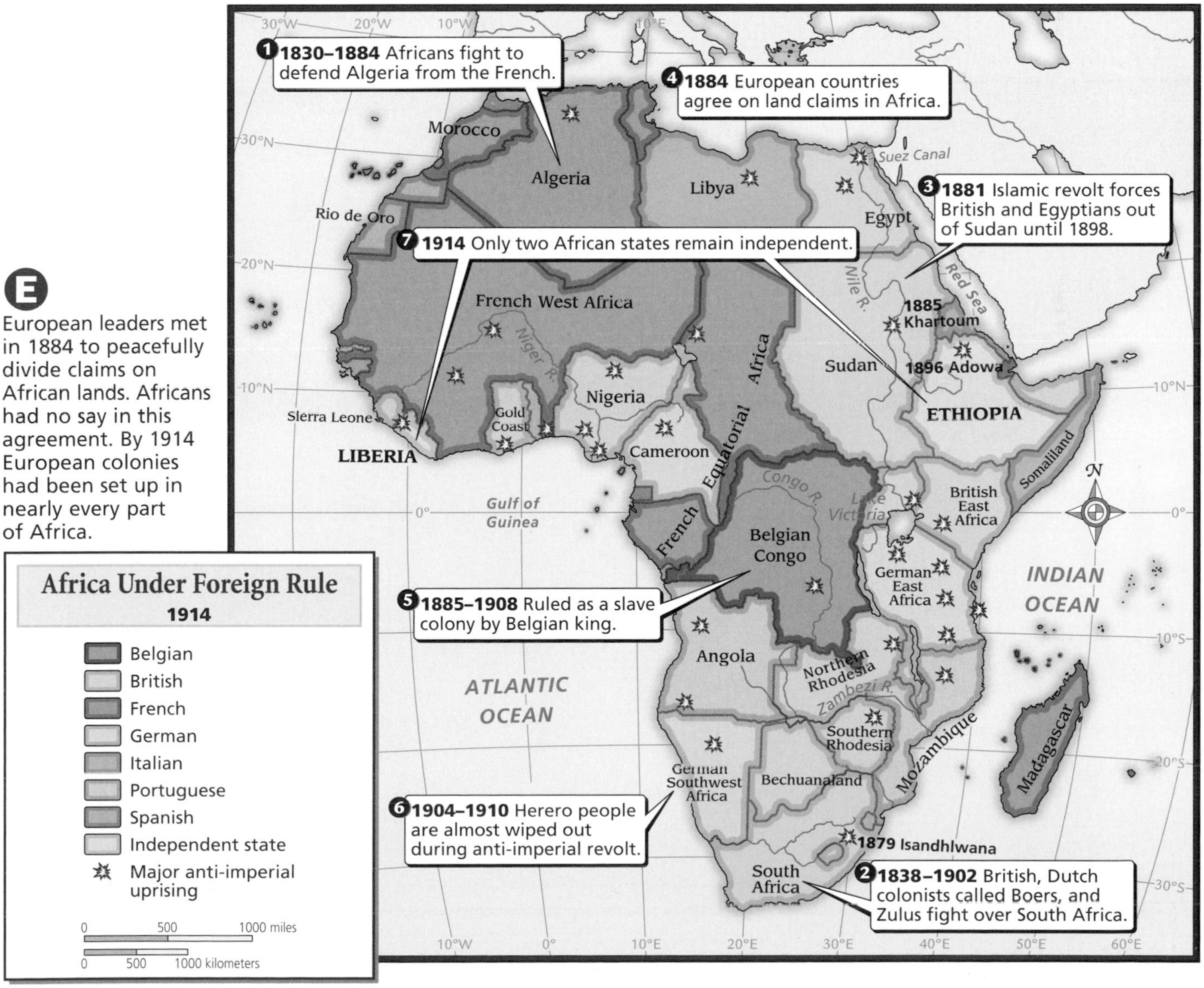

Africa Under Foreign Rule
1914
Belgian
British
French
German
Italian
Portuguese
Spanish
Independent state
Major anti-imperial uprising
0 500 1000 miles
0 500 1000 kilometers
1 1830–1884 Africans fight to defend Algeria from the French.
2 1838–1902 British, Dutch colonists called Boers, and Zulus fight over South Africa.
3 1881 Islamic revolt forces British and Egyptians out of Sudan until 1898.
4 1884 European countries agree on land claims in Africa.
5 1885–1908 Ruled as a slave colony by Belgian king.
6 1904–1910 Herero people are almost wiped out during anti-imperial revolt.
7 1914 Only two African states remain independent.
Morocco
Algeria
Libya
Egypt
Rio de Oro
French West Africa
Sierra Leone
LIBERIA
Gold Coast
Nigeria
Cameroon
French Equatorial Africa
Sudan
ETHIOPIA
Somaliland
British East Africa
Belgian Congo
German East Africa
Angola
Northern Rhodesia
Southern Rhodesia
German Southwest Africa
Bechuanaland
Mozambique
Madagascar
South Africa
1885 Khartoum
1896 Adowa
1879 Isandhlwana
Suez Canal
Nile R.
Niger R.
Congo R.
Zambezi R.
Red Sea
Lake Victoria
Gulf of Guinea
ATLANTIC OCEAN
INDIAN OCEAN
N
30°W
20°W
10°W
0°
10°E
20°E
30°E
40°E
50°E
60°E
30°N
20°N
10°N
10°S
20°S
30°S

UNIT 10 Twentieth Century and Beyond

1914 to the Present

1945	1947
UN is formed.	India is independent
1939–1945	1948
World War II	Israel is founded.

| 1910 | 1920 | 1930 | 1940 | 1950 |

| 1914–1918 | 1917 | 1922 | 1930 | 1946–1991 |
| World War I | Russian Revolution | Mussolini becomes prime minister of Italy. | Gandhi leads protests against British in India. | Cold War between East and West |

World War I Changes Europe

In 1914 an Austrian archduke was assassinated by a Serbian nationalist. Austria-Hungary declared war on Serbia, and military alliances soon brought most of Europe into the conflict.

■ The war was fought between the Central Powers and the Allies. The main Central Powers were Germany, Austria-Hungary, and the Ottoman Empire. The Allies included the United Kingdom, France, Russia, Serbia, and later the United States.

■ New technology, especially machine guns and chemical weapons, made World War I deadlier than previous wars.

■ New countries were formed out of the defeated empires.

Where was the front?
A **front** is the long battle zone that forms where two armies meet. The bloodiest fighting in World War I took place on the Western Front. There both sides fought from elaborate defensive trenches.

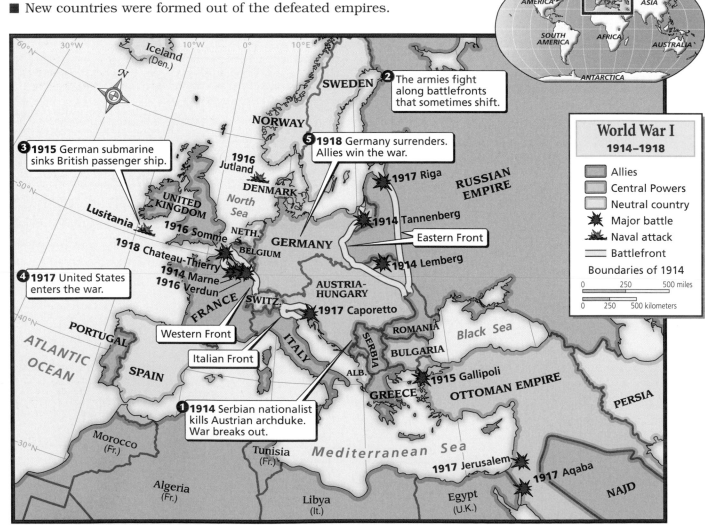

2 The armies fight along battlefronts that sometimes shift.

3 1915 German submarine sinks British passenger ship.

5 1918 Germany surrenders. Allies win the war.

1916 Jutland

1917 Riga

1914 Tannenberg

Lusitania

1916 Somme

Eastern Front

1918 Chateau-Thierry

1914 Lemberg

4 1917 United States enters the war.

1914 Marne
1916 Verdun

Western Front

1917 Caporetto

Italian Front

1915 Gallipoli

1 1914 Serbian nationalist kills Austrian archduke. War breaks out.

1917 Jerusalem

1917 Aqaba

World War I
1914–1918

	Allies
	Central Powers
	Neutral country
✸	Major battle
	Naval attack
—	Battlefront
	Boundaries of 1914

0 250 500 miles
0 250 500 kilometers

A Fighting along the Western Front, the most important battleground, was deadlocked. For over three years, the defensive strength of the trenches prevented the armies on both sides from gaining ground.

Timeline

| 1960 | 1970 | 1980 | 1990 | 2000 | 2010 |

1960–1980 Independence comes to dozens of former colonies.

1969 Apollo 11 lands on moon.

1980 Solidarity Union begins challenging communist rule in Poland.

1991 Persian Gulf War

2001 Terrorists attack World Trade Center and Pentagon.

2003 War in Iraq begins.

2005 Warmest year in a century

1961 Berlin Wall is built.

1965–1973 Vietnam War involves U.S. forces.

1975 Vietnam War ends.

1979 Smallpox is eradicated.

1991 Soviet Union collapses.

2011 South Sudan declares its independence.

B Both sides used poison gases that burned eyes, skin, and lungs, and killed thousands of troops. After the war, most countries agreed to ban chemical warfare.

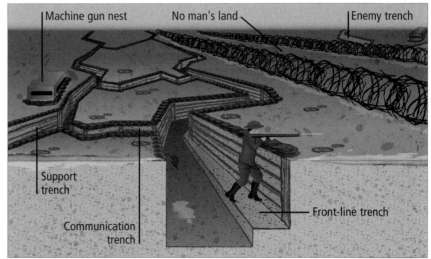

Machine gun nest • No man's land • Enemy trench • Support trench • Communication trench • Front-line trench

C Soldiers often lived for months in muddy, rat-infested trenches. Artillery, poison gas, and disease killed tens of thousands. Behind the front-line trenches shown here was a vast network of trenches that provided supplies and re-enforcements.

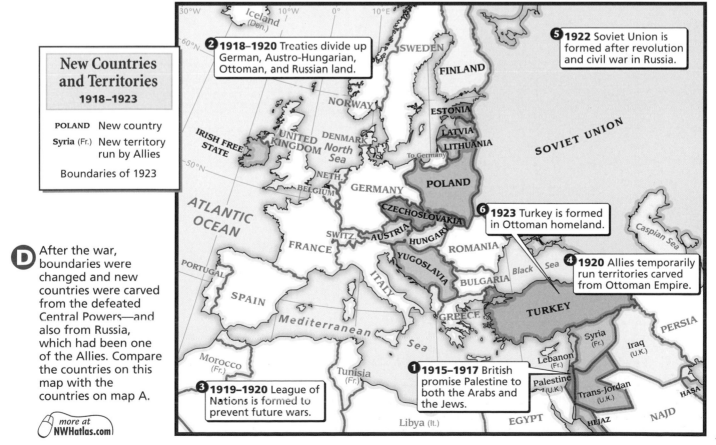

New Countries and Territories
1918–1923

POLAND New country

Syria (Fr.) New territory run by Allies

Boundaries of 1923

❷ **1918–1920** Treaties divide up German, Austro-Hungarian, Ottoman, and Russian land.

❺ **1922** Soviet Union is formed after revolution and civil war in Russia.

❻ **1923** Turkey is formed in Ottoman homeland.

❹ **1920** Allies temporarily run territories carved from Ottoman Empire.

❸ **1919–1920** League of Nations is formed to prevent future wars.

❶ **1915–1917** British promise Palestine to both the Arabs and the Jews.

D After the war, boundaries were changed and new countries were carved from the defeated Central Powers—and also from Russia, which had been one of the Allies. Compare the countries on this map with the countries on map A.

more at NWHatlas.com

111

Rise of Dictatorships

World War I left many Europeans poor and jobless. Money was often worthless. People were unhappy and looking for new leadership.

- In 1917 angry Russian soldiers, workers, and peasants overthrew the czar. Civil war followed.

- Communists won the war. Lenin took control and changed Russia into the Soviet Union.

- In the 1920s and 1930s, over a dozen other dictators won control of countries throughout Europe.

- Using brute force, dictators such as Mussolini, Stalin, and Hitler eliminated opposition within their countries.

B Lenin was the leader of the Bolshevik (or Communist) Party. His army and secret police crushed all opponents in Russia. This poster of him announces, "Lenin lived, Lenin lives, Lenin will live forever."

A The Bolsheviks (communists) also were called Reds. Their opponents, the anti-Bolsheviks, were called Whites. Reds and Whites battled for control of Russia.

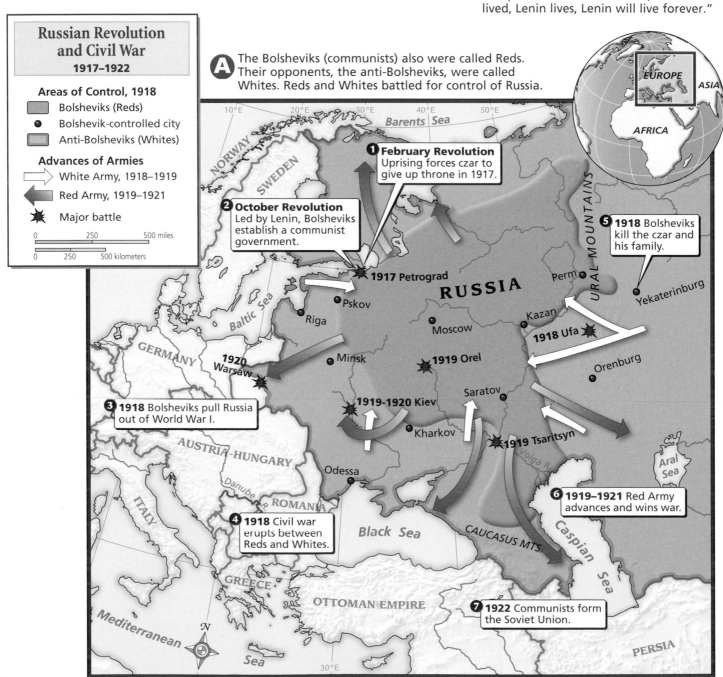

Russian Revolution and Civil War
1917–1922

Areas of Control, 1918
- Bolsheviks (Reds)
- Bolshevik-controlled city
- Anti-Bolsheviks (Whites)

Advances of Armies
- White Army, 1918–1919
- Red Army, 1919–1921
- Major battle

0   250   500 miles
0   250   500 kilometers

1 February Revolution Uprising forces czar to give up throne in 1917.

2 October Revolution Led by Lenin, Bolsheviks establish a communist government.

5 1918 Bolsheviks kill the czar and his family.

3 1918 Bolsheviks pull Russia out of World War I.

4 1918 Civil war erupts between Reds and Whites.

6 1919–1921 Red Army advances and wins war.

7 1922 Communists form the Soviet Union.

1917 Petrograd · RUSSIA · Perm · Yekaterinburg · Pskov · Riga · Kazan · Moscow · 1918 Ufa · Orenburg · 1920 Warsaw · Minsk · 1919 Orel · Saratov · 1919–1920 Kiev · Kharkov · 1919 Tsaritsyn · Odessa · Black Sea · Aral Sea · Caspian Sea · Mediterranean Sea · GREECE · OTTOMAN EMPIRE · PERSIA · NORWAY · SWEDEN · GERMANY · AUSTRIA-HUNGARY · ROMANIA · ITALY · Baltic Sea · Barents Sea · Danube · Volga R. · CAUCASUS MTS. · URAL MOUNTAINS

EUROPE · ASIA · AFRICA

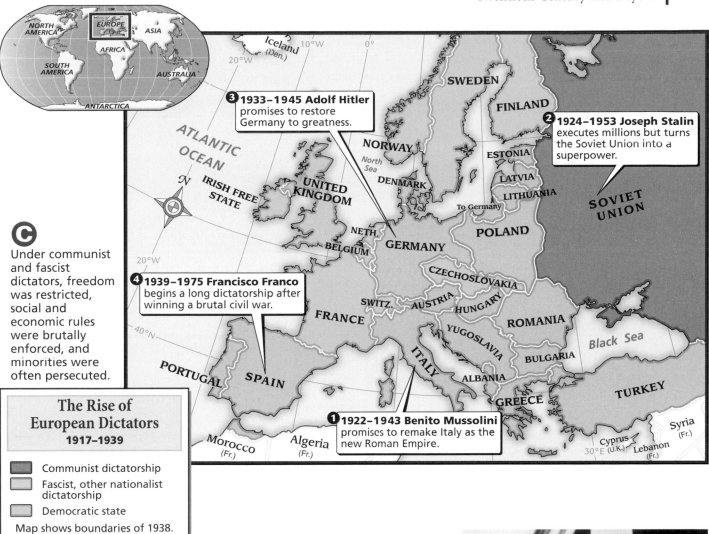

❸ 1933–1945 Adolf Hitler promises to restore Germany to greatness.

❷ 1924–1953 Joseph Stalin executes millions but turns the Soviet Union into a superpower.

❹ 1939–1975 Francisco Franco begins a long dictatorship after winning a brutal civil war.

❶ 1922–1943 Benito Mussolini promises to remake Italy as the new Roman Empire.

C Under communist and fascist dictators, freedom was restricted, social and economic rules were brutally enforced, and minorities were often persecuted.

The Rise of European Dictators
1917–1939

- ▨ Communist dictatorship
- ▨ Fascist, other nationalist dictatorship
- ▨ Democratic state

Map shows boundaries of 1938.

GOVERNMENT
Communists and Fascists

 more at NWHatlas.com

Communism		Fascism
Workers of the world unite; you have nothing to lose but your chains. —Karl Marx	**Founding Beliefs**	*All within the state, nothing outside the state, nothing against the state.* —Benito Mussolini
• Owned by the government	**Land and Factories**	• Privately owned under strict government control
• One-party rule	**Political System**	• One-party rule
• Virtually none • No freedom of religion	**Freedoms**	• Repression of select minority groups • Freedom of religion for most

D Communist and fascist governments relied on secret police to control their citizens. Radio stations and newspapers, run or controlled by the government, presented only communist or fascist views.

E In 1937 Mussolini (with his arm raised) and Hitler reviewed German troops in Munich. The visit convinced the two powerful fascist leaders to form an alliance.

World War II Engulfs the World

World War II was the most devastating war in history. It was fought between two groups of countries—the Axis and the Allies.

- Before the war, the Axis nations extended their territories by seizing nearby countries. Japan went into China, Italy into Albania, and Germany into Austria. Other nations joined forces as the Allies and tried to stop them.

- Early in the war, the Axis powers defeated every country they attacked. By 1940 only the United Kingdom was left to oppose Germany in Western Europe.

- In 1941 Germany attacked the Soviet Union, and Japan attacked the United States, causing these two powerful nations to join the Allies.

- By the time the Allies had defeated the Axis, Japan and much of Europe were in ruins.

WARFARE
Axis vs. Allies

 more at NWHatlas.com

Axis Powers	Allied Powers
Germany	United Kingdom
Japan	United States
Italy	Soviet Union
	China
	Australia
	Canada
Six other nations were allies of the Axis during the war.	There were 50 Allied nations from around the world.

A The Allies had greater resources than the Axis. The United Kingdom used troops and supplies from its colonies. The United States had vast industrial power.

B Unlike the Allies, the Axis was prepared for war and had conquered huge areas by 1942. But the Allies recovered and attacked by land, sea, and air.

more at NWHatlas.com

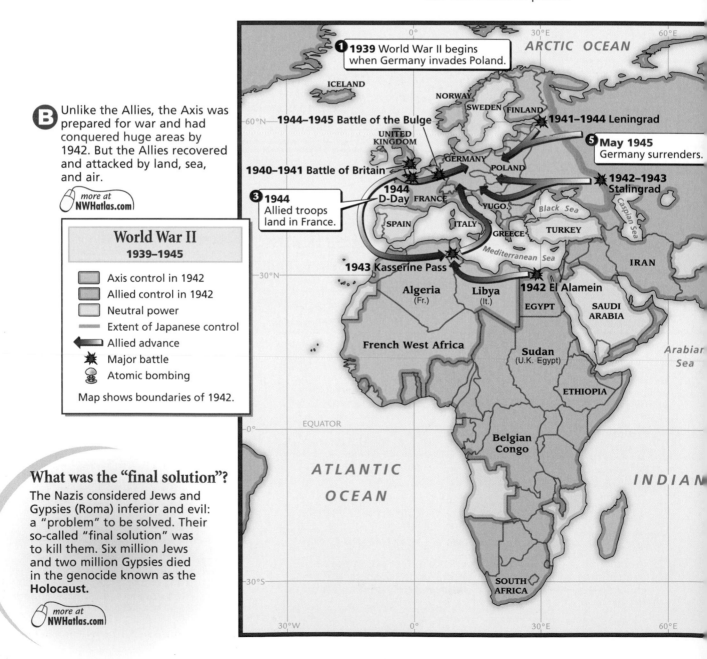

World War II
1939–1945

- Axis control in 1942
- Allied control in 1942
- Neutral power
- Extent of Japanese control
- Allied advance
- Major battle
- Atomic bombing

Map shows boundaries of 1942.

1 1939 World War II begins when Germany invades Poland.

1944–1945 Battle of the Bulge

1941–1944 Leningrad

5 May 1945 Germany surrenders.

1940–1941 Battle of Britain

1942–1943 Stalingrad

3 1944 Allied troops land in France.

1944 D-Day

1943 Kasserine Pass

1942 El Alamein

What was the "final solution"?

The Nazis considered Jews and Gypsies (Roma) inferior and evil: a "problem" to be solved. Their so-called "final solution" was to kill them. Six million Jews and two million Gypsies died in the genocide known as the **Holocaust**.

more at NWHatlas.com

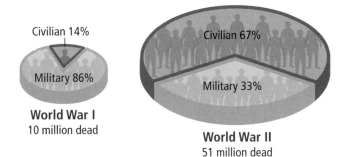

WARFARE
Lives Lost in World Wars

 more at NWHatlas.com

Civilian 14%

Military 86%

World War I
10 million dead

Civilian 67%

Military 33%

World War II
51 million dead

C Aircraft kept evolving throughout World War II. Planes were developed to fly faster and farther. Late in the war, jets were introduced. Here an American *Avenger* bombs a Japanese airstrip in the Pacific in 1944.

D Worldwide, World War II took the lives of more people, mostly civilians, than any other war.

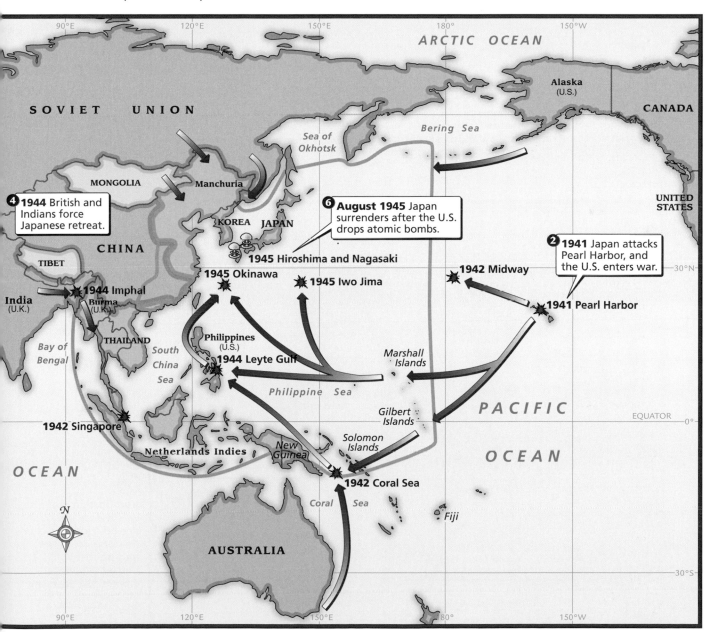

4 **1944** British and Indians force Japanese retreat.

6 **August 1945** Japan surrenders after the U.S. drops atomic bombs.

1945 Hiroshima and Nagasaki

1945 Okinawa

1945 Iwo Jima

1942 Midway

2 **1941** Japan attacks Pearl Harbor, and the U.S. enters war.

1941 Pearl Harbor

1944 Imphal

1944 Leyte Gulf

1942 Singapore

1942 Coral Sea

ARCTIC OCEAN

Alaska (U.S.)

CANADA

SOVIET UNION

UNITED STATES

MONGOLIA Manchuria

Sea of Okhotsk

Bering Sea

KOREA JAPAN

CHINA

TIBET

India (U.K.)

Burma (U.K.)

THAILAND

Bay of Bengal

Philippines (U.S.)

South China Sea

Marshall Islands

PACIFIC

EQUATOR

Philippine Sea

Gilbert Islands

Netherlands Indies

New Guinea

Solomon Islands

OCEAN

OCEAN

Coral Sea

Fiji

AUSTRALIA

The Cold War Threatens the World

After World War II, the communist and anti-communist nations of the world opposed each other in what came to be called the **Cold War**.

- The two main opponents were the Soviet Union and the United States, the superpowers that had been allies in World War II.

- The Cold War was mainly a political and economic struggle, but sometimes it erupted into regional shooting wars.

- The Cold War ended when the Soviet Union broke up in 1991.

A After World War II, Berlin was divided into sectors. In 1961 it was divided even further. Soviets built a wall to prevent East Germans from escaping to democratic West Berlin. The wall stood until 1989.

more at NWHatlas.com

B The United States and the Soviet Union had most of the world's nuclear weapons. Both countries often tested new bombs above ground until they agreed to ban such tests in 1963.

more at NWHatlas.com

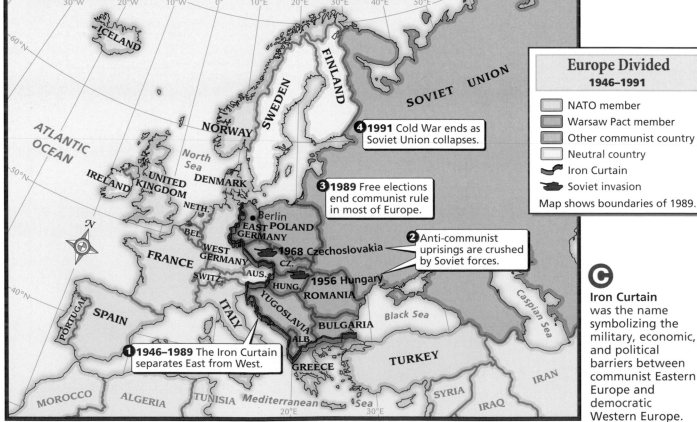

Europe Divided
1946–1991

- NATO member
- Warsaw Pact member
- Other communist country
- Neutral country
- Iron Curtain
- Soviet invasion

Map shows boundaries of 1989.

4 **1991** Cold War ends as Soviet Union collapses.

3 **1989** Free elections end communist rule in most of Europe.

2 Anti-communist uprisings are crushed by Soviet forces.

1968 Czechoslovakia

1956 Hungary

1 **1946–1989** The Iron Curtain separates East from West.

C

Iron Curtain was the name symbolizing the military, economic, and political barriers between communist Eastern Europe and democratic Western Europe.

D

The U.S.-led NATO alliance and the Soviet-led Warsaw Pact had enough nuclear weapons to kill every person on earth. Neither side could attack the other without risking complete destruction from a counterattack.

more at NWHatlas.com

No more nukes?

Nuclear non-proliferation means not allowing the spread of nuclear weapons or the technology to create them. Since 1968 about 190 countries have signed the Nuclear Non-Proliferation Treaty. It has helped limit the spread of nuclear weapons.

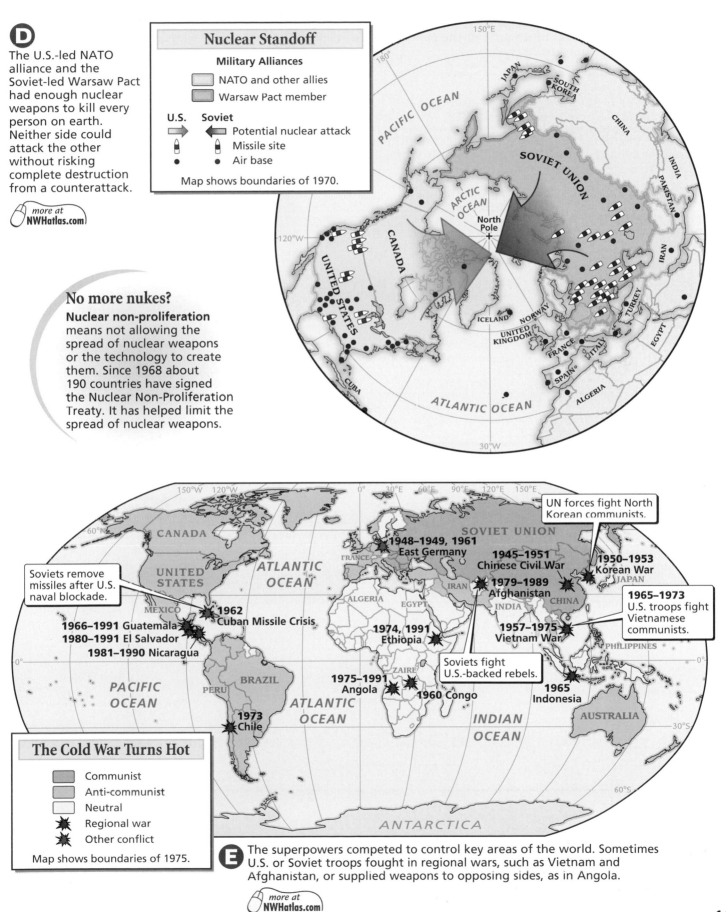

Nuclear Standoff

Military Alliances

- NATO and other allies
- Warsaw Pact member

U.S.   Soviet
- Potential nuclear attack
- Missile site
- Air base

Map shows boundaries of 1970.

The Cold War Turns Hot

- Communist
- Anti-communist
- Neutral
- Regional war
- Other conflict

Map shows boundaries of 1975.

Soviets remove missiles after U.S. naval blockade.

1962 Cuban Missile Crisis

1966–1991 Guatemala
1980–1991 El Salvador
1981–1990 Nicaragua

1973 Chile

1948–1949, 1961 East Germany

1945–1951 Chinese Civil War

1979–1989 Afghanistan

1974, 1991 Ethiopia

Soviets fight U.S.-backed rebels.

1975–1991 Angola

1960 Congo

1957–1975 Vietnam War

1965 Indonesia

UN forces fight North Korean communists.

1950–1953 Korean War

1965–1973 U.S. troops fight Vietnamese communists.

E The superpowers competed to control key areas of the world. Sometimes U.S. or Soviet troops fought in regional wars, such as Vietnam and Afghanistan, or supplied weapons to opposing sides, as in Angola.

more at NWHatlas.com

Communist Conflicts in Asia

Communists and anti-communists within countries also opposed each other. In no part of the world was this more common than in Asia.

- When the Chinese emperor lost power, China collapsed into chaos and civil war. After World War II, internal fighting resumed. Communists gained control in 1949.

- The following year, tensions between communist North Korea and anti-communist South Korea escalated into war.

- War between communist North Vietnam and anti-communist South Vietnam dragged on from 1957 to 1975.

- Today China, North Korea, and Vietnam are still communist.

War without end?

A peace treaty was never signed ending the Korean War. Years later North Korea is still communist, anti-communist U.S. troops are still in South Korea, and tensions still exist. For example, in 2010, North Korea sank a South Korean warship.

B Crowds welcomed communist troops into Peking (Beijing) in 1949, as nationalists evacuated the city. Troops carried portraits of their leaders, including Mao Zedong (center) who became Chairman of the People's Republic of China.

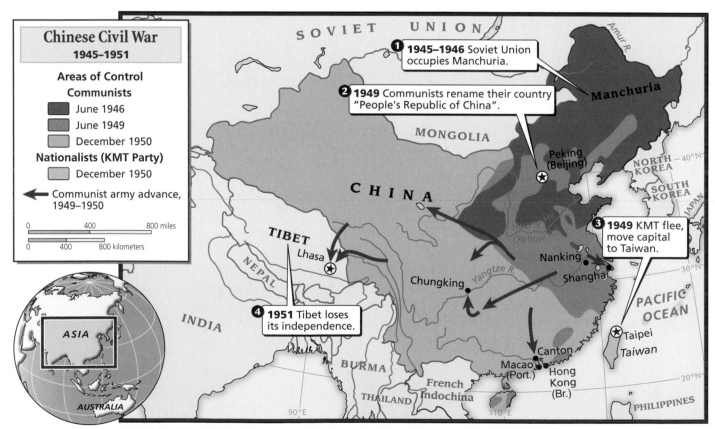

Chinese Civil War
1945–1951

Areas of Control
Communists
- June 1946
- June 1949
- December 1950

Nationalists (KMT Party)
- December 1950

← Communist army advance, 1949–1950

0   400   800 miles
0   400   800 kilometers

1 1945–1946 Soviet Union occupies Manchuria.

2 1949 Communists rename their country "People's Republic of China".

3 1949 KMT flee, move capital to Taiwan.

4 1951 Tibet loses its independence.

A After World War II, communists forced nationalists onto the island of Taiwan. Compare the areas under communist control by 1946 and by 1950.

more at
NWHatlas.com

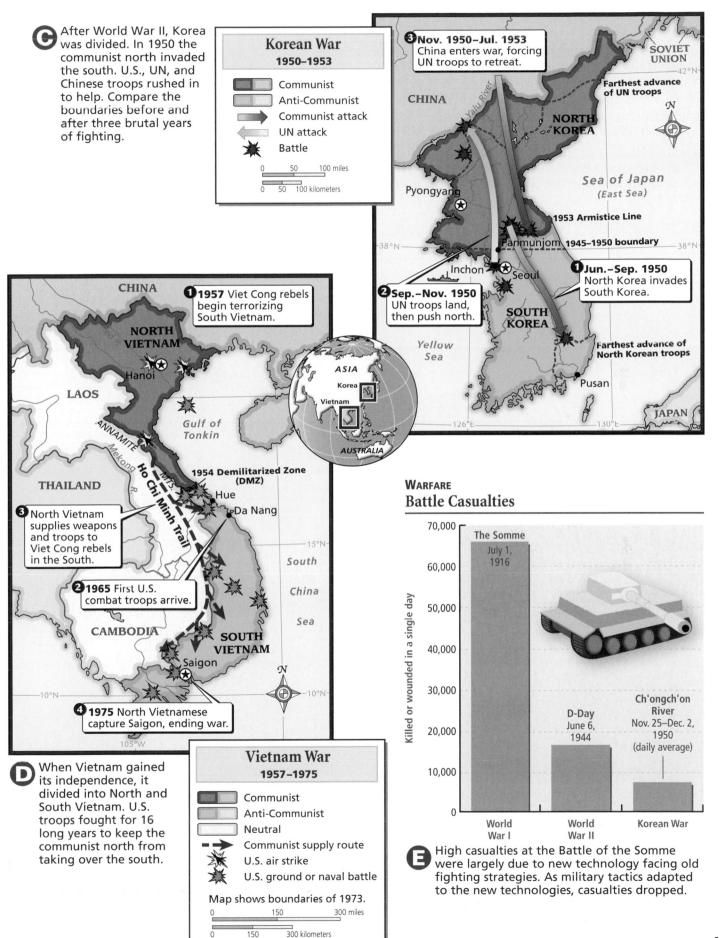

C After World War II, Korea was divided. In 1950 the communist north invaded the south. U.S., UN, and Chinese troops rushed in to help. Compare the boundaries before and after three brutal years of fighting.

Korean War
1950–1953

- Communist
- Anti-Communist
- Communist attack
- UN attack
- Battle

0   50   100 miles
0   50   100 kilometers

3 Nov. 1950–Jul. 1953
China enters war, forcing UN troops to retreat.

SOVIET UNION

42°N

CHINA

Farthest advance of UN troops

NORTH KOREA

Yalu River

N

Sea of Japan (East Sea)

Pyongyang

1953 Armistice Line

Panmunjom   1945–1950 boundary

38°N   38°N

Inchon   Seoul

2 Sep.–Nov. 1950
UN troops land, then push north.

1 Jun.–Sep. 1950
North Korea invades South Korea.

SOUTH KOREA

Yellow Sea

Farthest advance of North Korean troops

Pusan

126°E   130°E

JAPAN

ASIA
Korea
Vietnam

AUSTRALIA

CHINA

1 1957 Viet Cong rebels begin terrorizing South Vietnam.

NORTH VIETNAM

Hanoi

LAOS

ANNAMITE

Gulf of Tonkin

Mekong R.

THAILAND

Ho Chi Minh Trail

1954 Demilitarized Zone (DMZ)

Hue
Da Nang

3 North Vietnam supplies weapons and troops to Viet Cong rebels in the South.

15°N

South China Sea

2 1965 First U.S. combat troops arrive.

CAMBODIA

SOUTH VIETNAM

Saigon

N

10°N   10°N

4 1975 North Vietnamese capture Saigon, ending war.

105°W

D When Vietnam gained its independence, it divided into North and South Vietnam. U.S. troops fought for 16 long years to keep the communist north from taking over the south.

Vietnam War
1957–1975

- Communist
- Anti-Communist
- Neutral
- Communist supply route
- U.S. air strike
- U.S. ground or naval battle

Map shows boundaries of 1973.

0   150   300 miles
0   150   300 kilometers

WARFARE
Battle Casualties

Killed or wounded in a single day

70,000

The Somme
July 1, 1916

60,000

50,000

40,000

30,000

D-Day
June 6, 1944

Ch'ongch'on River
Nov. 25–Dec. 2, 1950
(daily average)

20,000

10,000

0

World War I   World War II   Korean War

E High casualties at the Battle of the Somme were largely due to new technology facing old fighting strategies. As military tactics adapted to the new technologies, casualties dropped.

Independence Sweeps the World

After World War II, European colonies in Africa, Asia, and the Caribbean began seeking independence. Most succeeded within the next 35 years. In the 1990s, after the fall of communism, a second wave of independence swept Asia and Europe.

- The war weakened the economies of the European colonial powers. They could no longer afford to run their overseas empires.

- The colonies felt they could manage their own resources to improve the lives of their citizens. But independence brought unexpected problems, including poverty and civil war.

A Mohandas Gandhi led the independence movement in India. In 1930 he led the Salt March to protest a British tax on salt. This march was an act of nonviolent civil disobedience.

more at NWHatlas.com

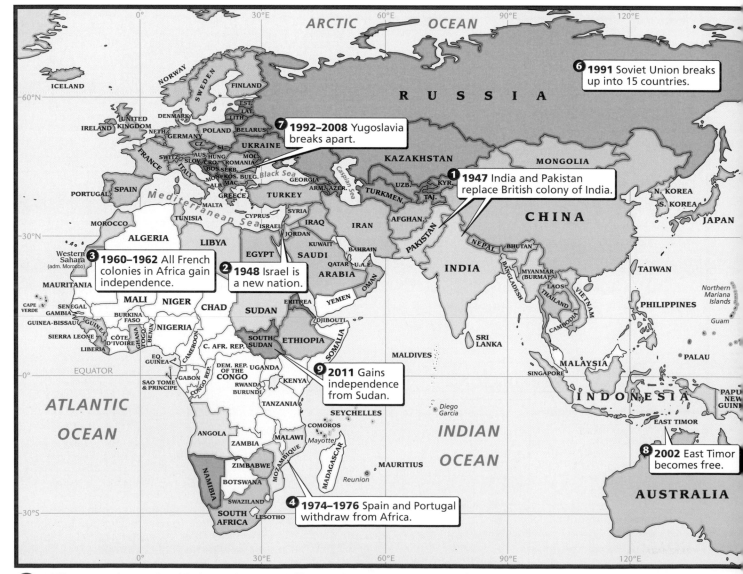

6 **1991** Soviet Union breaks up into 15 countries.

7 **1992–2008** Yugoslavia breaks apart.

1 **1947** India and Pakistan replace British colony of India.

3 **1960–1962** All French colonies in Africa gain independence.

2 **1948** Israel is a new nation.

9 **2011** Gains independence from Sudan.

8 **2002** East Timor becomes free.

4 **1974–1976** Spain and Portugal withdraw from Africa.

B Different regions gained independence at different times. It was common for many countries in the same region to gain independence within a few years of each other. Which regions gained independence in which decades?

POPULATION
People Under Foreign Rule

C The United Nations encouraged decolonization. After World War II, the United Kingdom, France, Germany, Spain, Portugal, and the United States began granting independence to their colonies in Africa, Asia, and the Caribbean.

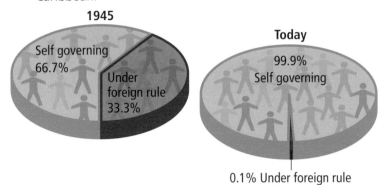

1945

Self governing 66.7%

Under foreign rule 33.3%

Today

99.9% Self governing

0.1% Under foreign rule

D Eritreans celebrate their independence from Ethiopia after 30 years of war.

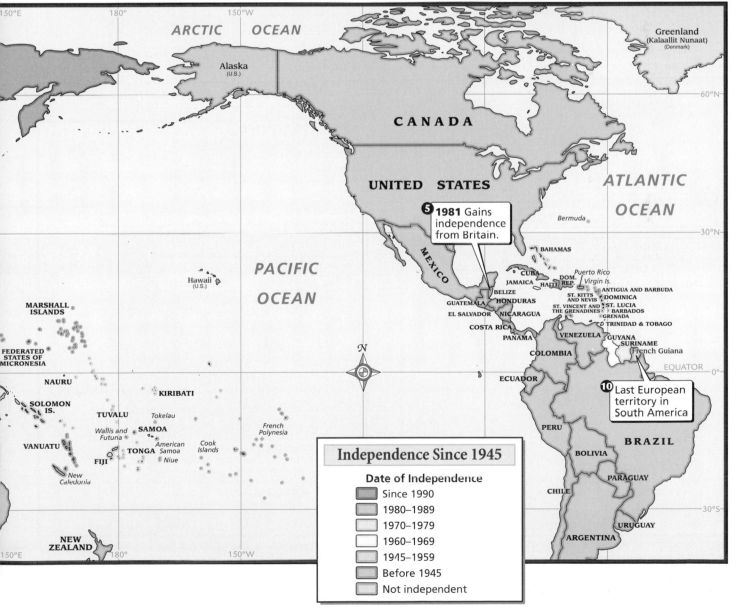

ARCTIC OCEAN

Greenland (Kalaallit Nunaat) (Denmark)

Alaska (U.S.)

60°N

CANADA

UNITED STATES

ATLANTIC OCEAN

5 **1981** Gains independence from Britain.

Bermuda

30°N

PACIFIC OCEAN

Hawaii (U.S.)

BAHAMAS

CUBA
DOM. REP.
Puerto Rico
Virgin Is.
JAMAICA HAITI
ANTIGUA AND BARBUDA
DOMINICA
BELIZE
ST. KITTS AND NEVIS
ST. LUCIA
GUATEMALA HONDURAS
ST. VINCENT AND THE GRENADINES
BARBADOS
EL SALVADOR NICARAGUA
GRENADA
TRINIDAD & TOBAGO
COSTA RICA
PANAMA
VENEZUELA
GUYANA
SURINAME
French Guiana

MARSHALL ISLANDS

COLOMBIA

EQUATOR 0°

FEDERATED STATES OF MICRONESIA

NAURU

ECUADOR

10 Last European territory in South America

KIRIBATI

SOLOMON IS.

TUVALU Tokelau

PERU

BRAZIL

VANUATU

Wallis and Futuna SAMOA
American Samoa
Cook Islands

French Polynesia

BOLIVIA

TONGA
Niue

FIJI

New Caledonia

Independence Since 1945

Date of Independence

Since 1990
1980–1989
1970–1979
1960–1969
1945–1959
Before 1945
Not independent

PARAGUAY

CHILE

30°S

URUGUAY

NEW ZEALAND

ARGENTINA

150°E 180° 150°W

Conflicts in the Middle East

Since the fall of the Ottoman Empire in 1918, the Middle East has seen almost continuous conflict.

- In 1948 the United Nations divided Palestine into Arab and Jewish sectors. The Jews called their sector Israel. Palestinians resented giving up their land.

- Israel has been the site of at least four wars and numerous uprisings and terrorist attacks since its creation.

- In 1990 Iraq sought to control the oil-rich Persian Gulf. First it attacked and conquered Kuwait. A United Nations coalition forced Iraq out of Kuwait.

- Islamic fundamentalist movements seeking to enact religious law have been growing in the Middle East and Islamic countries around the world.

A In 1948–1949 more than 700,000 Palestinians fled Israel and set up refugee camps in neighboring countries. Many Palestinians have lived in refugee camps their entire lives. This camp in Lebanon was rebuilt after heavy fighting.

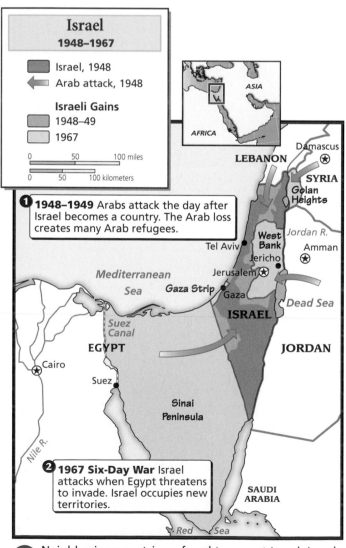

Israel
1948–1967

- Israel, 1948
- ← Arab attack, 1948

Israeli Gains
- 1948–49
- 1967

0   50   100 miles
0   50   100 kilometers

❶ 1948–1949 Arabs attack the day after Israel becomes a country. The Arab loss creates many Arab refugees.

❷ 1967 Six-Day War Israel attacks when Egypt threatens to invade. Israel occupies new territories.

B Neighboring countries refused to accept Israel. Israel defeated each Arab attack and gained more land.

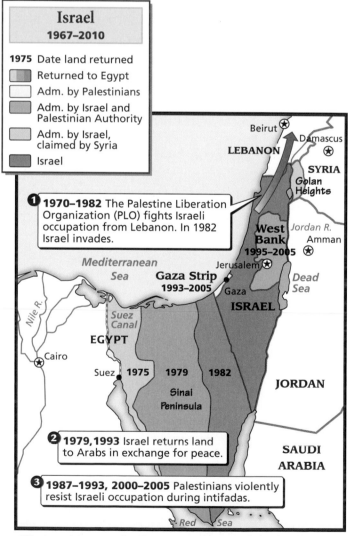

Israel
1967–2010

- **1975** Date land returned
- Returned to Egypt
- Adm. by Palestinians
- Adm. by Israel and Palestinian Authority
- Adm. by Israel, claimed by Syria
- Israel

❶ 1970–1982 The Palestine Liberation Organization (PLO) fights Israeli occupation from Lebanon. In 1982 Israel invades.

❷ 1979, 1993 Israel returns land to Arabs in exchange for peace.

❸ 1987–1993, 2000–2005 Palestinians violently resist Israeli occupation during intifadas.

C Israel has gradually returned most of the land gained in the Six-Day War to Egypt and the Palestinians. However, no agreement has been reached on final boundaries.

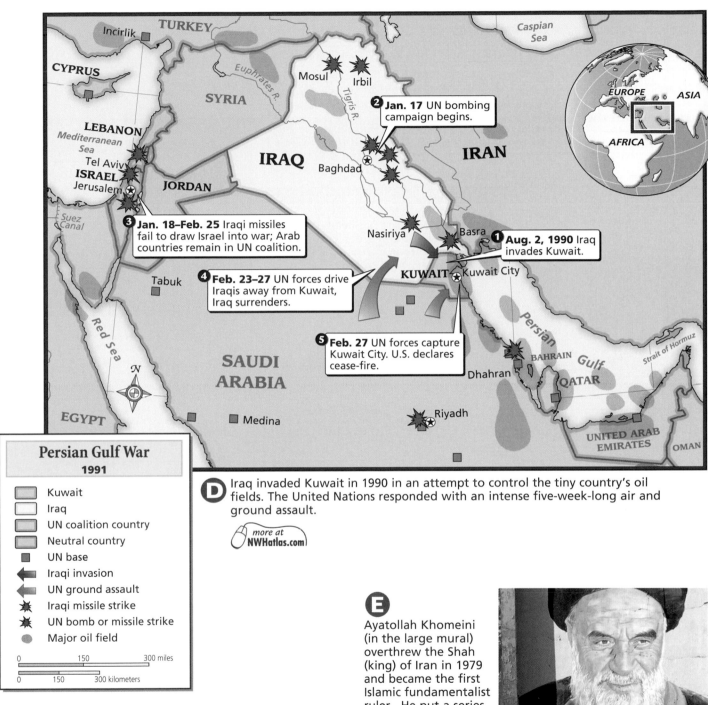

TURKEY
Incirlik
Caspian Sea

CYPRUS

SYRIA

Euphrates R.

Mosul   Irbil

2 **Jan. 17** UN bombing campaign begins.

IRAQ

Tigris R.

IRAN

LEBANON
Mediterranean Sea
Tel Aviv
ISRAEL
Jerusalem

JORDAN

Baghdad

3 **Jan. 18–Feb. 25** Iraqi missiles fail to draw Israel into war; Arab countries remain in UN coalition.

Suez Canal

Nasiriya

Basra

1 **Aug. 2, 1990** Iraq invades Kuwait.

Tabuk

4 **Feb. 23–27** UN forces drive Iraqis away from Kuwait, Iraq surrenders.

KUWAIT Kuwait City

5 **Feb. 27** UN forces capture Kuwait City. U.S. declares cease-fire.

Red Sea

SAUDI ARABIA

Persian Gulf

Strait of Hormuz

BAHRAIN

Dhahran QATAR

EGYPT

Medina

Riyadh

UNITED ARAB EMIRATES OMAN

Persian Gulf War
1991

- Kuwait
- Iraq
- UN coalition country
- Neutral country
- ■ UN base
- ◀ Iraqi invasion
- ◀ UN ground assault
- ✹ Iraqi missile strike
- ✹ UN bomb or missile strike
- ● Major oil field

0   150   300 miles
0   150   300 kilometers

D Iraq invaded Kuwait in 1990 in an attempt to control the tiny country's oil fields. The United Nations responded with an intense five-week-long air and ground assault.

more at NWHatlas.com

E

Ayatollah Khomeini (in the large mural) overthrew the Shah (king) of Iran in 1979 and became the first Islamic fundamentalist ruler. He put a series of Islamic laws into effect, including forbidding Western music and requiring women to wear a veil.

Middle of what?

In the 1800s European geographers used *Near East*, *Middle East*, and *Far East* to describe regions east of Western Europe. The Middle East is the region around the eastern Mediterranean Sea and the Persian Gulf.

123

Recent International Challenges

Today the world faces serious challenges, many of which can only be solved through global cooperation.

- Even after the Cold War, many regions are trapped in violence and war.

- Terrorists use violence against innocent people in hopes of forcing governments to change and eliminating foreign influence in their homelands.

- At the same time, nations are coming together to improve trade, health, nutrition, the environment, and international safety.

more at NWHatlas.com

A Global warming has been attributed to an increase in greenhouse gases, such as carbon dioxide. If the trend continues, much of the polar ice caps will melt, significantly raising sea levels.
more at NWHatlas.com

ECONOMICS
World's Largest Economies

more at NWHatlas.com

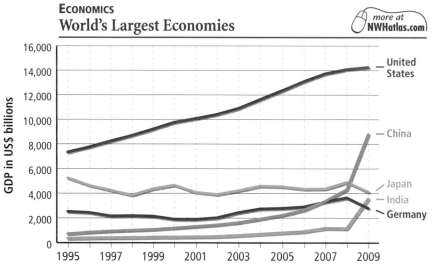

United States
China
Japan
India
Germany

B This graph measures Gross Domestic Product (GDP), the value of the goods and services produced in a country in a year. The United Kingdom, Russia, France, Brazil, and Italy also have large economies.

Where was it made?
Today it's not always easy to say. A car might be designed in Japan, made of U.S. steel, and assembled in Mexico with parts from all over the world. We now have a **global** economy.

Top 10 Cities, 2010

more at NWHatlas.com

C Urban populations in many countries have skyrocketed in the last 50 years. Compare this map and chart with the Top 10 Cities in 1900 on page 107. How many cities are still on the list?

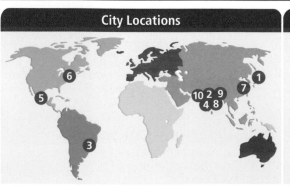

Rank/City (Modern Country)	Population
❶ Tokyo (Japan)	36,669,000
❷ Delhi (India)	22,157,000
❸ Sao Paulo (Brazil)	20,262,000
❹ Mumbai (India)	20,041,000
❺ Mexico City (Mexico)	19,460,000
❻ New York (United States)	19,425,000
❼ Shanghai (China)	16,575,000
❽ Kolkata (India)	15,552,000
❾ Dhaka (Bangladesh)	14,648,000
❿ Karachi (Pakistan)	13,125,000

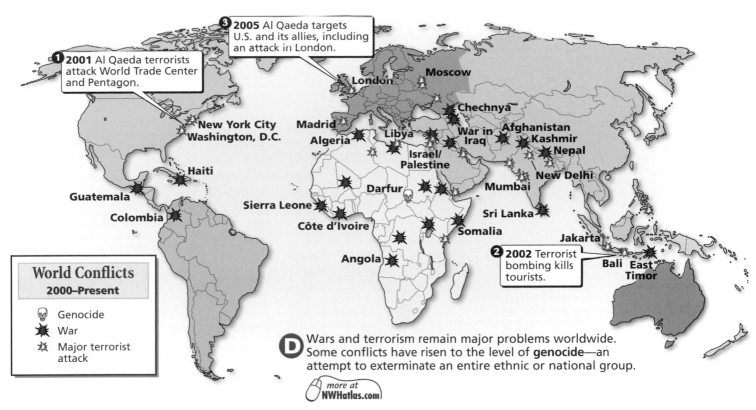

1 **2001** Al Qaeda terrorists attack World Trade Center and Pentagon.

3 **2005** Al Qaeda targets U.S. and its allies, including an attack in London.

2 **2002** Terrorist bombing kills tourists.

Moscow

London

Chechnya

New York City
Washington, D.C.

Madrid

Algeria

Libya

Israel/
Palestine

War in
Iraq

Afghanistan

Kashmir

Nepal

New Delhi

Haiti

Darfur

Mumbai

Guatemala

Colombia

Sierra Leone

Côte d'Ivoire

Somalia

Sri Lanka

Jakarta

Angola

Bali East
Timor

World Conflicts

2000–Present

☠ Genocide

✴ War

✷ Major terrorist attack

D Wars and terrorism remain major problems worldwide. Some conflicts have risen to the level of **genocide**—an attempt to exterminate an entire ethnic or national group.

more at **NWHatlas.com**

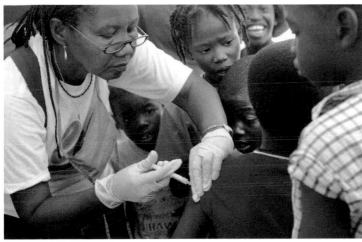

E Vaccines can now control and prevent many diseases that once killed millions. This doctor is giving tetanus and diphtheria vaccines to victims of the 2010 earthquake in Haiti.

SCIENCE & TECHNOLOGY
Innovations, 1970–2010

1970 Fiber optics	**1976** Video cassette recorder	**1984** CD-ROM	**1986** First use of DNA evidence	**1998** Portable MP3 player	**2008** Retail DNA testing		
1973 Cellular phone	**1981** Space shuttle		**1991** World Wide Web	**1999** Wireless fidelity			

1970   1975   1980   1985   1990   1995   2000   2005   2010

1971 Word processor, Microprocessors in calculators	**1977** Mass-produced personal computer, MRI scanner	**1983** Scientists isolate HIV	**1992** First text message sent	**1996** DVD, Dolly the sheep cloned	**2005** Streaming video	**2010** Tablet computer	

F This has been called the Information Age. Imagine living in 1970 without any of these innovations. How would your life have been different?

125

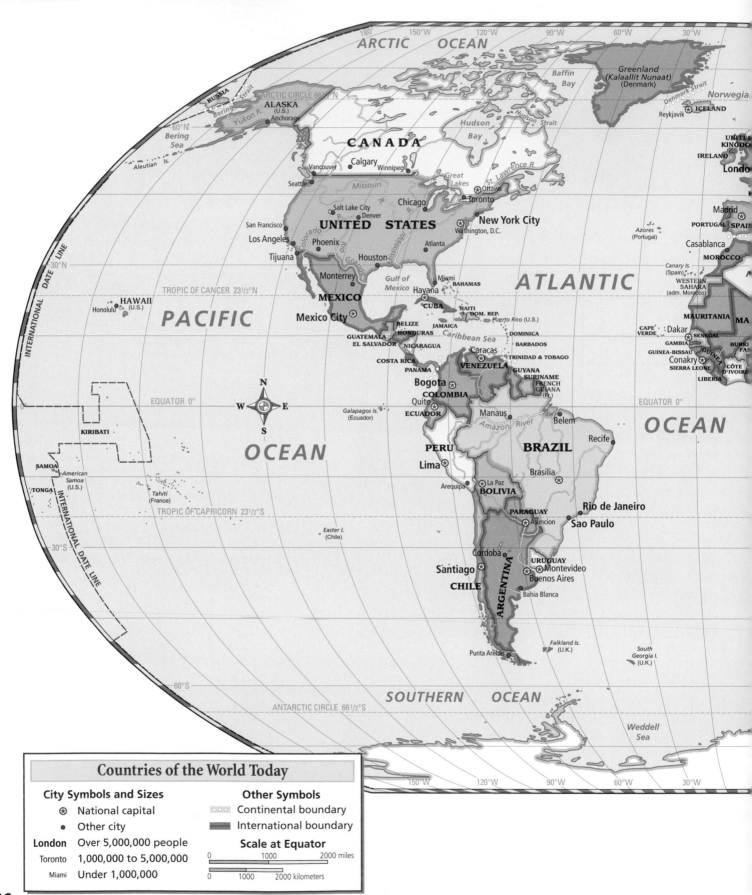

Countries of the World Today

City Symbols and Sizes

⊛ National capital

• Other city

London Over 5,000,000 people

Toronto 1,000,000 to 5,000,000

Miami Under 1,000,000

Other Symbols

ᴑᴑᴑ Continental boundary

▬▬ International boundary

Scale at Equator

0   1000   2000 miles

0   1000   2000 kilometers

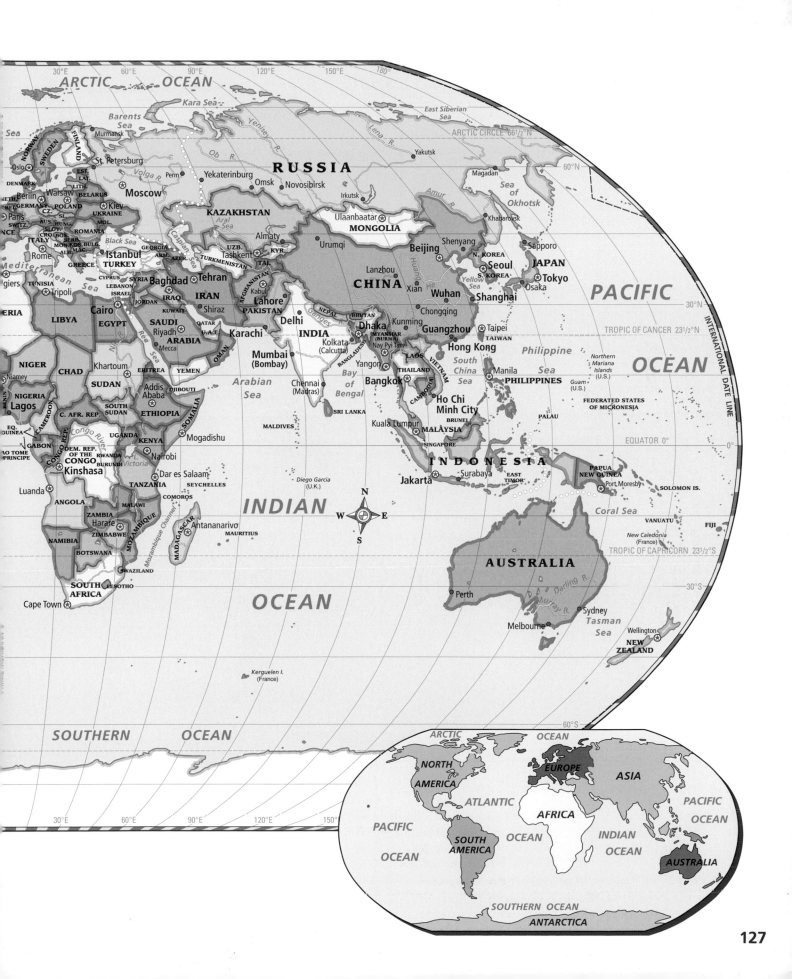

ARCTIC OCEAN
Polar ice mass
Banks I.
Victoria I.
Ellesmere I.
Baffin Bay
Greenland (Kalaallit Nunaat)
Denmark Strait
Norwegian
Iceland
ARC

ARCTIC CIRCLE 66½°N
Mt. McKinley 20,320 ft.
Bering Strait
Mackenzie R.
Interior Plains
Canadian Shield
Hudson Bay
Hudson Strait
Cape Farewell
British Isles
London

60°N
Bering Sea
Yukon R.
Kodiak I.
Aleutian Is.
Vancouver I.
Vancouver
Seattle
Rocky Mountains
NORTH AMERICA
Great Plains
Missouri R.
Great Lakes
St. Lawrence R.
Toronto
Montreal
Newfoundland
Iberian Peninsula
Madrid
Azores

Chicago
New York City
Appalachian Mts.
Strait of Gibraltar
Casablanca
Atlas

Los Angeles
Sierra Madre
Rio Grande
Mississippi
Cape Hatteras

30°N
Houston
Gulf of Mexico
Miami
ATLANTIC
Canary Is.
Atlas
S

TROPIC OF CANCER 23½°N
Cape San Lucas
Mexico City
Bahama Is.
Cuba
West Indies
Puerto Rico
Hispaniola
Caribbean Sea
Cape Verde Is.
Niger

Hawaiian Islands
PACIFIC
Central America
Panama Canal
Caracas
Trinidad
Guiana Highlands

EQUATOR 0°
Galapagos Is.
Bogotá
Amazon Basin
Amazon River
SOUTH AMERICA
EQUATOR 0°
OCEAN
Ascension I.

Samoa Is.
OCEAN
Andes Mountains
Lima
Brazilian Highlands
Brasília

Tuamotu Archipelago
Easter I.
Rio de Janeiro
Sao Paulo

TROPIC OF CAPRICORN 23½°S
Pitcairn I.

30°S
Juan Fernandez Is.
Santiago
Aconcagua 22,831 ft.
Buenos Aires
Pampas
Patagonia

Falkland Is.
Tierra del Fuego
Strait of Magellan
South Georgia I.
Cape Horn

60°S
SOUTHERN OCEAN

ANTARCTIC CIRCLE 66½°S
Antarctic Peninsula
Weddell Sea
Ice shelf

N W E S

150°W 120°W 90°W 60°W 30°W
180° 150°W 120°W 90°W 60°W 30°W

Physical World

Natural Regions

Tundra or ice Forest Grass Shrub or desert

Symbols

⚬⚬⚬ Continental boundary
— International boundary
• City
▲ Mountain peak

Scale at Equator

0   1000   2000 miles
0   1000   2000 kilometers

Timetables of World History

	Middle East and Africa	East and South Asia	Europe and Russia	Americas and Oceania
9000 B.C. (B.C.E.)–4000 B.C. (B.C.E.)	9000 B.C. Farming develops in the Fertile Crescent. 8000 B.C. First cities are built—Jericho and Catal Huyuk. 6000 B.C. Farming develops along the Nile River. 5000 B.C. Irrigation is used in Egypt and Mesopotamia.	6000 B.C. Farming develops along the Huang He, Indus, and Yangtze Rivers. 5000 B.C. Yangshao culture emerges in China.	5000 B.C. Farming spreads across Europe. 4500 B.C. Plow is used in southeastern Europe.	9000 B.C. People inhabit the southern tip of South America. 5000 B.C. Farming develops in Middle America and the Andes Mountains.
4000 B.C. (B.C.E.)–2000 B.C. (B.C.E.)	4000 B.C. Saharan herders move to West Africa. 3500 B.C. First bronze tools are made in Sumer. 3100 B.C. Egypt is unified. 3000 B.C. Sumerians begin using cuneiform symbols. 2900 B.C. Phoenicians become first sea-going civilization. 2650 B.C. Egyptians build first pyramid. 2350 B.C. Akkadians create world's first empire.	3000 B.C. Longshan culture emerges in China. 2500 B.C. First planned cities built in Indus Valley—Harappa and Mohenjo-Daro.	3000 B.C. Minoan civilization emerges in Crete.	3000 B.C. Corn (maize) is first cultivated in Middle America.
2000 B.C. (B.C.E.)–1000 B.C. (B.C.E.)	1800 B.C. Hammurabi of Babylon issues his law code. 1570 B.C. New Kingdom of Egypt begins. 1504 B.C. Egypt defeats Kush. 1500 B.C. Iron begins to be used in Anatolia. 1200 B.C. Hebrews start kingdom in Canaan. 1070 B.C. Libyan invasion ends the New Kingdom.	1766 B.C. The Shang start China's first dynasty. 1600 B.C. Chinese begin using pictographs. 1500 B.C. Aryan invasion ends Indus Valley civilization. Hinduism begins to spread through India. 1122 B.C. Shang dynasty is overthrown by the Zhou.	1600 B.C. Mycenaean civilization emerges in Greece. 1450 B.C. Mycenaens conquer the Minoans. 1200 B.C. Sea Peoples invade Greece. Mycenaean civilization collapses.	2000 B.C. People begin to colonize distant islands in the Pacific. 1200 B.C. Olmec farmers build permanent settlements. Maya civilization emerges.
1000 B.C. (B.C.E.)–500 B.C. (B.C.E.)	900 B.C. Phoenician ships reach the Atlantic Ocean. 724 B.C. Kush conquers Egypt. 664 B.C. Assyrians conquer Egypt. 612 B.C. Babylonians conquer Assyria. 586 B.C. Hebrews are exiled to Babylon. 539 B.C. Persia conquers Babylon.	1000 B.C. Hindus write down the world's oldest scriptures. 551 B.C. Confucius is born. 528 B.C. Siddhartha Gautama founds Buddhism.	750 B.C. Greek city-states begin colonizing the Mediterranean. Phoenician alphabet is introduced to Greece. 509 B.C. Rome becomes a republic. 508 B.C. Athens becomes a democracy.	700 B.C. Adena culture builds ceremonial mounds in North America.

	Middle East and Africa	East and South Asia	Europe and Russia	Americas and Oceania
500 B.C. (B.C.E.)–1 B.C. (B.C.E.)	**500** B.C. Bantu migrations begin in Africa. **331** B.C. Alexander the Great conquers the Persian Empire. **264** B.C. Punic Wars begin between Carthage and Rome. **146** B.C. Rome destroys Carthage. **30** B.C. Rome conquers Egypt. **4** B.C. Jesus Christ is born.	**500** B.C. Hindu kingdoms exist throughout India. **326** B.C. Alexander the Great reaches India. **321** B.C. Mauryan Empire begins in India. **260** B.C. Mauryan emperor Asoka becomes Buddhist. **221** B.C. China's first emperor takes control. **220** B.C. Construction begins on Great Wall of China. **206** B.C. Han dynasty expands Chinese empire. **150** B.C. Silk Road links China and Europe through trade.	**480** B.C. Persian invasion of Greece is defeated. **431** B.C. Peloponnesian War begins between Athens and Sparta. **399** B.C. Plato writes down the teachings of Socrates. **336** B.C. Alexander the Great becomes king of Greece and Macedonia. **264** B.C. Rome controls all of Italy. **146** B.C Rome conquers Greece. **27** B.C. Rome becomes an empire.	**400** B.C. Maya begin building pyramids.
A.D. (C.E.) 1–A.D. (C.E.)500	**29** Jesus Christ is crucified. **45** Paul begins to spread Christianity. **70** Jews flee Roman rule in Judea. **330** Axum adopts Christianity. **350** Kush falls to Axum.	**220** Han dynasty ends, Chinese empire declines. **320** Gupta dynasty begins in northern India.	**100** Rome is the world's largest city. **117** Roman Empire reaches its greatest extent. **303** Rome begins harsh persecution of Christians. **392** Christianity becomes official religion of Roman Empire. **395** Roman Empire divides into eastern and western regions. **476** Western Roman Empire falls to barbarians.	**1** Earliest settlers arrive in Hawaii. **300** Maya begin to record events on stone slabs.
A.D. (C.E.) 500–A.D. (C.E.) 1000	**622** Muhammad's journey to Medina begins spread of Islam. **639** Muslim armies invade North Africa. **700** Ghana is first empire in West Africa. **900** Baghdad is the world's largest city.	**500** Gupta Empire collapses after Hun invasion. **552** Buddhism reaches Japan. **751** Chinese expansion is halted by Muslim armies. **800** Khmer kingdoms emerge in Southeast Asia.	**500** Constantinople is the world's largest city. **540** Plague weakens the Byzantine Empire. **711** Moors conquer Spain. **789** Vikings raid England for first time. **800** Charlemagne is crowned Emperor of the West. **843** Charlemagne's empire breaks up. **936** Otto I of Germany begins the Holy Roman Empire.	**700** Anasazi begin building pueblos. **900** Maya Empire declines after crop failures. First people arrive on Easter Island.

	Middle East and Africa	East and South Asia	Europe and Russia	Americas and Oceania
A.D. (C.E.) 1000–A.D. (C.E.) 1500	1098 First Crusade takes Jerusalem from Muslims. 1169 Saladin conquers Egypt. 1200 Swahili culture emerges in East Africa. 1240 Sundiata founds the Mali Empire. 1270 Last Crusade ends. 1291 Last Crusader state falls to Muslims. 1335 Songhai Empire rises in West Africa. 1444 Atlantic slave trade begins. 1453 Ottomans conquer the Byzantine Empire.	1001 Chinese perfect gunpowder. 1100 Angkor Wat is built. 1127 Manchurian invasion pushes Chinese south. 1185 Shoguns take power in Japan. 1200 Hangchow is the world's largest city. 1279 Mongols conquer China. 1368 Ming dynasty starts in China. 1398 Timur invades India. 1433 Chinese government ends Zheng He's voyages. 1498 Portuguese reach India. 1500 Beijing is the world's largest city.	1066 Normans conquer England. 1095 Pope calls for crusades to Holy Land. 1215 Magna Carta gives rights to free Englishmen. 1346 Bubonic plague spreads from Asia to Europe. 1450 Gutenberg perfects the printing press. 1492 Muslim rule in Spain ends.	1000 Vikings settle in Newfoundland. 1200 Pueblo civilization builds cliff dwellings. Maori settle in New Zealand. 1325 Aztec people settle at Tenochtitlan. 1438 Inca begin to expand their empire in the Andes. 1492 Christopher Columbus reaches the Americas. 1500 Portugal claims Brazil.
A.D. (C.E.) 1500–A.D. (C.E.) 1700	1505 Portuguese start East African colonies. 1574 Ottomans complete North African expansion. 1591 Songhai is destroyed. 1652 Dutch settle at Cape Town, South Africa.	1526 Babur begins the Mughal Empire in India. 1565 Spain claims the Philippines. 1602 English and Dutch start trade colonies in India. 1644 Manchus end the Ming dynasty, begin ruling China. 1650 Dutch control most European trade in Asia. 1674 Maratha Kingdom established in India.	1503 Leonardo paints the *Mona Lisa*. 1517 Luther starts the Protestant Reformation. 1543 Copernicus proposes a sun-centered universe. 1585 Russians build their first settlement in Siberia. 1618 Thirty Years' War begins. 1651 Hobbes publishes *Leviathan*. 1683 Ottoman Empire is defeated at Vienna. 1698 First steam engine invented.	1521 Spain conquers the Aztec. 1532 Spain conquers the Inca. 1535 New Spain extends from Mexico to Chile. 1606 Europeans first encounter Australia. 1607 Jamestown is settled by the English.
A.D. (C.E.) 1700–A.D. (C.E.) 1850	1798 Napoleon leads French invasion of Egypt. 1815 Zulu kingdom is founded. 1838 Dutch (Boers) defeat the Zulus.	1707 Mughal Empire reaches its height. 1800 Beijing's population is over 1,000,000. 1803 British take control of Mughal Empire. 1818 British take control of Maratha Kingdom. 1839 Opium War begins between Britain and China.	1769 Improved steam engine speeds the Industrial Revolution. 1789 French Revolution begins. 1796 World's first vaccine is developed to fight smallpox. 1804 Napoleon crowns himself emperor. 1815 Napoleon is defeated at Waterloo. 1848 Revolutions sweep across Europe.	1750 Europeans claim most of the Americas. 1775 American Revolution begins. 1787 U.S. Constitution is written. 1788 Britain sends convicts to Australia 1810 Revolutions against Spain begin in Latin America.

Middle East and Africa	East and South Asia	Europe and Russia	Americas and Oceania
	A.D. (C.E.) 1850–A.D. (C.E.) 1900		1833 Slaves in British colonies are emancipated.
	1853 Perry's fleet opens way to U.S.-Japanese trade.	1850 Over 50 percent of the British live in cities.	
	1857 Indian troops mutiny against British commanders.	1861 Italy is unified.	1861 American Civil War begins.
			1863 Lincoln frees most slaves in the U.S.
1869 Suez Canal links Red Sea and Mediterranean Sea.	1867 Japanese emperor regains power from the shogun.	1870 Industrial Revolution spreads across Europe.	1867 Canada gains its independence from Britain. U.S. buys Alaska.
1884 Seven European nations agree to divide up Africa.		1885 Daimler and Benz build first gasoline-powered car.	1879 Edison invents the electric light bulb.
	1895 Japan wins Sino-Japanese War.		1888 Brazil frees the last slaves in the Americas.
			1898 U.S. annexes Hawaii.
	A.D. (C.E.) 1900–A.D. (C.E.) 1950		
	1900 Chinese attack foreigners in the Boxer Rebellion.	1900 London is the world's largest city.	1901 Australia gains its independence from Britain.
	1904 Japan wins Russo-Japanese War.		
1914 European colonies make up most of Africa.	1910 Japan annexes Korea. Last Manchu emperor is deposed in China.	1914 World War I begins.	1910 Mexican Revolution begins.
			1914 Panama Canal connects Atlantic and Pacific Oceans.
		1917 Russian Revolution overthrows the czar.	1917 U.S. enters World War I.
1920 Ottoman Empire is divided into several countries.		1919 New nations are created after end of World War I.	
	1930 Gandhi begins non-violent protests against British in India.		1929 Worldwide depression begins.
	1931 Japan invades Manchuria.	1933 Adolf Hitler becomes chancellor of Germany.	
1936 Ethiopia is conquered by Italy.		1939 World War II begins.	1941 Japan attacks Pearl Harbor. U.S. enters World War II.
	1945 U.S. drops atomic bombs on Japan, ending World War II.	1945 Allies defeat Germany.	1945 UN is formed.
1948 State of Israel is created.	1947 India gains independence.	1946 Cold War begins.	
	1949 Communists take control of mainland China.		
	A.D. (C.E.) 1950–Present		
	1950 U.S. troops enter Korean War.	1957 Soviet Union launches Sputnik, the first satellite.	1959 Castro leads communist revolution in Cuba.
	1954 Vietnam gains independence from France.	1961 Soviet Union sends first man into space. Berlin wall is built.	1962 Cuban Missile Crisis nearly leads to war.
1960 Eighteen African nations gain independence.			
1967 Israel takes control of the West Bank, Gaza, Sinai, and the Golan Heights.			
1969 Most of Africa is independent.			1969 U.S. lands first men on the moon.
1977 Last known outbreak of smallpox ends.	1975 Vietnam War ends with communist victory.		
1979 Iranian Revolution establishes an Islamic fundamentalist government.			1977 First mass-produced personal computers are sold.
		1980 Solidarity Union challenges Communist rule in Poland.	1981 Belize gains independence from Britain.
1991 UN coalition forces Iraq out of Kuwait.		1991 Soviet Union collapses and Cold War ends. World Wide Web is organized.	
	1997 China regains control of Hong Kong.		
2003 U.S. leads invasion of Iraq.	2008 China becomes the world's second largest economy.	2001 European Union introduces a single currency.	2001 Terrorists attack New York City and Washington, D.C.
	2010 Tokyo is the world's largest city.		

Glossary

barbarian

civil disobedience

Cold War

agriculture Practice of raising plants and animals for food and other products. Farming.

Arab Ethnic and culture group that originated in the Middle East and has spread to North Africa.

aristocracy Small ruling class that inherits its powers; may control the land and military in its country. Also called *nobility*.

astrolabe Device that calculates latitude based on the sun and stars. Important for navigation at sea.

Bantu Large family of ethnic and language groups that extends from West Africa to South Africa.

barbarian A word used by one group to describe another group thought to be less advanced. Often refers to people who invaded the Roman Empire.

bourgeoisie Social class based on money and education. Middle-class professionals and business owners and their families.

bronze Mixture of copper and tin; main metal used for tools and weapons in Europe and Asia until iron replaced it.

Buddhism Religion from India that includes the belief that happiness is found by eliminating all desires. Founded by Siddhartha Gautama, who was known as *Buddha* or the "Enlightened One."

caliphate Islamic country where the ruler is considered the political successor of Muhammad. Caliphates existed between 632 and 1250.

capital City where a country's government is located.

caravan Group of overland traders and the animals carrying their goods.

casualties People killed, wounded, missing, or taken prisoner in a battle or war.

Christianity Religion that arose in Israel during Roman times and includes belief in Jesus Christ as the Son of God.

church 1. Organization of Christians with shared beliefs, such as the Roman Catholic Church or the Lutheran Church. 2. Group of Christians who worship together. 3. Building where they worship.

citizen Person allowed to vote and participate in government in a democracy.

city Very large settlement of people. Unlike some of those in villages, people in cities do not farm.

city-state Independent city and its surrounding farms. Has its own rulers and is not part of any other country.

civil disobedience Acts to promote political change by peacefully disobeying unjust laws. First used on a large scale by Gandhi in British India after World War I.

civil war War between different groups or regions within a country, usually for control of the country.

civilization Society that has writing, cities, agriculture, artisans, and public monuments.

clergy People whose work directly serves a religion, especially Christianity. Includes cardinals, bishops, priests, nuns, monks, ministers, and pastors.

Cold War Armed rivalry from 1946 to 1991 between the United States and its allies and the Soviet Union and its allies.

colony Settlement or region usually governed by a distant parent country. Settling the area is called *colonization*.

communism System of government in which the government owns and controls the property and equipment used to produce goods and services.

Confucianism Philosophy from China that includes belief in government by an educated, moral elite. Based on the teachings of Confucius.

conscripted Term used to describe soldiers who are required by law to serve in their country's army. Sometimes called *drafted*.

Counter Reformation Efforts by the Catholic Church to counter or reverse the Protestant Reformation.

country Land with one government.

culture Beliefs, customs, and practices of a group of people.

culture group Ethnic, racial, or religious group.

culture region Where a particular culture is found; usually outlasts the countries established there.

czar One of the monarchs who ruled Russia until the revolution of 1917.

democracy Government by voting citizens, developed in Greece and Rome. Country with democratic government.

desert Dry natural region with little rain and few if any plants.

domestic Term used to describe tame animals or plants cultivated by people.

Dutch People from the Netherlands, a country in Europe.

dynasty Family of rulers, usually powerful for generations.

Eastern Orthodox Church Main branch of Christianity in Eastern Europe and the Middle East, originally the Eastern Christian Church. Often called *Orthodox*.

economy System of making, distributing, and buying goods and services.

emperor Man who rules an empire. A woman who rules an empire is an *empress*.

empire Separate nations or regions under a single ruler or government.

Enlightenment A philosophical movement that believed in examining everything according to reason and science. Inspired the American and French Revolution.

export Something that is sold to another country.

fascism System of government in which most rights are suppressed to support nationalist aims. Includes increasing military power and oppressing minority groups.

feudalism System of government that gives most power to large landowners. Common in Europe from 500 to 1500 and in Japan from 1100 to 1860.

free trade Economic system in which a country's government does not tax or restrict imports and exports.

fundamentalist 1. Term used to describe a religious or political movement that reads its holy book literally and seeks to impose religious law. 2. A person who holds these beliefs.

genocide Deliberate murder or attempted murder of every man, woman, and child from an ethnic or racial group.

globalization Modern process of connecting worldwide communications and trade for the benefit of corporations or of humanity, but not of specific countries.

Gross Domestic Product (GDP) The value of all goods and services produced in a country in one year.

hajj Muslim pilgrimage to Mecca. One of the main duties of all able Muslims.

Hinduism Religion from India based on belief in reincarnation and in spiritual connections between all things.

Holocaust Attempted genocide of Jews and others by Nazi Germany and its allies from 1933 to 1945.

Holy Roman Empire Weak government that ruled Germany and Italy from about 1000 to 1806.

hunting and gathering Way of life using only wild animals and wild plants for food.

imperialism Policy of expanding a country's power by gaining territory, by controlling other countries, or both.

import Something that is bought from another country.

independence State of being free from rule by another country.

Indies European name for the islands and mainland of Southeast Asia, India, and coastal China.

indigenous Coming from a particular area or environment.

Industrial Revolution Social change in the 1700s and 1800s caused by replacing goods made by hand at home with goods made with machinery in factories.

industrialization Process of changing a country's economy from one based on agriculture and manufacturing by hand to one based on factory production.

irrigation Artificially supplying water to land so that crops will grow.

Islam Religion from Arabia that includes belief in one god (*Allah* in Arabic) and the unity of all believers. Based on the life and teachings of Muhammad.

ivory Material from animal tusks, usually elephants.

Jew Believer in Judaism. Originally called *Hebrew*.

Jewish Diaspora Migration of Jews away from Israel to the rest of the Middle East, the Mediterranean lands, and Europe.

Judaism Religion from the Hebrews based on belief in one god and obeying the laws of Moses, especially the Ten Commandments.

kingdom Country ruled by an inherited ruler, often a king or queen.

Kurd Ethnic group in present-day northern Iraq.

manufacturing Making products in large amounts.

mercantilism Economic system in which the government taxes and regulates trade in order to get the maximum amount of money for itself.

merchant Person who makes a living by selling and transporting goods.

Middle East Region including Southwest Asia and Northeast Africa.

migration Mass movement from one region to another.

millet Grain domesticated in Africa and eastern Asia. Most commonly grown today in China, India, and West Africa.

monarchy Country ruled by one person whose position passes on to his or her children.

monastery Isolated religious community of men, called *monks*, dedicated to study and strict discipline. Women called *nuns* live in similar communities called *convents*.

Muslim Believer in Islam.

nationalism Belief that a people with similar language, religion, history, and customs should have their own country.

Nazi Related to the fascist political party that ruled Germany from 1933 to 1945 and that was responsible for World War II and the Holocaust.

noble Member of an aristocracy. Also called an *aristocrat*. Includes dukes, counts, barons, marquises, and lords.

nomad Person who lives by herding animals, moving from place to place in search of food, water, and grazing land.

Ottoman Empire Muslim Turkish empire that ruled much of the Middle East and Balkan Peninsula from 1307 to 1920.

Palestinian Arab whose family came from or lives in present-day Israel, the West Bank, or Gaza.

Palestinian Authority Government of the Palestinians established in 1994 to rule Gaza and the Arab areas of the West Bank.

pastoralism System of herding animals and moving them from place to place in search of grazing land and water. Sometimes called *nomadic herding*.

hajj

Industrial Revolution

monarchy

pictograph

Renaissance

village

peasant Member of a poor farming or laboring family that has little or no personal property.

persecution Violence and discrimination against a particular group of people.

pictograph Simple picture of an object, used as a symbol in early writing.

pilgrimage Religious journey to an important sacred site.

plague Highly infectious disease, often deadly. Bubonic plague, which struck Europe and Asia in the 1300s, is spread by rats and fleas.

plantain Starchy, domesticated fruit similar to a banana but eaten cooked. Common food in Africa, Latin America, Southeast Asia, and Pacific islands.

plantation Large tract of land where one labor-intensive cash crop is grown. Work on colonial plantations was usually done by slaves.

pope Head of the Roman Catholic Church.

porcelain Type of ceramic, or pottery, originally from China, known for its white color and lightness. Often called *china*.

Protestant churches Non-Catholic groups that grew out of Western Christianity.

Reformation Movement beginning in the 1500s to change Western Christianity; led to the emergence of Protestant Christianity.

refugee Person who has fled his or her home because of war or persecution.

region Large area that is different from the areas around it. Defined by a single feature or several features, either natural or cultural.

Renaissance Intellectual and cultural movement in Europe from 1300 to 1600. The rebirth of cultural progress after the Middle Ages.

republic Country governed by officials elected by citizens and their chosen representatives.

revolution 1. Overthrow of a country's government by its citizens. 2. Other enormous change in government or society.

Roman Catholic Church Largest branch of Christianity, originally the Western Christian Church, led by the pope. Its members can be called *Roman Catholics* or just *Catholics*.

Scientific Revolution Period between 1540 and 1800 when modern ideas of observation and experimentation allowed far more accurate descriptions of the universe than ever before.

Sea Peoples Groups of people of unknown origin who attacked eastern Mediterranean civilizations in the 1200s and 1100s B.C.

Semite Member of a culture group that began as herders in the ancient Middle East and included Assyrians and Babylonians. Modern Semitic groups include Jews and Arabs.

serf Member of a poor farming family required to farm specific land for a feudal landowner. Similar to peasant, but serfs cannot legally leave their farm.

settlement 1. Community, usually small, with permanent residents. 2. The act of establishing homes in a new place.

shogun Military ruler of Japan, a position that lasted from 1192 to 1867.

Silk Road Ancient overland trade route between China and Europe.

slavery Practice of owning people and forcing them to work without pay. A person treated this way is a *slave*.

sorghum Grain from Africa. Grown in Africa and India for humans, and in the United States for animal feed.

sovereign 1. Monarch. 2. Word to describe any person or group that holds final authority in a country.

specialize To concentrate on a specific type of job, while trading with others for all other goods and services.

state 1. Area with its own government, not ruled by outsiders. 2. Part of a country, such as the United States of America, with laws and leaders of its own.

stele Single carved piece of stone standing upright as a monument.

superpower Country with widespread political and military power. The United States or the Soviet Union during the Cold War.

Swahili 1. Civilization that developed in East Africa combining Bantu, Arabic, Persian, and Indian cultures. 2. The language of Swahili civilization.

taro Starchy root from Southeast Asia. Most commonly grown in tropical areas of Africa, Asia, and Pacific islands.

terrorism Use of deliberate attacks on civilians, usually by non-military groups, to cause fear in order to advance a cause.

textiles Woven or knitted cloth. Textiles are made from wool, cotton, silk, or other fibers.

trade Exchanging goods and services for other goods and services or for money.

trench Long, narrow ditch used to protect soldiers in war.

United Nations Organization of countries set up in 1945 to promote peace and improve the standard of living for the world's people. Nearly all countries are members.

vaccine Medicine used to prevent disease that uses a weakened or dead version of the disease-causing germs.

vassal Person who receives land in exchange for military service in feudalism.

verdict Decision in a court of law.

village Settlement, usually small, where most people work on nearby farms.

Index

O

P

Q

R